ETHNOTHEATRE

QUALITATIVE INQUIRY AND SOCIAL JUSTICE

SERIES EDITORS

Norman K. Denzin
University of Illinois at Urbana-Champaign

Yvonna S. Lincoln
Texas A&M University

Books in this series address the role of critical qualitative research in an era that cries out for emancipatory visions that move people to struggle and resist oppression. Rooted in an ethical framework that is based on human rights and social justice, the series publishes exemplary studies that advance this transformative paradigm.

VOLUMES IN THIS SERIES

Betweener Talk: Decolonizing Knowledge Production, Pedagogy, and Praxis
Marcelo Diversi and Cláudio Moreira

Body, Paper, Stage: Writing and Performing Autoethnography
Tami Spry

Ethnotheatre

RESEARCH FROM PAGE TO STAGE

Johnny Saldaña

Left Coast
Press Inc.

Walnut Creek, California

Left Coast Press Inc.

LEFT COAST PRESS, INC.
1630 North Main Street, #400
Walnut Creek, CA 94596
www.LCoastPress.com

ISBN 978-1-61132-035-0 hardcover
ISBN 978-1-61132-036-7 paperback
eISBN 978-1-61132-037-4

Library of Congress Cataloging-in-Publication Data
Saldaña, Johnny.
Ethnotheatre : research from page to stage / Johnny Saldaña.
    p. cm. -- (Qualitative inquiry and social justice)
Includes bibliographical references and index.
ISBN 978-1-61132-035-0 (hardcover : alk. paper) -- ISBN 978-1-61132-036-7
(pbk. : alk. paper) -- ISBN 978-1-61132-037-4 (ebook)
1. Drama--Social aspects. 2. Theater--Social aspects. 3. Theater and society.
4. Literature and society. I. Title.
PN1643.S25 2011
792--dc23
                          2011033087

Printed in the United States of America

The paper used in this publication meets the minimum requirements of
American National Standard for Information Sciences—Permanence of Paper
for Printed Library Materials, ANSI/NISO Z39.48–1992.

CONTENTS

I don't care about realism—I care about reality.

—Augusto Boal

ILLUSTRATIONS

ACKNOWLEDGMENTS

Thanks are extended to:

Mitch Allen, editor of Left Coast Press, Inc., for commissioning this work.

Ryan Harris, editorial assistant of Left Coast Press, Inc., for his prepublication guidance.

Anne Brown, copyeditor, and Lisa Devenish, designer/production manager, for their meticulous care with the manuscript.

Norman K. Denzin and Yvonna S. Lincoln, series editors, for their inspirational writings, mentorship, and support.

Tom Barone, Mary Lee Smith, Amira De la Garza, and Sarah J. Tracy, my qualitative research instructors at Arizona State University, for teaching me the methods and literature of the field.

Brian Schlemmer, Charles Vanover, Harry F. Wolcott, Susan Finley, Macklin Finley, Joe Norris, Sandra Stauffer, Philip J. Taylor, and Kip Jones for their invitational and collaborative ventures with me as an ethnodramatist and ethnotheatrical director.

An Introduction to Ethnotheatre and Ethnodrama

What a verbatim play does is flash your research nakedly.
It's like cooking a meal but the meat is left raw. . . .

—Max Stafford Clark[1]

The following dramatic text is the beginning of a one-man play about competition in a high school band titled *Second Chair*. Notice how the italicized stage directions specify the actor's movements and describe the simple yet carefully chosen visual and aural elements of the theatrical presentation.

> *(setting: two metal folding chairs with metal music stands in front of each one; the music stands hold all necessary props for the production; first chair appears shiny and pristine; second chair appears worn, rusty, and beaten)*

> *(pre-show music: various selections composed by W. Francis McBeth (The Feast of Trumpets, Praises, Caccia, Flourishes); lights rise; JOHNNY enters at the beginning of Flourishes, looks longingly at first chair, then sits in second chair and looks occasionally toward the empty first chair; music fades out; he speaks to the audience)*

JOHNNY: In high school band, Tammi Jo thought she was *so* special. She played an ebony wood Selmer clarinet with a glass mouthpiece, while all I had was this cheap-ass plastic Bundy. Her family was typical middle-class and she was the only child, thus receiving all of the attention and all of the spoils. My family was transitioning from lower class to middle, but that was kind of hard with so many children to take care of.

In our junior year, I was second chair;

> *(looks at and scowls at the chair next to him)*

and Tammi Jo was first chair.

> *(brief pause; to audience)*

And I think you know where this story is going.

(adapted from Saldaña, 2008, p. 179)

This format is quite typical of the beginning of many one-person plays, but its content is quite different from fictional dramatic works. This is a true story. It was performed by the actual person who lived the experience. And everything that will be told to the audience really happened—though the names of others have been changed to maintain their anonymity. This is an example of a literary genre called *ethnodrama*. And its performance on stage in front of a live audience makes it *ethnotheatre*.

Ethnotheatre: Research from Page to Stage is a playwriting textbook for the *ethnodramatic* genre of literature. The content is geared toward a broad readership in fields such as sociology, psychology, anthropology, education, human communication, health care, theatre, media, and performance studies.

It is very difficult, even for full-time theatre practitioners, to stay current with the ethnodramatic and ethnotheatrical literature. Sometimes a new play script becomes known through word of mouth, and sometimes through systematic searches of online catalogs. At other times, an ethnodrama appears in a journal to which you just happen to subscribe, and at still other times you find one serendipitously through a nonrelated Internet search. It is difficult to document all that happens in this unique field because ethnotheatrical productions are sometimes local performances or *signature works* whose scripts never get published. I hope to provide in this book some guidance to accessible, published plays because you become a better playwright by reading exemplary scripts.

An individual also becomes a better playwright by writing monologues, scenes, and extended play scripts. Throughout this book is a series of playwriting exercises I strongly encourage you to explore. They will attune you to the craft and art of writing for the stage, especially when adapting qualitative data or empirical materials such as interview transcripts, field notes, and written documents for ethnodramatic work.

Terms and Definitions

I define two key terms as follows:

> *Ethnotheatre,* a word joining *ethnography* and *theatre,* employs the traditional craft and artistic techniques of theatre or media production to mount for an audience a live or mediated performance event of research participants' experiences and/or the researcher's interpretations of data. The goal is to investigate a particular facet of the human condition for

purposes of adapting those observations and insights into a performance medium. This investigation is preparatory fieldwork for theatrical
production work.

An *ethnodrama*, a word joining *ethnography* and *drama*, is a written play
script consisting of dramatized, significant selections of narrative collected
from interview transcripts, participant observation field notes, journal
entries, personal memories/experiences, and/or print and media artifacts
such as diaries, blogs, e-mail correspondence, television broadcasts, newspaper articles, court proceedings, and historic documents. In some cases,
production companies can work improvisationally and collaboratively to
devise original and interpretive texts based on authentic sources. Simply
put, this is dramatizing the data (adapted from Saldaña, 2005, pp. 1–2).

Ethnodrama is a specific genre of dramatic literary writing, yet its
ethnotheatrical performance on stage or through media permits various artistic interpretations and styles.

Notice that this chapter's introductory quote included a related
term: *verbatim play*. A specific definition exists for this form, but it depends on which text you read and which artist or scholar you're listening to. In my research about the genre, I've located approximately
eighty unique terms (and I've developed a few on my own) that relate
to ethnodrama or ethnotheatre, or suggest variations on the form. My
goal is not to review each term's origin and its nuanced definition, but
to make you aware that the literature contains an abundance of these
which can be considered siblings or distant cousins of what this book
is about. Filewod (2009) calls these "a rhizomorphic archive of pro-
cedures and perceptions rather than a genealogy of forms" (p. 62). In
alphabetical order, these terms follow.

autodrama

autoperformance

commemorative drama

conversational dramatism

conversational performance

docudrama

documentary theatre

docu-performance

dramatic commentary on interview
    data

dramatized report

embodied methodological praxis

ethnodrama

ethnodramatics

ethnodramatology

ethnographic drama

ethnographic performance text

ethnographic theatre

ethno-mimesis

ethnoperformance

ethnostorytelling

ethnotainment

ethnotheatre

everyday life performance

everyday theatre

factual theatre

generative autobiography
heritage theatre
historical drama
historical reenactment
informance
interview theatre
investigative theatre
life review
life writing
lifeworld theatre
living newspaper
living theatre verbal art
memory theatre
metadrama
metatheater
mystory
narradrama
natural performance
nonfiction playwriting
nonfiction storytelling
oral history performance
performance anthropology
performance ethnography
performance science
performative inquiry
performative social science
performative writing
performed ethnography
performed theory

performing autobiography
presentational theatre
public voice ethnography
reality theatre
reflexive anthropology
reminiscence theatre
research as performance
research staging
research-based theatre
scripted research
self-revelatory performance
self-performance
semidocumentary play
social drama
stand-up storytelling
stand-up theory
testimonial theatre
theatre as representation
theatre of actuality
theatre of fact
theatre of re-enactment
theatre of reportage
theatrical documentary
theatrical research-based performance
transcription theatre
tribunal play
verbatim theatre
word-for-word theatre

The common thread that weaves through all of these terms is that the script or performance text is solidly rooted in nonfictional, re-searched reality—not realism, but *reality*. Be aware that if you conduct a literature review about this subject on a search engine, you may have quite a task ahead of you. I will presumptively label all plays I discuss in this book as ethnodramas, though their original playwrights may prefer other terms for their unique work.

I should also mention that the terms *drama* and *theatre* will each be used purposefully throughout this book, for there are distinct dif-ferences between the two. Theatre most often refers to the formal play production process and performed product, while drama usually refers to dramatic literature and improvisational studio work. And for those who may be wondering about spelling differences, theat*er* generally refers to a building or production company; theat*re* generally refers to the art form itself. These distinctions are generally preferred among the theatrical community but are not standardized in any way.

Why Ethnodrama and Ethnotheatre?

An ethnodramatic play script and its ethnotheatrical production are deliberately chosen as representational and presentational methods of ethnographic fieldwork or autoethnographic reflection because the researcher or artist has determined that these art forms are the most appropriate and effective modalities for communicating observations of cultural, social, or personal life.

You can find out what's happening in the world through several methods: printed newspapers with photographs, and their online editions; televised news programs with live coverage and video footage; radio broadcasts; Internet home pages; news-related websites; and simply word of mouth. But which one of these forms, or in what combination, is the "best" way to get world news? Many will say it depends on the story, the media format's capacities for delivering it, and the receiver's preferences for learning new information. But it ultimately comes down to the *people* initiating the reportage in the first place deciding which format(s) to adopt to spread the news. In most cases, that decision will be made for them if they work for an organization that requires particular methods and modes of communication.

Researchers face a comparable decision. With a variety of ways available to disseminate research, when is a play script and its performance—rather than a series monograph, academic journal article, book chapter, fifteen-minute conference session paper, or even a poem or visual art rendering, and so forth—the best way to communicate with others what you observed and learned about the human condition? Many audience members who attend an effective theatre production, even if the play is a fictional work, testify afterward that the live performance event made things seem more "real"—a paradox, if you think about it. Yet if the art form has this ability, this power, to heighten the representation and presentation of social life, and if our research goal with a particular fieldwork project is to capture and document the stark realities of the people we talked to and observed, then the medium of theatre seems the most compatible choice for sharing our findings and insights.

But we must not forget that theatre artists create theatre productions for their own reasons. You may hear quite lofty purposes for the art form such as "a mirror held up to human nature" or "a manifestation of our innate desire to make-believe." What drives me as a playwright, director, actor, and designer is nothing more complex than a deep love for the art form itself. Theatre is my preferred field of study and creative medium of expression because I have been indoctrinated into its craft since young adulthood and find great personal satisfaction from my involvement and accomplishments. And when I fell in love with qualitative inquiry decades later and learned there had been others before me, like anthropologist Victor Turner, who shared those same two passions and created fascinating hybrids of *performance ethnography*, it seemed so sensible, so natural, to employ the medium of theatre to tell nonfictional stories about real people. "Both disciplines, after all, share a common goal: to create a unique, insightful, and engaging text about the human condition" (Saldaña, 2005, p. 29).

Several professional organizations have embraced and endorsed the arts as legitimate interests of their members who integrate traditional research with human participants and expressive forms of documentation and reportage. For example, the American Educational Research Association includes special interest groups such as Arts-Based Educational Research as well as Narrative Inquiry. One of the American Counseling Association's recognized divisions is The Association for Creativity in Counseling, whose professional journal explores mental health treatment through "psychodrama, art, dance, music, theater, and other modalities." And the American Anthropological Association includes sections such as the Society for Humanistic Anthropology and the Society for Visual Anthropology. Artists are involved not only within their own disciplines but within the social sciences, for not everyone who acts in a high school play production goes on to become a theatre major in college or pursue a professional acting career in Hollywood. Many of them are drawn to nontheatrical fields of study such as sociology, health care, and law. But many of those same people will testify that they have never forgotten the power of theatre and its potential for influencing others' lives as much as it has their own (McCammon & Saldaña, 2011).

Approaches to Ethnodramatic Playwriting

Following are four distinct approaches to ethnodramatic playwriting to give an idea of the form and how it may differ from conventional, fictional dramatic literature.

Ethnodramatic Dramatization of Interview Transcripts

The opening narrator's monologue in Moisés Kaufman and the Tectonic Theater Project's 2001 production *The Laramie Project* explains that the sources for the play script included over two hundred interviews conducted by production company members, their own journal entries, and "other found texts" (p. 21). Interviews (and, to some degree, participant observation field notes) can become the primary source material for performance adaptation or *dramatization* by a playwright. Some choose to preserve the precise language of the interviewee from an audio recording or written transcript for the adaptation, thus maintaining a *verbatim* approach. Other playwrights will take the unedited material yet select portions of and rearrange the original text into a more aesthetically shaped *adaptation*. And still other playwrights may develop an *original* dramatic composition based on or inspired by raw interview materials. A *composite character* may be created when several interviews with different participants refer to similar themes or stories. Thus, the composite character is a fictional creation that nevertheless represents and speaks the collective realities of its original sources.

Though not the originator of ethnotheatre, Anna Deavere Smith is perhaps the field's first playwright-performer "superstar" who crystallized the genre and demonstrated its artistic possibilities and social impact for both the academic and commercial worlds. She burst onto the theatrical scene with two landmark productions: *Fires in the Mirror: Crown Heights, Brooklyn and Other Identities* (Smith, 1993, 1997) and *Twilight: Los Angeles, 1992* (Smith, 1994, 2003). Both play scripts use verbatim excerpts from her interviews with everyday citizens and major social and political figures. Smith's classical acting training focused her on the intricacies and nuances of language, and that knowledge transferred into her analyses of conversations with people and the performances of their words. Her social consciousness attuned her to the "character of America," and her cultural goal through theatre is to represent the spectrum of its diverse citizens on stage and to weave the fragments of its people for critical examination and audience dialogue.

Fires in the Mirror profiles various perspectives about the 1991 conflict and riots in Crown Heights between African Americans and Jews when an accidental death and retaliatory murder fueled ethnic tensions. Figures portrayed range from cultural icons such as Angela Davis and the Reverend Al Sharpton to Anonymous Young Man #1. *Twilight: Los Angeles, 1992* profiles citizens' perspectives about the city's riots following the acquittal of the police officers who beat Rodney King. The interviewee characters are Korean, Latino, white, and black, and range from shop owners to trial jurors to Reginald Denny, the truck driver whose retaliatory beating during the riots was broadcast live nationally.

In her production notes for *Twilight*, Smith (2003) advises audience framing for the documentary theatre event by showing slides and videos of key news footage about the riots, and a special slide that reads: "This play is based on interviews conducted by Anna Deavere Smith soon after the race riots in Los Angeles of 1992. All words were spoken by real people and are verbatim from those interviews" (p. 4). Smith refers to the actors of this play's real people as "cultural workers" and encourages them to research the historic events and the specific people they portray, paying particular attention to the lines as written, including all "uh"s, incomplete sentences, and phrase repetitions: "The theory of the play is that an actor has the ability to walk in another person's 'words,' and therefore in their hearts" (p. 7). One example of verbatim text is from Smith's interview with Reginald Denny himself:

I mean,
does anyone know
what a riot looks like?
I mean, I'm sure they do now.
I didn't have a clue of what one looked like
and
I didn't know that the verdict had come down.
I didn't pay any attention
to that,
because that
was somebody else's problem
I guess I thought
at the time.
It didn't have anything to do with me.
I didn't usually pay too much attention of what was going on in California
or in America or anything
and, uh,
I couldn't for the life of me figure out what was going on.[2]

(Smith, 1994, pp. 104–105)

Notice that Smith arranges the monologic form into a poetic-like structure. Part of this is her belief that people speak in "organic poems," but this technique also *parses* the interview text into distinct phrases of meaning where the briefest hint of a pause comes at the end of each line. Some ethnodramatists like Paul Brown (2001) attest that verbatim adaptation is not only more authentic, it also creates a sense of "character": "It is indeed the repetitions, convolutions, pauses, malapropisms, idiom, vocabulary and non-word sounds that make each character's voice as distinctive as a fingerprint" or a "voiceprint," as Brown labels it (p. xiv).

Smith (2000) further documents her career and play development process in *Talk to Me: Listening Between the Lines*. She asserts that her audio tape recorder is her "camera" because *language is identity*. During her interviews she listens for those moments when language fails her participants, "in the very moment that they have to be more creative than they would have imagined in order to communicate. It's the very moment when they have to dig deeper than the surface to find words, and at the same time, it's a moment when they want to communicate very badly" (p. 53). These portions of an interview tend to be the richest and most significant, and thus find their way onto the page and onto the stage.

Smith's productions are available on VHS and DVD, and selections from her work can be accessed on YouTube. An exceptional sample of her work can be accessed on the website TED: Ideas worth spreading at http:// www.ted.com/talks/anna_deavere_smith_s_american_character.html.

Steve Cosson, artistic director of a professional New York City theatre company called The Civilians, produces occasional ethnotheatrical or "investigative theatre" work as part of the troupe's repertoire. But unlike Anna Deavere Smith's meticulous interview methods, The Civilians' methods rely more on informal rather than documented fieldwork, as Cosson (2010) describes in the production notes for *Gone Missing*, a charming one-act ethnodrama about things people lose and find:

> Over a period of several months, the members of the company gathered stories first hand in coffee shops, at bus stops, in retirement centers. Some of the subjects were relatives, some are friends, but most were complete strangers. . . . These interviews became the text for the show, and the actors of the company play the people they've interviewed. It's important to mention that as part of this process we didn't take notes or record anything during these interviews. Whatever's spoken is committed to memory and written down later, and the words are inevitably altered somehow by the listener. So we don't identify anyone by name, as the character is not exactly them. It is an impression of them interpreted by a performer, as accurate as possible but—like all perceptions—subjective. (p. 38)

Gone Missing consists not only of monologic stories (which have quite an authentic ring of truth to them) but also original songs composed by Michael Friedman. Whether selected lyric portions are extracted verbatim from various sources or freely adapted is unknown.

Nevertheless, it is worth noting that even songs can be ethnodramatically-inspired, creating a hybrid form of Musical Ethnotheatre. Below is a sample of lyrics from the song "The Only Thing Missing," sung by the character identified as a Korean Deli Woman:

> I'll admit I have a problem holding onto things
> A sock, a book, a clock, a look, a chance.
> And the moment that a fella
> Lends me his umbrella
> It's just another doomed romance.
> I've learned to never worry about losing things.
> A car, a pin, a star, some gin, a bet.
> But when you said that we were through
> And suddenly I knew
> There was one loss I'd regret.
>
> (Cosson & Friedman, 2003, p. 46)

Ethnodramatic Adaptations of Documents and Published Accounts

Most of us are familiar with the phrase that prefaces a number of films and television specials: "based on a true story." But a critical perspective to the dramatization can make us skeptical about the "truth" of what we're watching and hearing. Some leeway and dramatic license are usually taken when autobiographical, biographical, official, and historic textual materials, whether primary or secondary sources, are adapted by a playwright. The actual words spoken by a historic person may not be documented, but his letters, diaries, and other handwritten documents give us more authentic insight into his ways of thinking. Sometimes, though, we do have access to rich historic documents as well as contemporary writings and, like interview transcript adaptation, the playwright must make decisions as to whether to adapt the material faithfully or with artistic interpretation.

Below is an excerpt from a narrative inquiry about homeless youth in pre-Hurricane Katrina New Orleans. Susan Finley and Macklin Finley (1999), mother and son and ethnographer and poet, respectively, collaborated to compose a research story based on her fieldwork and his lived experiences. Roach is a 19-year-old streetwise male who meets covertly with a drug dealer to work as his runner. This text was one source for its ethnodramatic play script adaptation, which follows.

Roach leaves the others listening and, waiting around the corner from the Bourbon Pub, he meets his dealer connection. For every hook-up he makes with a horse customer, he takes a $10 cut, whatever size the sale. "Thas' OK. There's nobody lookin' to me for more than an evening's entertainment anyways," Roach agrees with the deal. The hook-up is a short, nervous Jamaican, about 30 and going bald, who keeps looking both ways down the alley where they talk. His nerves indicate that he uses what he sells and that it's about time for a fix. He gives Roach a telephone number for his scores already neatly written out on a corner of paper. Roach maintains his usual easy-going manner with the guy and, after they've settled business, the hook-up relaxes, pulls a tight little jib from his pocket and lights it. The jib passes to Roach who fixes on the little red glow of the end. He draws deeply, makes an effort not to cough.

"You use?" the hook-up asks him, taking his turn at the joint.

"No," Roach answers, but keeps talking, "Well, I have. I don't anymore, not now." He pauses, watching the Jamaican bogart the joint a little longer. "Tell you the truth, I'm back on that shit all the time." He speaks quietly, talking more to himself than to the Jamaican.

The Jamaican reaches inside his sport coat pocket and places a tiny vial in Roach's hand. He keeps the J that he's no longer passing lighted with an occasional deep drag, and tells Roach through a rising cough, "That one's on the house. Gift to newcomers from your Neighborhood Club." He laughs at his own joke as he flicks the roach of the jib down the alley way. "Meet me here tomorrow night. Same time. Same place. We'll settle accounts then." He turns on his heel and is gone without a reply from Roach.

Roach waits to be sure the guy is really gone, then surveys the ground of the alley around him, looking for the butt-end of the jib the guy threw off. He gives the search a minute or two and then shrugs it off, leaving the alley. (p. 330)

Dialogic exchanges within a prose narrative can easily be extracted and adapted into a two-character scene for the stage, with careful consideration as to whether some dialogue passages may be superfluous and thus unnecessary for the play script. Any passage that mentions something that was talked about might inspire a new spoken line. Physical and gestural action described in the narrative can be incorporated into italicized stage directions and thus movement on stage. In conjunction with these fundamental adaptation principles, additional sources and the playwright's or director's vision might enter the picture to create more evocative staging.

Macklin Finley's (2000) haunting poetic collection, *Street Rat*, chronicles in angry verse the harsh lives of the homeless youth he befriended. This additional literary source was perused along with the Finleys' joint narrative for dramatic adaptation. "Mack," the street poet, was incorporated into the ethnodrama as an omniscient narrator and critical commentator on the action unfolding around him. Poems that related to the characters' dilemmas were extracted from his anthology and woven throughout the play, as in the following scene entitled "Needles in Veins" from Saldaña, Finley, and Finley's (2005) *Street Rat*:

> (*lights up; as MACK recites, the DEALER, a short nervous Jamaican, about 30 and going bald, enters and waits nervously; ROACH enters; they meet covertly and mime talking to each other; Cajun music fades out*)

MACK: Lobotomizing without tools,
    tubes in noses,
    paper on tongues—
    Constant escape,
    circular streets
    around and down,
    scraping gutters,
    sleeping in abandoned homes
    watchful of peripheral motion—
    Always taking chances
    With motions like
    a train.

> (*the DEALER passes ROACH a baggie of heroin packets, a cell phone, and a piece of paper with phone numbers written on it and mimes talking the directions for hook-ups*)

Needles in veins
Needles in veins
Needles in veins.
Pink blood, diluted
blood, blocking the
works blood, cramming the
artery blood. Metallic tastes
numb tongues, prickly eyes
watery walls—
unaware a thousand
tomorrows rusty machines
around like turnstile justice.

(the DEALER pulls out a joint from his pocket and lights it, drags, passes it to ROACH who also takes a hit)

Like a train rhythm—money
burning—like a train rhythm—
bondsmen and pushers
bondsmen and pushers
bondsmen and pushers—
Insane on floors—
Spinning—Hot hairy Middle-
Aged hands—Gotta pay somehow—
like a train rhythm:
Shaking at dawn
for another,
another,
another.

DEALER: *(keeps and continues to drag on the joint)* For every hook-up you make with a customer, you take a ten dollar cut, whatever size the sale.

ROACH: Thas' OK. There's nobody lookin' to me for more than an evening's entertainment anyways.

DEALER: You use?

ROACH: No. Well, I have. I don't anymore, not now. *(laughs)* Tell you the truth, I'm back on that shit all the time.

DEALER: *(reaches in his coat pocket, pulls out a packet of heroin and places it in ROACH's hand)* That one's on the house. Gift to newcomers from your Neighborhood Club. *(he laughs through his cough and flicks the joint down on the ground)* Meet me here tomorrow. Same time, same place. We'll settle accounts then. *(he turns and walks away briskly, exits)*

> *(. . . ROACH looks at the heroin, slips it in his pocket, picks up the joint the DEALER flicked to the ground, snuffs it out to save for later)*

(pp. 152–154)

Qualitative inquiry sometimes employs a technique called *triangulation*, which relies on more than one information source or type to collect, compare, and corroborate information. Triangulation might also be employed by ethnodramatists to gain a broader spectrum of perspectives or richer dimensions to the story. Jessica Blank and Erik Jensen (2004), in the trade book edition of the play script for *The Exonerated*, explain that their primary sources for monologue and dialogue originated not just from interviews but also from public records such as court transcripts, documentation stored on microfiche files, and hard copy documents such as affidavits, depositions, official letters, and police reports.

The Exonerated and *The Laramie Project* went through yet another iteration of adaptation when they were each transformed into teleplays for network made-for-television movies. The stage, television, and film art forms each have their own performance and presentation conventions, and film and television media obviously permit more visual scope and scale. But the television adaptation of *The Exonerated* maintained the reader's theatre simplicity of the off-Broadway stage work, while the television adaptation of *The Laramie Project* incorporated the magnitude of feature films. As availability permits, it is wise to read the acting edition play scripts for each of these works, then compare them to their mediated adaptations.

Original Autoethnodramatic Work

A third variant of ethnodramatic writing is the playwright's personal memories, experiences, and perceptions as sources for the dramatic text. The autobiographical—preferably performed by the writer himself or herself—now becomes *auto*ethnodramatic. As audience members, we place our faith in the autoethnotheatrical performer that what he or she tells us will indeed be true. But the writer/performer also has an ethical responsibility to tell us nothing but the truth as an understood "contract" between the actor and the audience. Unlike the experience of fictional theatre, we are not as audiences "suspending disbelief"; in autoethnodrama, we are "assuming belief."

In *Second Chair* (Saldaña, 2008), my one-man autoethnodrama about my high school band days (a commissioned performance for a Narrative Inquiry in Music Education conference), I describe my attempts to become first chair clarinetist. The play is primarily about competition but also about the marginalization and second-class status of being a lower class, overweight, gay person of color. In the excerpt below, Tammi Jo is first chair clarinetist and I am second chair; Mr. Garcia is the band director (their names are pseudonyms). Notice the stage directions' prompts for the actor to assume a different character voice when needed. One-person autoethnodramas sometime include the solo actor portraying multiple roles when significant characters enter the story.

JOHNNY: Now, Tammi Jo and I were actually quite good friends. We had been sitting next to each other as first and second chair for almost a year already, and we would often joke and laugh—quietly of course, while Mr. Garcia worked with or *(snickers)* yelled at the brass and percussion sections. And since I was also involved with high school theatre at the time, and quite the closeted drama queen, Tammi Jo and I made a secret pact: as soon as I would win the Academy Award for best actor, she would win the Nobel Prize for medicine.

She was the genius of our school. You know her kind: straight A-pluses on every report card, first on the honor roll, reading Charles Darwin's *Origin of the Species* without being required to, and eventually becoming valedictorian of our graduating class.

She was smart. And skinny—thin as a rail! Me?

(rises)

My top weight in high school was 310 pounds.

(to audience members who may be reacting to that)

No, really. I was so large that my mom had to custom-sew a new pair of pants for my band uniform because there were none in stock that fit me. Boy, did she jump all over me for that—as she stuffed me with those potato, egg, and flour tortilla tacos.

(as his mother, in a thick Hispanic dialect)

"Aye, Johnny, you're too fat!"

(normal voice)

And, because it had probably been drilled into her, it was also drilled into me:

(as his mother)

"¡Aye, Juanito, mejicanos son pendejos!"

(pause; normal voice)

Growing up, I was frequently called "stupid" by my mother.

(pause)

Fat *and* stupid. Needless to say, my self-esteem issues were pretty raw back then.

(pp. 181–182)

Alecky Blythe, an autoethnodramatic playwright and performer, discloses in some of her onstage work the research process as well as the product: "I was ... letting the audience in behind the scenes and involving them in a way that they weren't used to. This technique of showing the audience how the play was made helped a great deal in gaining their trust" (Hammond & Steward, 2008, p. 89). Ethnodramas needn't always include the backstage or offstage accounts of a play's origins, but whether in the script itself, through a program note, or from promotional publicity, somehow the audience must be made aware that what they are about to watch is nonfictional.

Intriguing one-person autoethnodramas have been written that range from breast cancer survivorship to difficult teaching experiences in inner-city schools. Performance artists such as Tim Miller draw from their own personal experiences and cultural backgrounds as the basis for their some-times-absurdist yet reality-based work. Noted celebrities such as Elaine Stritch, Spalding Gray, and John Waters have also developed one-person shows that are unabashedly autobiographical for stage performance, though they most likely did not label their preparatory work "research." And the genre of *autoethnography* has developed rich prose narratives in print that almost read as one-person play scripts. With a few minor adjustments, some can be transformed easily into extended monologues for the stage.

All of these variants do raise some interesting questions to ponder: When does written autobiographical or autoethnographic work become auto*ethnodramatic*? When the text meets certain content and dramatic format conditions? When the work is mounted on a stage and performed live in front of an audience? I am a theatre artist by training and my understanding of the term *performance* has specific parameters, unlike its eclectic use today across several disciplines (Saldaña, 2006). As traditional and conventional (if not conservative) as it may seem to you, I do not identify anything in print—even a play script—as a performance. Nor do I consider someone seated in a chair, sitting behind a table, reading aloud poorly from a written text a performance—even if he or she declares at the beginning of the paper, "My work is a performance." To me, only live or electronically mediated embodied work, with thoughtfully crafted quality and artistic form presented in front of others serving as an audience, merits itself as performance.

Collective Creation of Ethnodrama—Devised Work

A fourth variant on the development of ethnodramatic work is generally called *devising*. This is the collection of empirical materials by a company of actors under a facilitator/director's guidance. The theme is selected be-

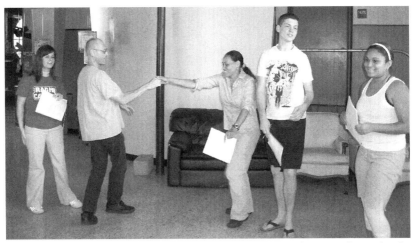

Figure 1.1. Actors in rehearsal for Keith Dorwick and John Patrick Bray's ethnodrama, *Dancing with the Virus* at Cité Des Arts, 2006. Production supported with funds from the Acadiana Center for the Arts and the Lafayette Consolidated Government.

forehand or negotiated by the company according to their or the community's interests. The material is explored by the ensemble's members for dramatic adaptation into monologic forms, and/or improvised to generate dialogic renditions. Improvisational exploration can lead to representations and presentations of the major findings through choral speaking, found poetry, dance, song, and other performative modalities. For example, Emily Freeman and Leah Page, two theatre teaching artists, work with high school students during semester-long residencies to facilitate devised work. After a series of ensemble-building activities, they progress to a brainstorming session that generates a list of topics that interest or concern the students and their communities. (Freeman and Page remark that teenage pregnancy is a frequent subject raised by adolescents.) The group debates and eventually votes on one topic to explore, yet the theme can be a broad one such as "scars" (e.g., physical, emotional, psychological). The adult facilitators encourage students to think before they choose the final subject, "Which topic has the strongest stories?"

Once the core topic has been selected, the group brainstorms further about the subtopics, phrases, images, and other ideas suggested. Next, specific individuals and communities that may have relevance to the topic are listed (for example, for the concept of scars, these communities may include people with tattoos, burn victims, abuse survivors, and so on). Then, possible interview questions are formulated by the students—for example, "What kinds of physical scars might you have?" and "What's the story behind that scar?"

The students then practice interviewing each other in pairs with digital voice recorders to learn basic interaction techniques such as listening attentively, affirming, encouraging, supporting, and so on. They also learn note-taking and transcription techniques and are taught to look for "golden moments" that arise during the practice interview. These moments are particular words, phrases, or even gestures from the experience that seem to stand out and merit documenting in a theatrical way. For example, a participant may be asked, "If an emotional scar had a physical appearance, what would it look like?" The participant might reply "It looks like a heart with a jagged line through it" as she makes a quick zigzag motion with her finger. The "golden moment" for the interviewer is the zigzag gesture, which is then repeated over and over as a way to embody—to perform—an emotional scar.

The group negotiates a standardized interview protocol of specific questions to ask all participants so they can be thematically linked during the rehearsal and devising process. They then learn how to schedule an interview and manage the contract that is signed between the interviewers and participants. Freeman and Page recommend that high school students work in pairs when interviewing others for comfort and security. The adult facilitators also note that one of the students who interviews a particular individual will most likely portray that individual on stage if his or her material is chosen for dramatization.

During the devising rehearsal process, students share their "golden moments" and interview experiences with each other to explore common themes and ideas for dramatization and adaptation. Some portions of the research may be developed into verbatim monologues or joined into composite narratives as poems. Some moments may be combined for realization through movement or dance. Everything is eventually assembled and plotted into a format that represents a revue or performance collage of the research. The adult co-facilitators serve as directors and *dramaturgs* (i.e., playwriting mentors) for the students as they explore how to transform their research from page to stage.

Several excellent books are available that explain the devising process with an acting company (e.g., Weigler, 2001), and Bowles (1997) and Bailey (2010) document their recommended methods of working with gay/lesbian street youth and disabled youth, respectively. The best title that illustrates the connections between research and theatre through devising is Joe Norris's (2009) *Playbuilding as Qualitative Research: A Participatory Arts-Based Approach*. One of the projects with his university company of actors in drama education involved power and its negative uses among adolescents:

> For our scene on sexual pressures we went into our data-collection phase with a product/form in mind . . . and we wanted to demonstrate the barrage of messages young teens receive about sex. A "quote collage" of comments that pressure adolescents would be a useful form.
>
> On file cards we listed a large number of comments on sexuality that we recalled hearing. . . . [We] looked at statements for and against premarital activity. We also looked for pro and con statements from both teens and adults. (p. 94)

Norris then explains how the characters representing teens, their peers, and adults would be caught in a "verbal tug of war." He also notes that during the rehearsal phase "through the improvisation, other phrases and insights emerged. The improvisation itself was a form of data generation and collection" (p. 95). Below is a scene from *What's the Fine Line?*, their "touring research" production to secondary schools:

MALE PEER GROUP: Do it. Go on and do it. . . .

FEMALE PEER GROUP: Yeah, everyone's doing it.

MALE PEER GROUP: You're a nerd if you don't.

MALE TEEN: Yeah, the guys will finally respect me.

FEMALE TEEN: Do I really want to do this?

MALE & FEMALE PEER GROUP: *(chant softly)* Do it. Do it. Do it.

FEMALE TEEN: I'd like to but . . .

MALE TEEN: I want to but . . .

FEMALE TEEN: Maybe, but what would mom and dad say?

FEMALE ADULT: It's wrong.

MALE ADULT: It's natural, but make sure you use protection.

FEMALE ADULT: It's dirty.

FEMALE ADULT & MALE PEER GROUP: *(chant softly twice)* It's dirty. It's wrong. Use protection.

MALE TEEN: I don't want to, but . . .

FEMALE TEEN: No, but I do want to kiss him.

MALE TEEN: What if she thinks I'm chicken if I don't?

FEMALE TEEN: What if he thinks I don't like him if I don't?

MALE PEER GROUP: Virgin, Virgin, Virgin.

FEMALE ADULT: Tramp. Slut.

FEMALE PEER GROUP: He's a girly man.

MALE ADULT: Show women some respect.

MALE TEEN: What should I do?

MALE ADULT: Son, we should talk. *(pause)* Later.

FEMALE TEEN: What should I do?

MALE PEER GROUP: Do it or you'll lose him.

MALE & FEMALE ADULT: Read a book.

MALE & FEMALE PEER GROUP: We wish we could do it.

MALE & FEMALE TEEN: Who can we talk to?

FEMALE ADULT: You're not old enough.

MALE ADULT: 16 is a good age.

MALE TEEN: I'm 14.

FEMALE TEEN: I'm 14.

FEMALE PEER GROUP: Wait for marriage.

MALE ADULT: Sex is natural, let them go.

MALE TEEN: What if she gets pregnant?

FEMALE TEEN: What if I get pregnant?

(pp. 97–99)

Jo Carson (2009), oral historian and dramatist, succinctly sums up the ethnodramatic writing process thusly:

> First, the [transcripts] you will read come from real people and real oral histories, but oral histories are people's memories, and memory is a notoriously bad historian. What is caught in memory is another kind of truth besides the facts, often just as valid.
>
> Second: a few of the [plays] began with two or three lines in an oral history about something else besides the story, and the digression was compelling enough that I made something of it that surprised everybody.
>
> Or often, I have condensed twenty or thirty pages of rambles into two or three minutes of cogent story.
>
> Or, I have combined different people's stories to make a more interesting piece for the stage.
>
> Or, most likely, some combination of all of the above. (p. 6)

Ethnodrama's Purposes

The preceding examples of ethnodramas profiled suggest a range of purposes to the genre. Devised work, for example, can have an *educational* or *pedagogical* agenda, teaching young people as participants how to research social life, and how to artistically shape that research for public performance. Ethnodrama can also have a *social awareness* agenda, making adults and young people as performers and audiences attuned to the issues that impact their lives and communities. Ethnodramatist Emily Mann and others provide important *historic* or *ethnographic documentation* in much of their ethnodramatic work, and create space and time for *marginalized voices to be heard*. Autoethnodrama provides a *public forum for the individual* who feels that his or her story must be told in a theatrical way. Anna Deavere Smith and The Tectonic Theater Project hope that constructive community *reflexivity and dialogue* can emerge among audiences after viewing their productions. Many of these playwrights also maintain explicit *social justice* or *social change* agendas, hoping that their events serve as cautionary tales for the public to never let the inequities portrayed in their plays ever happen again. Though some may not wish to acknowledge this, if the professional theatre explores ethnodramatic productions in their seasons, they must also maintain a *commercial* agenda that produces work with broad audience appeal for sufficient box office revenue. Fortunately, quality ethnotheatrical work with its risk-taking approaches can provide audiences and creators with an intellectually and emotionally satisfying *aesthetic experience*.

Figure 1.2. The reader's theatre cast of the ethnodrama, *Breaking the Silence* by Cheryl L. Kaplan. Photo by Cheryl L. Kaplan.

Ackroyd & O'Toole (2010) in *Performing Research: Tensions, Triumphs and Trade-Offs of Ethnodrama*, offer a provocative research-based rationale for the genre:

> Re-creating a research site through performance makes particularly good sense from a post-structuralist perspective. The phenomena of human behaviour are so complex, so dynamic, so protean and so negotiable, involving the ongoing lives of the subjects and the shifting and variable meanings made out of these by the observers. So a form of reportage that maintains all the dimensions of the original interaction or observation can perhaps provide a valuable holding form. (p. 4)

Overall, the purpose of ethnodrama and ethnotheatre is *to progressively advance its source participants, creators, body of dramatic literature, readers, audiences, and the broader communities they involve, to new and richer domains of social and artistic meaning*. Both the social and artistic are necessary. You can have an outstanding ethnodramatic play script about a riveting social issue, but if it's poorly mounted and performed, audiences will be unlikely to care about its content. And, you can have an outstanding production company with first-rate actors, but if the content of their script has little to no socially conscious merit and artistic quality, then the purposes of ethnotheatre are all for naught.

Ethnodrama's Potential

This leads to a conundrum about ethnodrama's playwrights and their playwriting. The academic world has probably produced more ethnodramas than the commercial world, but the latter's play scripts are much better as dramatic literature. Jessica Blank and Erik Jensen were not criminal justice majors, sociologists, or social workers when they researched and wrote *The Exonerated*. They were actors with a strong sense of social consciousness. Their theatrical knowledge gave them an insider's edge when it came time to adapt the stories of six exonerated people for their play. They also had the skills and resources necessary to try out and fine-tune their work as it progressed through workshop development and rehearsals. Of course, having a professional director, actors, and designers for an off-Broadway New York City production certainly gave the effort a sense of occasion and increased the likelihood of artistic as well as commercial success. But the novelty for audiences, quite frankly, was that the play was about real people and their real stories of injustice.

But what really "changed," as ethnodrama scholars and theatre practitioners sometime claim happens when audiences see impacting theatre? Certainly the lives of the exonerated featured in the play, the playwrights, and perhaps some of the production company members may have changed in minor to major ways for the better as a result of their participation. But how might individual audience members have been changed—if at all? Did some feel motivated to investigate and intercede in suspicious court cases and convictions, while others saw it as nothing more than a good evening's entertainment? Short of surveying or interviewing them immediately after they'd seen the production and with a follow-up inquiry months later, we will never know.

Ethnodramatists without a theatre background need to be aware that research in the field of general mainstream theatre suggests that audience change after viewing just one theatrical performance is somewhat possible but most likely minimal. Certainly, it depends on what type of play is shown and its relevance to the spectators' lives. But too many variables exist in audience analysis that factor into the equation: acting quality, audience member alertness, audibility and decoding of language, seating proximity to the stage, gender and age of the protagonist and audience member, physical attractiveness of the actors, amount of previous theatre viewing experience, perceived similarities with characters and action, an individual's capacity to sympathize and empathize, and so on.

Seasoned theatre practitioners have learned how to manipulate bodies, voices, light, color, spectacle, music, and other theatrical elements to increase the *likelihood* of achieving a certain audience effect. And seasoned playwrights know of certain conventions and well-documented "tricks of the trade" for script writing that *may* affect audience members in a particular way to evoke a laugh or tug at the heart. Simply acknowledge that the theatrical medium is a venture which may have a well-intentioned social change agenda and goals by its artists, but there is no guarantee that the work will actively and positively change each and every audience member who attends the production. After four decades as a theatre practitioner and audience member, I've learned that the *art* comes first; the *message* comes second.

Ethnodramatists need to remember that *"Theatre's primary goal is to entertain—to entertain ideas as it entertains its spectators*. With ethnographic performance, then, comes the responsibility to create an entertainingly informative experience for an audience, one that is aesthetically sound, intellectually rich, and emotionally evocative" (Saldaña, 2005, p. 14).

Social change is an admirable goal, and we should never give that up as citizens of the world. But I respectfully ask you to be realistic about your expectations when it comes to ethnotheatrical representation and presentation. I myself have been admittedly guilty of producing creaky ethnotheatre now and then. But I've also had a few artistic successes, and my actors and a few audience members testified that they were indeed changed for the better through the production experience. I have been aesthetically "wow-ed" and charged up from just a handful of live theatre productions, DVDs, and play scripts. Most times after I've seen what I personally felt was a mediocre attempt at ethnotheatre, I was polite and collegial to the company and supportive of their efforts. But the event and whatever outcomes they intended were soon forgotten. If I am not motivated toward social action, I hope, at the very least, to be artistically satisfied. Ultimately, the final arbiter of change rests with the individual audience member.

Bad Ethnodramatic Scholarship and Artistry

One of the major knowledge deficits of nontheatre academics is that most are unacquainted with the majority of published ethnodramatic play scripts available from commercial play leasers for the arts and entertainment industry. This is not due to lazy scholarship or an unwillingness to learn what's available; it's simply a matter of insider knowledge bases and time limitations. It's difficult to keep up with the vast amounts of literature being published every day—even within one's own academic discipline. This book references some of the most accessible published titles in ethnodrama, and I hope you have both the time and resources to read them. You become a better playwright by reading exemplary scripts, and Dani Snyder-Young (2010) wisely reminds scholars that we could learn a thing or two from the high quality aesthetic, literary, and production standards of professional theatre artists who have staged award-winning, internationally recognized ethnodramatic work.

Those in academia in nontheatre subject areas such as education, sociology, communication, health care, and so on, sometimes stay close to their respective field's peer reviewed research literature found in journals, handbooks, and other scholarly ventures (see Appendix B). There is certainly nothing wrong with that. But when it comes to accessing materials about ethnodrama, most will stay within what they may find published within their own or allied disciplines, or limit themselves to accessing scholarship from the field of *performance studies*, thinking that this automatically means theatre as well. Performance studies and theatre certainly share a body of theoretical and critical thought, but the practical literature of theatre is where you'll find pragmatic guidance in such areas as playwriting, directing, acting, design, and other production matters.

As a theatre artist coming into the very welcoming field of qualitative inquiry and its inclusive colleagues, I am sometimes leery of what I perceive as unhealthy, incestuous inbreeding when it comes to their citations of the scholarly literature related to performance studies. I see the same names over and over again—writers who have given us superior foundations for performance in its broadest sense, but who have little to offer when it comes to the mechanics of writing an ethnodrama. I have insider knowledge of decades of theatre practice, but I am also humble enough to acknowledge that I do not possess the intricacies of such disciplines as sociology, communication, and psychology. Nevertheless, I wish that my colleagues would recognize that performance studies is a discipline that has limited advice to offer when it comes to mounting an ethnotheatrical production. Read a playwriting textbook. See professional theatre productions. Meet and collaborate with reputable theatre practitioners. Don't just write *about* performance, write a play script.

Tara Goldstein, one of the field's most published ethnodramatists in education, grew exponentially as an artist after she voluntarily enrolled in a university playwriting course. Performance studies scholar Tami Spry is an outstanding performer because she reflects thoughtfully on both theory *and* practice. Jim Mienczakowski brought years of theatre production work to clinical settings for brave and innovative ethnodramatic explorations of mental health care. Criminologist and social advocate Martin Glynn (of the U.K.) works with and rigorously researches black youth and men's experiences as solid foundations for his ethnodramatic adaptations. And Norman K. Denzin (1997), one of the world's most renowned research methodologists, champions ethnodrama for social science as "the single, most powerful way for ethnography to recover yet interrogate the meanings of lived experience" (pp. 94–95).

I applaud (please excuse the pun) those scholars who venture into ethnodramatic projects. They are progressive and willing to listen to the artist within themselves to risk how social science research can be represented and presented through theatrical modalities. But I notice that it's quite difficult for some who've been indoctrinated into the culture of academia with its expectations of rigor, APA manual format guidelines, and sometimes vicious peer review processes, to stop thinking like a social scientist and start thinking like an artist.

More mediocre plays are written than superior ones. I've read my fair share of bad plays—and admittedly, I've written my fair share of them, too. Not everything penned is destined to become a classic. But there are some principles to be aware of to keep you from descending into the reject pile. One of these is the "talking heads" play—a common flaw of novice playwrights who use the dramatic medium to advocate for their philosophical attitude, value, and belief systems rather than composing a character-driven story. I do not wish to publicly embarrass anyone by quoting a bad example from an actual play script, so I've constructed one that typifies some of the worst playwriting I've read by academics:

(two scholars sit in a faculty lounge grading papers)

SCHOLAR #1: Our graduate students today seem to be having a difficult time grasping the notions of post-structuralism—this wasn't an issue with our earlier classes.

SCHOLAR #2: Indeed. As Foucault (1969) writes, truth and meaning are contextual to time.

SCHOLAR #1: Yes. The discursive traditions should be critically deconstructed for their historic and contemporary applications.

SCHOLAR: #2: But how can humans ever know the real truth? Our ontological and epistemological paradigms in this post-post-modern era …

SCHOLAR #1: If that is indeed our era.

SCHOLAR #2: True. Wait—I just said "true." How can I claim what is "truth" anyway? (Michel Foucault enters the room; the scholars are blinded by his brilliance)

FOUCAULT: Enchanté!

SCHOLARS #1 and #2: Who are you?!

FOUCAULT: I'm Michel Foucault, and I've come to set the record straight about post-structuralism, oui?

A play is not a journal article. They are two completely different genres of writing, each with its own distinctive traditions, elements, and styles. I am usually the kind of mentor who encourages people to find their own creative direction, but I will be quite unwavering on this point: Don't even think about including any footnotes or citations of the related literature in your play script. A play is not a journal article; you do not need references after the play is over. If the play can't speak for itself, then you either need to rewrite the script until it does, or find a more accommodating literary genre to say what you have to say. You may also be in trouble if you envision your stage setting to include a lectern, or if the action is set in a university classroom or faculty office. *A play is not a journal article. So stop thinking like a social scientist and start thinking like an artist.*

Good Ethnodramatic Scholarship and Artistry

Margarete Sandelowski, Frank Trimble, Elizabeth K. Woodard, and Julie Barroso (2006) collaborated to create one of the most qualitatively rigorous *and* artistically successful ethnodramas in print and on DVD, titled *Maybe Someday: Voices of HIV-Positive Women.* Interviews and an exhaustive literature review served as source material to develop documentary narrative and composite monologues of HIV-positive women's experiences. In one scene, a narrator's voice-over informs health care workers (one of the intended audiences for the work):

> Some women struggle with issues beyond their HIV status. These include the extra stigma and discrimination connected with being a woman, being a minority woman, and being a mother. Sometimes women are looked down upon because people make assumptions that their illness is related to drug use, prostitution, promiscuity, poverty, or homelessness. (p. 1363)

Maybe Someday profiles how the themes of stigma associated with HIV status influence and affect women's perceptions, as in this monologue, spoken by an actor to an off-camera interviewer:

WOMAN #4 (African American): People talk about minority this and minority that. Well, let me tell you somethin'. You try bein' a Black woman with HIV and see how far you get. See the men, well, they HIV *victims.* You know, they may face some discrimination, but mostly there's concern and money and support. Then there's the people who caught HIV, you know, because they was doin' somethin' they shouldn't been doin' and got "caught," you know? Yeah, them's mostly minority women, or poor women, or women with too many children, whatever "too many" is. I am sick of that shit! I am physically sick and then I have to handle all that other shit on top of it. It's too much. It's just too much. So what if a HIV person ain't always been good, or maybe is still doin' some of that junk? Sure, a woman needs to change her life if it hurts her and maybe other people, but we have all been hurt by this disease and need to help make things better. But I keep doin' the best I can. Have to. Just have to. Because . . . my children, you know? You

don't know me. No one knows me. But my children . . . they know
me. And I want to keep it that way. (p. 1364)

Maybe Someday succeeds as ethnodrama for two primary reasons:
(1) the subject matter was rigorously researched by Sandelowski,
Woodard, and Barroso; and (2) the research was adapted and scripted
by a sensitive and seasoned theatre artist, Frank Trimble. You do not
have to be a trained theatre artist to write ethnodrama and produce
ethnotheatre, but collaborative ventures between social scientists and
theatre practitioners are more likely to produce higher quality research-
based work on stage.

Securing Participant Permissions

A publicly performed ethnodrama is subject to legal scrutiny, as are
all performed and published works, regardless of content, purpose, or
venue. Thus, it is legally and ethically necessary to secure some type of
permission from people you interview or observe if you plan on adapting their words into ethnodramatic play formats, and especially if you
mount those works for public performance or publish the play scripts.

If you work in a setting such as a university that has Institutional Review Boards (IRBs), check with their offices about ethnodramatic pro-
tocols. Some institutions may (wrongly) perceive ethnotheatre as strictly an artistic venture, not as social and behavioral research, and thus
will exempt the project from their review and oversight. But educate
them, nevertheless, on the genre, what types of data collection methods you plan to employ, and how participants will be represented and
presented in public performance and in print. The IRB can then evalu-
ate whether the project merits a formal submission for board review
and can even offer some methodological and legal guidance. When in
doubt, apply to an IRB for any ethnotheatrical venture (see Appendix A
for a sample consent form).

Institutions such as independent theatre production companies
and individual freelance artists not bound by IRB regulations may
have an easier time securing participant permissions but are still liable
for how their research is represented in a script and presented on stage.
Permissions can range from being as simple as a verbal understanding before a conversation or formal audiotaped interview begins, to
as complex as a formal attorney-composed contract with spaces for
required signatures from the interviewer and interviewee, especially
if any of the parties is a minor. We live in a litigious society and the

potential for libel and slander is always present. When in doubt, consult with an office of legal counsel to protect yourself and your work. Regardless of what type of permission form or written agreement you write, include a section that specifies that the empirical materials may be transformed into dramatic format then performed for live audiences, video recorded during performance, and published in journals or books or as a separate play script.

If you are writing your own autoethnodrama, you of course needn't secure your own permission to tell your own story publicly. But if you make references to other living people or actual settings in your story, you should replace the names with pseudonyms to protect their identities and to keep yourself from encountering any problematic legal issues. If you need to use actual people's names, or if the content of what you say about them is substantive or may be interpreted negatively, it is best to run the play script past them (if possible) for their review, signed consent, and release.

One subtopic that segues between the legal and ethical is ownership of the ethnodramatic work. Decisions between the artists and participants regarding copyright of the play and the distribution of any financial profit from the production should be negotiated beforehand and included in any written releases. These are slippery matters with no specific answers or concrete guidance. Ethnodramatist Paul Brown (2010) advocates that each verbatim theatre project's ownership issues should be negotiated on a case-by-case basis between the parties concerned.

The Ethics of Representation and Presentation

After legal matters have been addressed, one of the most contested tensions of writing ethnodrama is the ethics of representation and presentation—in other words, the moral and authentic use of participant materials in the form of interview transcripts, field notes, writings, and so forth as the basis for dramatic adaptation and performance. I often muse that with all the reflexive angsting, fretting, and hand wringing over such matters these days, it's amazing researchers ever get anything written at all. I sometimes want to ask my colleagues who seem, from what I perceive, obsessed over these matters, "What part of 'But first, do no harm' do you not understand?" Rather than needlessly navel gaze about these issues and paralyze yourself into stalemate or writer's block over whether you *should* write an ethnodrama, or whether you are or aren't representing your participants fairly and ethically, collaborate instead with your participants on *how* it can best be done.

If you know during fieldwork that one of the outcomes of your study will consist of a theatrical production, devote some interview time with participants to that portion of the project. Inform them of your performance goals and ask them such pertinent questions as:

- What is important for me to remember or to include about you as I write the play?
- What do you *not* want included or mentioned in the play?
- What concerns you about your words and actions being dramatized on the stage and performed by someone else?
- What do you hope audiences might take away with them after seeing the production?
- What ideas about the script or its performance on stage do you have at this time for me to consider?
- Let's discuss what we should do just in case there are any disagreements about the script that might come up before or during rehearsals.

The final discussion topic above might be perceived by some as a door some are afraid to open, or as a bridge not to be crossed until you might come to it. I myself prefer to address these issues during the early stages of ethnodramatic fieldwork because it lets the participants know that they are an active part of the artistic process. It also frames me as a playwright for what might be considered contested passages of monologue or dialogue as I write them. The conundrum for an ethnodramatist is to balance the authentic with the artistic. It is also a matter of perception. An action or sentence I feel is nonproblematic may be interpreted by a participant as a troublesome issue.

For my ethnodramatic projects, I give a copy of all play script drafts to my participants before and during rehearsals to keep them apprised of the work in progress. When possible, I send video recordings of rehearsals to key participants if they are unable to attend them live. The participants function as dramaturgs and offer me valuable feedback on my script's accuracy and how they are (or would prefer to be) represented in the play. Some have even provided me with some wonderful staging ideas such as appropriate background music choices.

I have yet to read *any* backstage, behind the scenes account by *any* ethnodramatic playwright that didn't make some mention of struggling about what to leave in, what to leave out, "tweaking" the verbatim text, creating composite characters, fictionalizing to some degree, and so on. Such tensions are not anomalies but givens of the ethnotheatrical enterprise. The resolution is not to shy away from these matters but *how* you deal with them.

Cautionary Notes

Some ethnotheatrical productions are not without controversy. The nature of being "real" with what we publicly perform may push the buttons of certain audience members. I believe that no ethnodrama is intentionally written to shock or offend, but a few projects that began in good faith were interpreted as inappropriate by selected constituents. Below are just three examples.

First, Cozart et al. (2003) described a multiyear evaluation research project presented as a performance ethnography to key personnel (teachers, administrators, artists, and so on) of a North Carolina arts integration project called the "A+ Program." Space does not permit a full description of the production, but it was the negative audience response that merits discussion here. The play was previewed for a small audience of professionals at an American Educational Research Association (AERA) conference where it was well received. But when it was performed for the stake-holding constituency, the research team observed in North Carolina that

> Some of the A+ Fellows' additional comments were critical of the performance. . . : (1) some were unsettled by the suggestion that the implementation of A+ was flawed; (2) some were disturbed that a prior audience at AERA had seen what they considered to be a negative portrayal of A+; (3) some maintained that the research team had misunderstood the A+ Program; (4) some challenged our methodology, suggesting our misunderstanding of the program was the result of having spent inadequate time in schools; and (5) some critiqued the quality of the performance itself and offered to help make it more polished.
>
> The critical nature of some of the comments made it difficult for [the researchers/performers] to engage in conversation with the A+ Fellows. Their responses were unexpected, and we were shocked. In our responses back to them, we spent considerable time in a defensive posture attempting to explain our reasoning and restating our purposes. At the same time, we demonstrated our willingness to listen to their interpretations and to reconsider our own. Afterwards, we stopped at a restaurant on the way home to process the interaction and console each other. . . . Later we found out that the Fellows argued about our performance for the rest of their weekend meeting. Some found that it resonated with their experience, while others remained convinced that we had misunderstood and misrepresented the program. (pp. 60–61)

As a second example, my ethnodramatic adaptation of Harry F. Wolcott's (2002) "sneaky kid" trilogy dramatized his professional then sexual relationship with a nineteen-year-old drifter. The original pieces themselves were controversial, setting off debate within the research community about the ethics of Wolcott's involvement with a young man who eventually became emotionally unstable and violent due to emergent paranoid schizophrenia. When the trilogy was performed as a keynote for an international research methods conference, several audience members at a reflection session the next day reacted furiously to the ethical issues the play raised and the "abuse of power" exhibited by the ethnodrama's central protagonist. Other audience members perceived those who took offense to the play as people struggling with their own personal histories of sexual abuse and their unresolved emotions triggered by the performance. And still others simply saw the play as a well-produced, poignant love story that ended tragically for its characters.

As a third example (with a happy ending), the Wilton (Connecticut) High School 2007 production of *Voices in Conflict* gained national media attention after a school administration official cancelled the performance before it was scheduled to open. The perceived controversy centered on the play's content—authentic yet mostly negative testimonies from U.S. military service members about the Iraq war, collected from various sources. The professional theatre community and several major celebrities, perceiving this as a censorship issue, rallied in support of the educational company and offered both financial and venue support for the play. The production was eventually mounted in a prestigious venue and the script was even published through a national play leaser for other theatre companies to perform (Dickinson, 2008).

What these three ethnotheatrical stories share in common is unexpected response and reaction to the "realities" portrayed on stage. They are also testimony to the strong influences and affects on audience members, each one with a particular set of background experiences and values, attitudes, and beliefs. No two people see and hear the same play and performance. What an ethnodramatic playwright might think will be well received may be condemned by others because it is either "too" real or misrepresents their personal perceptions of reality and thus truth. Max Stafford Clark's observation that a verbatim play "flashes your research nakedly" means that some readers and audience members may be intrigued and even titillated with ethnodramatic revelation, while others may take offense to the disrobement and baring of life's messiness on stage.

As a writer I sometimes struggle with freedom of expression versus tactful discretion. I self-censor myself at the computer keyboard and monitor when I feel my audience may react negatively to what I've written—sometimes in anger or in haste. But when it comes to ethnodrama, there is one principle I've learned the hard way and now always try to hold onto: participants first, playwrights second, and audiences third. This means that no matter what I as a playwright or director want to see and hear on stage based on my ethnographic fieldwork, the participants' desires for how *they* wish to be represented and presented on stage take precedence. No playwright wants an audience to hate his or her work, but an ethnodramatist's first responsibility is to the people he or she interviewed and observed. The second responsibility is to one's self as a researcher and artist, maintaining personal integrity and standards of excellence. The audience, our third responsibility, then witnesses what the first two parties have collaborated on and becomes a group of new collaborators in the ethnotheatrical event. They will each attend to, respond, and react in ways that we may or may not be able to predict. But they are an important and essential part of the performance trinity. Without spectators, there is no purpose to theatre.

Some researchers and artists ponder, "What is our ethical responsibility toward our audiences?" I feel that my ethical responsibility as an ethnotheatrical producer is to make them aware in advance through advertising, promotion, news releases, and program notes as to what the play is about. Since I'm aware that everyone has different sensibilities and needs, I caution them if the performance includes profanity, violence, or special effects such as strobe lighting or artificial smoke that may trigger adverse physical reactions in some people. But I feel my responsibility ends there, for I cannot control or monitor what every single audience member will think and feel during the performance.

I ask you to consider this question as well: "What is the *audience's* ethical responsibility toward the production?" I have my own code of conduct as a spectator: I will support theatrical productions attempted in good faith and I will show courteous respect toward the production company during and after the performance. If I'm asked by them for my opinions about their work, I will praise what I found as significant accomplishments, and critically but tactfully express how the work could continue to develop through further rehearsals and rewrites. I also take responsibility for what I choose to attend. Audience members are not passive spectators but active consumers of art. If I don't like what's on TV, I change the channel or turn the set off. If I don't want to attend a certain play production for whatever reason, then I simply do not go. And if I do attend a live performance and I don't like what I'm watching and hearing on stage, then I try to put aside my own values for awhile to listen to what's being said. But if I cannot endure the work, then I leave the theatre. If motivated, I will contact the production company to express my specific concerns. Ethnodramatists, in collaboration with their participants, have an ethical responsibility to represent and present reality on stage as they perceive it. Audience members, in turn, have an ethical responsibility to take personal responsibility for their own reactions and responses to the production. See Madison (2005) for a more extensive discussion on ethical issues in performance ethnography.

In summary, this chapter introduced just a few fundamentals of ethnodramatic writing and ethnotheatrical production. The next chapter explores the researcher *and* artist within you to transform qualitative work from page to stage.

RECOMMENDED READINGS

Arts-Based Research

These sources provide excellent introductions to art forms as modalities for qualitative research representation and presentation.

Bagley, Carl, and Mary Beth Cancienne (Eds.). (2002). *Dancing the Data.* New York: Peter Lang. This chapter collection with an accompanying demonstration CD-ROM offers a glimpse into unique approaches to arts-based research.

Barone, Tom, and Elliot W. Eisner. (2012). *Arts Based Research.* Thousand Oaks, CA: Sage. Two pioneers of the genre offer their perspectives on the purposes and aesthetics of artistic approaches to inquiry.

Cahnmann-Taylor, Melisa, and Richard Siegesmund (Eds.). (2008). *Arts-based Research in Education: Foundations for Practice.* New York: Routledge. A variety of arts-based educational researchers offer their personal ways of working in the field.

Knowles, J. Gary, and Ardra L. Cole (Eds.). (2008). *Handbook of the Arts in Qualitative Research: Perspectives, Methodologies, Examples, and Issues.* Thousand Oaks, CA: Sage. This outstanding collection provides a broad spectrum of artistic approaches in qualitative inquiry.

Leavy, Patricia (Ed.). (2009). *Method Meets Art: Arts-based Research Practice.* New York: Guilford. Case study chapters by noted contributors include rich profiles of arts-based projects with various populations.

Introductions to Ethnodrama and Related Forms

These sources provide readers with excellent theoretical and practical guidance on ethnodramatic development (also see Appendix B: A Bibliography of Academic Resources in Ethnodrama and Arts-Based Research).

Ackroyd, Judith, and John O'Toole. (2010). *Performing Research: Tensions, Triumphs and Trade-offs of Ethnodrama.* Stoke on Trent: Trentham Books. Eight case studies of ethnotheatrical projects from Australia provide a rare behind-the-scenes look at how ethnodramatic play scripts get devised and written. Editors Ackroyd and O'Toole also offer insightful commentary on ethical issues in performance ethnography.

Biewen, John, and Alexa Dilworth (Eds.). (2010). *Reality Radio: Telling True Stories in Sound.* Chapel Hill, NC: The University of North Carolina Press. Informal essays by radio documentary producers present intriguing artistic visions and backstories that can inform ethnodramatic researchers and playwrights.

Blank, Jessica, and Erik Jensen. (2005). *Living Justice: Love, Freedom, and the Making of* The Exonerated. New York: Atria Books. Blank and Jensen offer a detailed account of their research, writing, and rehearsal processes for their landmark play about six exonerated citizens.

Brown, Paul (Ed.). (2010). *Verbatim: Staging Memory & Community.* Strawberry Hills NSW, Australia: Currency Press. This series of essays provides educators and secondary school students resources for studying *The Laramie Project* and some of the most well-known verbatim plays from Australia (e.g., *Aftershocks, Minefields and Miniskirts*). Workshop ideas for creating verbatim theatre are also included.

Denzin, Norman K. (2003). *Performance Ethnography: Critical Pedagogy and the Politics of Culture.* Thousand Oaks, CA: Sage. Denzin's foundational work offers rich theoretical and critical perspectives on performance as a research modality.

Favorini, Attilio (Ed.). (1995). *Voicings: Ten Plays from the Documentary Theater.* Hopewell, NJ: Ecco Press. Favorini provides a historic overview of the genre and anthologizes such play titles as *The Investigation, Quilters,* and *Unquestioned Integrity: The Hill-Thomas Hearings.*

Forsyth, Alison, and Chris Megson (Eds.). (2009). *Get Real: Documentary Theatre Past and Present.* New York: Palgrave Macmillan. Chapters on the history, theory, and criticism of the genre examine such playwrights as Joan Littlewood, Emily Mann, and Doug Wright.

Hammond, Will, and Dan Steward (Eds.). (2008). *Verbatim Verbatim: Contemporary Documentary Theatre.* London: Oberon Books. Interviews with U.K. verbatim theatre playwrights such as Robin Soans and David Hare reveal their playwriting processes.

Kazubowski-Houston, Magdalena. (2010). *Staging Strife: Lessons from Performing Ethnography with Polish Roma Women.* Montreal: McGill-Queen's University Press. The author presents a meticulous account of her play production process based on fieldwork with oppressed women. The text includes the final script, titled *Hope.* Co-winner of the 2011 Outstanding Book Award from the International Congress of Qualitative Inquiry.

Madison, D. Soyini. (2005). *Critical Ethnography: Method, Ethics, and Performance.* Thousand Oaks, CA: Sage. Chapter 7 "Performance Ethnography" provides a solid theoretical foundation with reference to Dwight Conquergood's contributions to performance studies.

Miller, Lynn C., Jacqueline Taylor, and M. Heather Carver (Eds.). (2003). *Voices Made Flesh: Performing Women's Autobiography.* Madison, WI: University of Wisconsin Press. Performance processes and several play scripts are included from multiple contributors on feminist approaches to solo and collaborative work.

Morey, Oma. (2010). *Caring for a Loved One with Dementia: From Phenomenological Findings to Lifeworld Theatre.* Ph.D. Dissertation, Bournemouth University. Morey's meticulously detailed document illustrates how her medical research transitioned into a poignant dramatic account.

Pollock, Della (Ed.). (2005). *Remembering: Oral History Performance.* New York: Palgrave Macmillan. This collection of chapters provides readers examples of how oral history research projects transformed into performed work.

Saldaña, Johnny (Ed.). (2005). *Ethnodrama: An Anthology of Reality Theatre.* Walnut Creek, CA: AltaMira Press. This anthology presents nine examples of monologic, dialogic, and unique approaches to ethnodramatic work, written primarily by theatre artists.

Smith, Anna Deavere. (2000). *Talk to Me: Listening Between the Lines.* New York: Random House. Smith provides an eloquent account of her social agenda and ways of working to develop her performance pieces for the stage.

ENDNOTES

1. In Hammond & Steward (2008), *Verbatim Verbatim: Contemporary Documentary Theatre*, p. 51.
2. From *Twilight: Los Angeles, 1992* by Anna Deavere Smith, copyright © 1994 by Anna Deavere Smith. Used by permission of Doubleday, a division of Random House, Inc., and reprinted by permission of Anna Deavere Smith and the Watkins/Loomis Agency.

Ethnodramatics—Studio Exercises

*I've long thought that teaching and learning anthropology should
be more fun than they often are. Perhaps we should not merely
read and comment on ethnographies, but actually perform them.
. . . How, then, may this be done? One possibility may be to turn
the more interesting portions of ethnographies into playscripts, then
to act them out in class, and finally to turn back to ethnographies
armed with the understanding that comes from "getting inside the
skin" of members of other cultures. . . .*

—Victor Turner[1]

Ethnodramatics, a term coined by anthropologist Victor Turner (1982,
p. 100), explores or "workshops" fieldwork documentation through
dramatic and theatrical modalities. The academic classroom is transformed into a rehearsal studio where on-your-feet adaptations of field
notes, interview transcripts, and ethnographic narratives are improvised
and dramatized. The goals are, as Turner advocates, to come to a deeper
understanding of other cultures, plus to realize the artistic possibilities
of staging research. Through replicating participants' words and actions
and immersing yourself in their emotional worlds and values systems,
we may gain new perspectives and empathetic connections with the
various social worlds we study.

I instructed my own course in Ethnodrama and Ethnotheatre at
Arizona State University, and course readings of texts, articles, and
play scripts ranged from works by Norman K. Denzin to Anna Deavere
Smith. Viewings of ethnodramas in media format (e.g., *The Exonerated,
The Laramie Project, United 93*) were also assigned. But what happened
during class—the ethnodramatics—were some of the most intriguing
and exciting moments I've encountered as an instructor.

This chapter provides individuals in a playwriting, performance
studies, or qualitative/ethnographic research methods class some recommended studio exercises for ethnodramatic exploration. Some are
improvisational activities; others are small-scale script writing projects.
If you are an individual reader not currently enrolled in a class, I provide alternative writing exercises for you based on the content. No prior
theatre or performance experience is necessary to participate in these

activities, but I acknowledge that those without this background may feel intimidated by the risk-taking that comes from "putting yourself out there." A common phrase heard from novices to the art form goes, "The thought of doing drama scares me to death" (Wright, 1999). You needn't mindset yourself with the idea that you're "performing." What you're doing instead is staging reality—and reality is something you're already quite expert at.

As you go through these exercises, it's important that you try to represent and present the participant/characters as authentically and believably as possible. Try not to venture toward stereotypes or caricatures, or to let your nervousness provoke you to "play for laughs." The goal is not to entertain others but to capture a sense of truthfulness within yourself.

Conversational Dramatism
—Rebekah Nathan's *My Freshman Year*

Conversational dramatism is a technique for replicating verbatim talk from everyday life on the stage. The primary purpose of this exercise is to attune yourself to the seemingly mundane yet inference-laden language of informal conversation. Rebekah Nathan's (2005) ethnography, *My Freshman Year: What a Professor Learned by Becoming a Student*, serves as the primary source material for this dramatic activity.

Nathan, an anthropology professor, covertly observed undergraduate life at "AnyU" by enrolling as a student. Her fieldwork ranged from classrooms to dormitories to dining halls, and she interviewed selected students plus gathered written documentation about their ways of working and perceptions of university life. Below is an excerpt from Nathan's ethnography that describes what students (mostly underclassmen) talked about before and after their nonmajor, general studies class sessions.

> The time before and after classes, when teachers were not within earshot, was instructive. It was a time for academic and social small talk, including stories about the recent weekend, the "fun" things that were done, or how tired or "wasted" the speaker was at the moment. Academic discourse was limited to a narrow sort of mutual questioning. "Did you do the reading for today?" and "Did we have anything due today?" were both common pre-class queries. Shared complaints about the way a course was going ("I can't believe he hasn't turned back either of our last two assignments") or the prospect of the upcoming class ("I hope he doesn't do that in-class writing thing again") were also heard.

What wasn't mentioned struck me as significant. One would never hear, "Did you like that reading?" or "That paper assignment really made me think." It's not that students didn't like the reading or find the assignments provocative; it's just that these weren't acceptable or normative topics to introduce in informal conversation. When academic assignments *were* mentioned, the discourse converged on a couple of main themes. Students either talked about reactions and comparisons of evaluations received ("How did you do on that paper?" "What did you put for number 19?" "Man, what does that guy expect?") or they focused on the effort or attention given to academic assignments—usually emphasizing the lack thereof ("I mean, I didn't know what he wanted—I just guessed and b.s.-ed my way through this"; "I was down in the city for the weekend and I was fucking drunk the whole time. Wrote this paper totally wasted at three in the morning"; "I couldn't believe I got an A—I hardly studied!"). (p. 96)

Replication and Improvisation Exercise

With a partner, reminisce about the types of classes you took as a college/university freshman. Recall the before-and-after class activities, conversations, and feelings. Improvise a 30-second exchange of dialogue incorporating some of the actual quotations from the text above, and/or your own memories of the topics you may have discussed as a student. Share these improvised scenarios with a research methods class and, as a group, discuss what struck you as recurring themes or significant pieces of dialogue.

Fieldwork for Ethnodramatic Work

1. After all necessary clearances and permissions have been secured, conduct participant observation in one or two different college/university classrooms before and after the formal class session begins. Large lecture hall settings for undergraduate general studies courses work best. Document the conversations overheard among students. Compare your notes with Nathan's descriptions. In groups of two or three, improvise or script a 30–60 second exchange of dialogue that replicates or adapts what you heard. Memorize it and present it for a research methods class. As a group, discuss what was gained from recreating and observing these scenes.

2. Under a theatre director's guidance, stage and collage the individual scenes into a mosaic script that the class "performs" for a video recorder. Watch the video and discuss how the learnings from this

exercise in conversational dramatism can transfer to the playwriting and staging of an ethnodramatic text.

3. Observe other facets and settings of college/university life and dramatize slices of the everyday conversations exchanged between students. An interesting and publicly accessible way to gather empirical material is to follow two or more students talking to each other as they walk across campus, or to sit close to two or more people seated and talking in a dining area. Or, dramatize additional excerpts from Nathan's *My Freshman Year* that lend themselves to improvised or scripted work—for example, female "Dorm Talk":

> . . . almost one-third of all discussion topics reported were about boys, meeting boys, and sex. Other frequently reported topics fell into the following categories, in order of their frequency of mention:
> - bodies, bodily functions, and body image
> - relationships and relationship problems
> - one's childhood, personal history, and future
> - TV, movies, games, and entertainment
> - alcohol and drug experiences
>
> Together these six topics represented three-quarters of all the topics reportedly discussed among friends. (p. 98)

If you are an individual not enrolled in a research methods class, observe and document in play script format 30–60 seconds of natural talk you overhear in various public settings such as restaurants, stores, and malls. Develop a series of vignettes collected together as a short piece entitled, "Scenes from a _____ (Starbucks, Wal-Mart, and so on)."

The Presentation of Self—and Others

The purpose of this exercise is to attune yourself to the varieties of ethos (values, attitudes, and belief systems) in people. How each individual acts, reacts, and interacts with others depends on his or her identity, worldview, cultural conditioning, personal experiences, and other complex factors. Rather than venture here into extended discussions about the sociology, psychology, and anthropology of human behavior, simply explore the activities described below and discuss with classmates how your experiences and observations might transfer into ethnodramatic character development, representation, and presentation on the stage.

Casting the Improvisation

Reflect on and identify three actual and *specific* people whom you know very well; at least one of them should be the opposite gender from your own. Some people chosen, such as a relative or former teacher, may have been involved in your life long ago and may now be deceased.

Select:

A. a good/best friend;

B. an immediate family member or close relative such as a spouse, sibling, parent, child, grandparent, and so on; and

C. a particular teacher from your past

Each student writes down the names of the three individuals, their gender, and their approximate age. Students should choose an approximate age at the time they best knew the person. They then jot down at least three to five descriptive adjectives or phrases for each person that best capture their personalities and/or physical characteristics. For example, my three individuals for this exercise might consist of:

A. Jacob, best friend, male, late 50s: easy-going, private, slow moving due to excessive weight

B. Sandy, my niece, female, late 30s: mother of four children, energetic, street-wise, loud, loving and giving

C. Mrs. Markinson, high school English teacher, female, late 20s: pretty, has her act together, no-nonsense, sharp as a tack, passionate about literature

For the ethnodramatic exercises below, there is no need to stereotype or exaggerate when playing someone of the opposite gender. The goal is to capture the essence and essentials of these actual people, not to parody the portrayal of the opposite sex.

Embodying the Characters Through Movement

After the class has had sufficient time to write character sketches, with all students seated, the facilitator prompts the following for everyone:

Right now, you're sitting as yourself. But change your body and sit as you think your good or best friend might sit. *(observe class)* Now change your body as if you're seated as your family member might sit. *(observe)* And now change your body and sit as if you're the former teacher you've selected. *(observe)* Relax and sit as yourself. What did you notice about body positioning, or what else may have struck you when portraying three different individuals? *(class discussion)*

Now stand up as yourself. Now sit back down as you think your best friend would return to the chair. *(observe)* Now stand up as your family member or relative might rise. *(observe)* Now sit back down as you think your teacher might return to the chair. *(observe)* Relax and sit as yourself. What did you notice about body movements, or what else may have struck you when portraying three different individuals? *(class discussion)*

If a large open space is available for this walking exercise, divide the class into smaller groups of four to five people. The facilitator prompts the following for each group:

> Walk across the space from one end to the other as yourself, just to get used to the distance. *(observe)* Now, walk across the space from one end to the other as you think your good friend would walk. *(observe)* Now, walk across the space as your family member might walk. *(observe)* And now walk one more time as your former teacher might walk. *(observe; repeat for remaining groups)*

Facilitate a class discussion on observations and experiences of walking as three different people.

Embodying the Characters Through "As If" Dialogue

The next step is to explore improvised dialogue that might emerge from these three specific people. Students get into pairs (for an odd number of students, one group of three will be needed), avoiding combinations in which one of the partners may know the people who will be portrayed. Each partner sits facing the other.

Students first take on the role of the good friend. In pairs with all groups dialoguing simultaneously, students will chat in role as they believe the friend might speak. One of the partners begins the scene by saying, "Let's go to a restaurant." (Work under the assumption that these are two people who are already acquainted with each other.) The partners then dialogue to negotiate where they will go, their favorite eateries, food preferences, and so on. After one to two minutes of improvised dialogue, stop the exercise and ask students, out of role, to discuss their experiences about language choices and vocal tones while portraying their friends. Ask one or two groups to volunteer a sampling of their improvised dialogue for the rest of the class to observe.

Next, ask students to switch so they are working with a different partner. Each one will assume the persona of the family member.

The same process described above applies to this round of improvisation. In role, students will dialogue a short improvisation that assumes they are both strangers in an airport terminal waiting for a flight, and they are killing time by talking about their families. The scene begins with, "Family is really something, isn't it?" After one to two minutes of improvised dialogue, stop the exercise and ask students, out of role, to discuss their experiences about language choices and vocal tones as their family members. Ask one or two groups to volunteer a sampling of their improvised dialogue for the rest of the class to observe.

Finally, ask students to switch again so they are working with a third partner. The same process described above applies to this round. In role, students will dialogue a short improvisation that assumes they are both teachers waiting for a session to begin at a professional educators' conference. The scene begins with one teacher saying to the other, "Kids today!" The dialogue centers on teacher talk or shop talk. After one to two minutes of improvisation, stop the exercise and ask students, out of role, to discuss their experiences about language choices and vocal tones as their former teachers. Ask one or two groups to volunteer a sampling of their improvised dialogue for the rest of the class to observe.

Embodying the Characters by Writing in Role

Writing in role is another method of embodying the character, and is a preliminary step for playwriting. The facilitator prompts the following:

> On paper, write as if you are your good friend sending *you* a tweet, text message, Facebook posting, or e-mail. What would he or she write?

> Next, write as your family member sending a greeting card or a short, handwritten letter to you.

> Finally, write as your former teacher writing a private journal entry in his or her grade book or teacher's log about *you* and your work.

After the writing period, discuss as a class the inner processes of writing from another person's perspective. Ask for volunteers to share a few compositions. Discuss how ethnodramatic monologue and dialogue originate from a character's point of view with an emphasis on action, reaction, and interaction.

If you are an individual not enrolled in a research methods class, do the "Writing in Role" exercise above, but extend the length of the communications.

Living Newspaper

The U.S. Federal Theatre Project's "Living Newspaper" program from the 1930s staged dramatizations of current news events for audiences— sometimes accompanied with biting social commentary to supplement the factual reportage. Today's news stories—whether in print, broadcast, or online—provide rich material for classroom reading, improvisation, and social critique. A few journalists have also become ethnodramatists, creating vivid full-length plays based on their experiences. Two examples are Anne Nelson's (2002, 2003) meetings and collaborative eulogy-writing efforts with a New York City fire captain after the September 11 terrorist attacks in *The Guys*, and George Packer's (2008) field reporting and covert interviews with Iraqi citizens assisting the U.S. military effort in *Betrayed*. Nelson did not audio-record her meetings but took copious notes on legal pads; Packer states that approximately half of his play's dialogue is taken directly from interview recordings. It is important to note that neither journalist had a professional theatre background, but they both entered their dramatic projects as avid patrons of the art form. This love and knowledge of theatre, coupled with their passion and investment in the issues they addressed, are what made their first-time ethnodramatic ventures so outstanding.

In my own work I have found that local stories, rather than national and international news, lend themselves better to ethnodramatic exploration. Other criteria for news articles that generate effective drama include: articles with multiple people referenced or interviewed; an unresolved problem or issue; a sense of story-line to the article; and matters of importance or relevance to the class participants. Each one to two paragraphs of a news story generally functions as a unit for pair or small group dramatization.

The facilitator should be flexible to accommodate different approaches to the story—e.g., as a news conference, TV news broadcast, radio/TV talk show. Also explore how different print publications such as *The New York Times*, *The National Enquirer*, and *Time* magazine might approach the same story with its own unique slant.

Following is a fictional news story that composites the types of articles that might be used for ethnodramatics. The numbers at the beginning of a section indicate a unit with a playable scenario or an idea for improvisation.

Homeless Youth Shelter Faces Closure

by Rianna Lowenstein

(1) Homespace, a youth shelter in the city dedicated to assisting runaway and homeless kids for the past five years, may close its doors permanently within the next two weeks if adequate funding sources cannot be secured.

"We've been operating in the red for months already," sighed Homespace director and social worker Matthew Williams, "and it looks as if the financial help we need is not on the way. (2) We had to let go of our full-time teacher last month because there was just no money to pay her."

(3) Private and corporate donations have decreased over the past year, forcing Homespace staff to budget their meager state and grant monies for the bare essentials to keep the shelter's doors open at its rented property.

"It's frustrating," said senior staff counselor Rita Jenkins, "when we have to turn away these poor kids because there's no more beds. We can barely afford to feed the kids we're taking care of now." (4) Volunteers have solicited food donations from the community and stocked the Homespace kitchen as best as they can, but available resources have been tapped to the maximum.

(5) The Jensen Foundation, one of Homespace's largest annual contributors since the shelter's beginning, unexpectedly withdrew its support for the current fiscal year. Administrators for the foundation declined to comment on their decision, merely to say that there were other urgent priorities for funding.

Homespace, a short-term residential unit for homeless teenagers located in mid-city, is a simple but comfortable facility with 30 beds—a drop in the bucket when an estimated 200,000 to 300,000 teens are living homeless in the U.S. today.

(6) "I'm really, really worried," said one young runaway who wishes to remain anonymous because her family is searching for her. "If Homespace closes, I have nowhere to go, no family who can help me." Rita Jenkins has been counseling the young teen for a traumatic incident, and says, "Now is not the best time for this place to shut down. This girl—and everyone else in here—needs a lot of help before we can even think of shutting down."

(7) One of the homeless youths turned away, a 16-year-old boy who calls himself Sundance, said that he and his friend Moondog haven't eaten a decent meal in three days. "We've been pullin' stuff from fast food dumpsters and trash cans—leftover burgers and fries, but it's not always fresh."

Moondog added, "And the people around here don't wanna give up their spare change when you ask 'em for some. Homespace doesn't have any food, so what can we do?"

(8) "They're a nuisance to the neighborhood," says Paul Thomson, elderly longtime resident of the area where Homespace has operated for the past five years. "These young punks are just lazy, looking for a free handout from anyone they can con, and trashing the place for decent, hardworking folks who live here." Thomson and his wife, Evelyn, say they are afraid to leave their home at night for fear of getting robbed by homeless youth roaming the area.

(9) City police regularly patrol the Homespace neighborhood looking for suspicious activity among teens. Sergeant Denise Ortega is sympathetic to the young people's plight, but must also uphold local ordinances, which include a prohibition on loitering. "Me and my partner would rather talk to the kids to get them some help, rather than arrest them because they have no place else to go."

(10) Director Matt Williams acknowledges that Homespace receives numerous complaints from hostile neighbors. "They want us to pack up and get out of here. Some people living in this 'hood would rather see these kids die than get the social and medical services they desperately need."

(11) Lilypad, a 16-year-old girl who appears six months pregnant, was given top priority for one of Homespace's limited number of beds. But the father of her child, a thin 17-year-old boy called Bearcub, voluntarily sleeps outdoors at night in the alley behind the Homespace facility. "As long as she's OK," says Bearcub, "I can tough it out. She's got my baby inside her, and they come first."

Warm-up Discussion and Reading

The ethnodramatic activities below are written as if any news story was selected for exploration, though the fictional one above can be dramatized using these guidelines.

Select and prepare a dramatizable newspaper story or article with the sections/units pre-numbered by the facilitator. Distribute copies to students. Begin with one or both of the following ideas:

A. Ask questions about or discuss relevant issues suggested by the newspaper story or article.

B. If any photos accompany the news story, discuss what the people in them might have been thinking, feeling, or saying just before or at the moment the photo was taken.

Have the class read the story aloud, exchanging readers for each unit.

Creating Photographs

If the news story has just a few or no accompanying photographs, ask players, "If a photojournalist had been present throughout this story, what photographs might have been taken to accompany each unit? Who would have been in them? What would they have been doing or saying?" As players suggest photograph ideas, ask for volunteers to form the number of people needed for each photo/unit. Possible photos and events not directly mentioned but inferred from the news article are also possible. Provide two to three minutes for each group to create a tableaux (frozen picture) representing its assigned unit of the news story. Each group then shares its tableaux, with observing participants developing possible captions for each photo.

Other questions from the facilitator could include: "What kinds of emotions or internal thoughts do the body language and facial expressions suggest?" "What do you think was said by or to these people at the moment this photo was taken?" Assess the work and discuss what insights may have been made about the issue or the people involved.

Devising Unit Improvisations

Select a few units from the story and discuss the possibilities for extracting or adding characters, constructing a scenario (i.e., what the scene is about), and playing the conflict or tension. For example, in the "Homeless Youth Shelter" news story, Unit 1 could involve director Matthew Williams confronted by a landlord for overdue rental payments for Homespace; Unit 5 could portray executives and board members from The Jensen Foundation debating whether or not to fund Homespace for another year. Discuss how this kind of improvisational work will be what players will develop with their assigned units of the story—a thirty-second to one minute vignette that is verbally improvised and shows a "slice of life." A linear "beginning, middle, and end" is not necessarily needed for this type of scene.

Note that if the number of participants in each photo group lends itself to dramatizing or improvising the assigned unit of the news story, the casting is complete. If needed, redistribute the participants so a minimum of two players dramatize each unit of the news story.

Provide players approximately ten minutes to develop their scenes. Strongly encourage specific beginning and ending lines for their improvisations. Circulate among the groups to assist as needed. Encourage groups to get on their feet and practice the scene several times, not to just sit and talk about what they will say. End the practice period when all groups seem ready to share.

The Living Newspaper

Arrange the groups in a circle around the room so they are numbered sequentially according to their assigned units. Have each group arrange chairs or other properties, as needed, in the space for their presentations. The facilitator recommends: "When you're finished with your improvised work, don't say 'That's it.' Just freeze briefly and look toward the next group to give them a non-verbal cue to begin their scene."

Have each group present its scene in predetermined order. The facilitator intervenes or facilitates only when needed (e.g., if a group loses commitment to the action).

End the presentation with all groups returning to and creating their original tableaux of photos simultaneously.

Reflection and Assessment

1. Reflect on the issues raised by the news story, such as the multiple or contradictory perspectives from the people involved, the complexity of the problem, possible solutions, or speculation on the outcome. Explore the rights and responsibilities of community citizens suggested by the story.

2. Discuss how this news story might be presented as a TV news feature or told by a different newspaper or magazine with a particular journalistic slant. Discuss how the improvised work could transfer into the development of an ethnodramatic play script.

3. Discuss the types of participatory action research, investigative journalism, or critical qualitative inquiry studies that could emerge from the news story.

4. For additional ideas on interpreting and improvising newspaper stories and articles, see Augusto Boal's (1998) *Legislative Theatre*, pp. 234–246.

If you are an individual not enrolled in a research methods class, rewrite the "Homeless Youth Shelter Faces Closure" news story as a short, one act play script, or as a reporter's script copy for a brief TV broadcast news feature.

Stage to Page and/or Page to Stage

The exercises in this chapter are primarily improvisational ways to explore how humans might act, react, and interact in simulated real life contexts, and how those observations and discoveries could transfer reverberatively from stage to page and/or page to stage.

Most playwrights do not deliver an original play script that's production-ready for rehearsal and performance to a director or actors. Good playwrights take the time to first hear and assess the quality and effectiveness of their text through a workshop reading—a trial run of the play with actors seated, reading aloud from the manuscript as the playwright and director take notes on what works and what doesn't. An invited audience might be present to offer responses to the play production team after its reading as to what engaged them, what confused them, and even what bored them. Actors would also be asked to share their perceptions of the characters they portrayed and whether they understood the playwright's intent and whether they felt comfortable interpreting the lines.

Depending on the nature of the play or its development stage, some playwrights and directors might work with actors in an informal studio setting to improvise with hypothetical scenarios or portions of unfinished play text to flesh out the characters or to explore possible directions for the storyline. Playwrights might adapt what actors say improvisationally during these studio exercises into finished monologue or dialogue.

Regardless of what developmental stage a play is in, I require that my student playwrights voice out loud privately every line from a play script draft they've written, nonstop, before it proceeds to the next writing or production level. If the playwright doesn't "feel right" saying aloud what he or she has written, then how can we expect the actors and audiences to "feel right"? This recommendation is surprisingly skipped by too many playwrights, yet it is one of the most revealing tests of a play's initial potential that can lead to significant rewrites. Scholars who write research-based dramatic texts for journal publications rather than actual production and performance should also voice out loud their scripts, nonstop, before submitting them for peer review.

The overall point here is that most plays do not transfer smoothly and directly from page to stage. A classic theatre saying goes, "Plays are not written—they are *re*written." There is an iterative process of moving back and forth from page to stage to page to stage as drafts of scripts are revised and tried out in rehearsal and even during the performance run. The exercises in this chapter are intended to do likewise—moving from the pages of this book to the studio stage of your improvisation then back to your own pages for writing what you discovered. I hope that these playwriting exercises attuned you to the nuances of characters and how they might speak believably and purposefully. The next two chapters focus on writing specific forms of dramatic texts: monologue and dialogue. These are foundation structures for a full-length play and will also require that you move iteratively from page to stage then stage to page then page to stage until what you've written "feels" right.

RECOMMENDED READINGS

The following selections will provide more ethnodramatic and related exercises.

Boal, Augusto. (2002). *Games for Actors and Non-actors* (2nd ed.). New York: Routledge. Groups interested in theatre for social change as well as politically conscious ethnotheatre will find an array of dynamic games in this collection.

Janesick, Valerie. (2011). *"Stretching" Exercises for Qualitative Researchers* (3rd ed.). Thousand Oaks, CA: Sage. Janesick's eclectic collection of intriguing writing exercises and resources enables researchers to explore the artist within.

Kelin, Daniel A., II. (2005). *To Feel as Our Ancestors Did: Collecting and Performing Oral Histories*. Portsmouth, NH: Heinemann. Though geared for facilitation with young people, Kelin's methods are quite applicable to adults exploring devised work for performance.

Norris, Joe. (2009). *Playbuilding as Qualitative Research: A Participatory Arts-Based Approach*. Walnut Creek, CA: Left Coast Press. Norris expertly illustrates devised theatre processes through a qualitative researcher's lens. Winner of the 2011 American Educational Research Association's Qualitative Research SIG's Outstanding Book Award.

Rohd, Michael. (1998). *Theatre for Community, Conflict and Dialogue: The Hope is Vital Training Manual*. Portsmouth, NH: Heinemann. Rohd's book contains excellent theatre games and drama structures for exploring social change.

RECOMMENDED DVDS

The Fourth Kind, Universal Studios, 2009. This film about alien abduction is not a cinematic ethnodrama, but purports and shows that its screenplay is based on "true" cases and "actual" footage of therapy sessions. The Internet Movie Data Base (www.imdb.com) documents that the filmmakers' claims are a clever hoax. Nevertheless, it is worth viewing to see how supposedly authentic footage of reality is split-screened with the filmic adaptation and dramatization.

Howl, Oscilloscope Laboratories, 2011. The cinematic ethnodrama of Allen Ginsberg's revolutionary poem and its consequent obscenity trial begins with: "Every word in this film was spoken by the actual people portrayed." Interview and court transcripts plus the text of the poem itself provide the monologue and dialogue for the screenplay. The reading of "Howl" is accompanied by striking animation.

Quitting, Sony Pictures Classics, 2001. Chinese actor Jia Hongsheng and his family play themselves in this cinematic ethnodrama. The actor's career is cut short by heroin addiction, and the film dramatizes his descent and recovery. Watch for a stunning visual moment when the camera pulls back to transition from a heated family argument in their home to reveal them as actors on a stage set.

Studs Terkel's Working, Image Entertainment, 1982. The popular musical integrates monologues adapted from Terkel's classic book. Performers on the DVD include Barry Bostwick, Barbara Hershey, Charles Durning, and Eileen Brennan. Terkel himself appears in the production.

United 93, Universal Pictures, 2006. Paul Greengrass's masterpiece was a meticulously and ethically researched project to create a plausible account of what may have happened on the doomed September 11 flight. Selected key individuals, from military personnel to air traffic controllers, portray themselves in the film. Listen to the director's commentary with the soundtrack for background information on dialogue sources and rationale.

The Up Series, First Run Features, 2007. This classic seven-part documentary series tracks a group of individuals at ages 7, 14, 21, 28, 35, 42, and 49. The films demonstrate how voice-over narration, interviews, and observational footage weave together to profile an amazing array of longitudinal case studies. Current director Michael Apted notes about this work: "Every life is an act of courage, and everybody has a story. . . . These are ordinary lives, ordinary stories. But they're told in such a dignified way, and they elevate the ordinary life to real drama and real dignity."

ENDNOTE

1. In *From Ritual to Theatre* (1982), pp. 89–90.

Writing Ethnodramatic Monologue

*I wouldn't say that verbatim theatre gives [a participant] a voice—
he has a voice already—but it does provide his voice with listening
ears: mine when he tells me his story, and those of the audience
when the actor tells it to them.*

—Robin Soans[1]

This chapter reviews the basics of monologue construction from participant sources such as interview transcripts and pre-existing texts such as diaries, journals, or published accounts. A section is also included on autoethnodramatic monologue development—generating and writing stories about one's self, performed for others. An exemplar of monologic writing—scenes from Joe Salvatore's ethnodrama *open heart*—concludes the chapter.

A monologue is an extended, one-person, dramatic narrative—a rendering of a character's portrait in miniature. Playwriting instructors frequently employ the monologic form as a beginning writing exercise since the condensed unit serves as an excellent way to hone the craft of dramatic construction (i.e., plotting and storylining), characterization basics, and appropriate word choices. Since most ethnodramas are monologic in structure, it is important to review the unique components of this theatrical storytelling format. The individual case study or autoethnography is just an adaptation away from the solo performance piece.

A Curtain Raiser Monologue

A *curtain raiser* refers to staged action and/or narrative that serves as a prologue to the play and/or the production. For example, at the beginning of a performance of Shakespeare's *Macbeth* and the opening scene with the three witches, a curtain raiser may include special lightning, thunder, smoke effects, and haunting music while the witches enter onstage with dancelike, unnatural movements. Another example of a curtain raiser is an extended introductory monologue from a narrator that establishes the setting, tone, and given circumstances of the play.

As a curtain raiser for this chapter on monologic writing, following is an excerpt from Alan Haehnel's (2010) ethnodrama, *What I Want to Say But Never Will*, which features an ensemble of adolescents voicing their most private thoughts about self, friends, teachers, and family members. The young participants first wrote their pieces which were then work-shopped by Haehnel's high school actors for performance. Character #6, presumably a son or daughter speaking to and about his or her mother, offers the rant that follows. The monologue is *self-standing* or *self-inclusive*, meaning that no other thoughts by Character #6 are presented before or after this vignette in the full-length play. Also notice that Character #6's monologue is a fluent series of sentences. The original work was written, not spoken aloud during an interview, so there is nothing orally verbatim about it. But it *is* an authentic text written by an adolescent that was adapted and edited as necessary by the adult playwright.

> #6: Dad is dead, dead so long I don't even remember him, so you have no right to say things like, "You're such a lazy piece of crap; what would your father think of you now?" I never even got to know him, so how do I know, or how do you know, for that matter, what he would think of me? It really pisses me off when you say that. Oh, and by the way, what would Dad think if he knew that you, the only big influence left for me, yells at me 24/7? What would he think about me having to clench my jaw and tighten my fist every time I walk in what used to be his house? Oh, and one last thing: Tell your boyfriend I'm not interested in his lectures. He's the last person to have any right to lecture me. (p. 11)

As the chapter continues, references will be made to this monologue to illustrate several playwriting principles. For now, simply reflect on the first impression impact this selection may have made on you as a reader.

Elements of Monologues

The monologue, as a literary genre, is composed of particular dramatic elements and structural forms. Knowledge of these enable a writer to craft a more aesthetically shaped work for the stage.

Point of View and Audience Relationship

Most qualitative research studies collect empirical materials through interviews with individual participants, so the majority of written transcripts will include one person speaking in extended passages of text. Perhaps this is why most ethnodramas are primarily monologic in structure—the solo voice telling his or her story from one or more of five staged points of view:

Figure 3.1. David Barker portrays his father and mother in his one-man auto-ethnodrama, *Dodging Bullets*. Photos by Larry Stone.

- speaking directly to an audience
- speaking aloud to one's self but not directly to the audience (also known as *soliloquy*)
- speaking directly to another character(s) on stage
- speaking on stage as if to an unseen character (such as an interviewer)
- speaking as a voice-over (usually through a sound system), unseen on stage

When a participant/character in performance makes eye contact with and speaks directly to an audience, we are presumably brought closer into his or her world. The connection is more intimate, immediate, and an unspoken contract that naturalism is suspended (yet a sense of realism can still be maintained). The audience might serve as a collective witness to the story, or function as the presumed interviewer.

Soliloquy is the audience omnisciently eavesdropping on the participant/character's inner thoughts voiced aloud. Generally, no eye contact is made with the audience, so spectators become witnesses to the participant/character's perspectives and can thus exercise more analytic judgment in addition to (or instead of) emotional involvement.

When a participant/character speaks to another character on stage, we are witnesses to the individuals in interaction, particularly if and when the onstage character reacts to the monologue. (From an acting standpoint, it also generates more belief within the performer when he/she "plays off of" or speaks to another actor on stage.) Should another character not be present on stage, a heightened focus obviously shifts toward the speaker, and the audience must imagine the circumstances surrounding the contexts of the narrative.

Voice-overs, especially when amplified through a sound system, provide a sense of magnitude to the participant/character and heightened audience attunement to the text. What is visually absent on stage is compensated through aural richness. The effect should be used sparingly and selectively, however, because audience members can lose interest from extended voice-over passages unaccompanied by visual novelty.

An ethnodramatist and director strategically select the point(s) of view that will best serve the goals and style of the play, and the kind of interaction between the performer and audience that generates the most appropriate relationship. Monologue writing for a participant/character considers not just who is speaking, it also considers *to whom* he or she is speaking.

Consider Character #6's monologue in the curtain raiser to this chapter. The playwright makes no specific recommendation as to how the piece should be delivered, so it is up to the actor and director to decide which one (or more) of the five performance points of view would be most appropriate. What is your choice and why?

What Monologues Reveal

Monologues are colloquially called "portraits in miniature." In an economic slice or span of time, a playwright presents an individual participant/character sketch that captures the essence and essentials of the person and his or her story. Monologues can be as short as one minute or less to as long as a full-length, two-hour performance. But regardless of duration, what are usually rendered by the solo narrative—or at least suggested—are the participant/characters':

- objectives (also known as "motivations")
- conflicts (also known as "obstacles" or "tensions")
- tactics (also known as "strategies")

In performance parlance, playwrights, actors, and directors will ask themselves, "What does the character want (objectives), what stands in his/her way (conflicts), and what will he/she do to get it (tactics)?" Some dramas also attribute *tragic flaws* to selected characters—aspects of personality that are weaknesses or faults that prevent them from successfully achieving their objectives. Interview selections with participants may not always overtly contain objectives, conflicts, and tactics in their theatrical sense. Depending on the topic and the types of questions we ask, we may hear more descriptive biographical information and reflective anecdotes about values, attitudes, and beliefs rather than linear, tension-infused vignettes.

If the researcher as ethnodramatic playwright knows beforehand that interviews will be adapted and transformed into dramatic narratives, the questions posed and the stories asked for should generate a repertory of tales from participants that include descriptions of the types of problems, tensions, troubles, glitches, annoyances, and so on they encounter, as well as how they go about dealing with them. An interview prompt as simple as "Tell me a story about . . ." evokes potentially engaging ethnodramatic content. We should seek participants' success stories and triumphs as well as those in-progress, still unresolved issues. Some researchers may hesitate to open what they feel might be a Pandora's box of woe, yet many participants find talking about their problems to an invested and sympathetic listener somewhat cathartic and therapeutic. Emily Mann (2000), who interviewed people ranging from a Ku Klux Klansman to a psychologically scarred Vietnam veteran for her plays, advises:

> A good interview consists of setting up the situation and the environment for someone to finally let go and reveal to you who they really are and what they really need to say and what their story really is. That means you have to learn how to shut up. The impulse, as people reveal more and more, is to have that conversation, but the key is to be quiet and be able to deeply listen. (pp. 3–4)

If you ask tough questions, you need to be ready for the tough answers you may get. But don't open a door you can't close.

Objectives, conflicts, and tactics are traditional and major constructs of playwriting and performance. But what also emerges from the narrative, an actor's rendition of the monologue, and/or audience inference-making, are the participant/characters':

- attributes (e.g., gender, ethnicity, social class, sexual orientation)
- general personality traits
- cultural world(s) and experiences
- values, attitudes, and beliefs
- emotions
- subtexts (i.e., what is inferred by an audience from what is suggested by the performance, or what is not directly said by the participant/character)

Some of the factors above are the playwright's job, but what monologues also overtly or subtly reveal about a participant/character is a collaborative venture between an actor's performance and an audience's interpretation of it.

Consider Character #6's monologue in the curtain raiser to this chapter. The playwright provides no other details about him or her, so the actor and director must imagine the young person's life profile suggested by only 146 words of text. Reread the monologue and reflect on what is directly revealed through the narrative, and what is inferred or interpreted about the participant/character by you as a reader. Answer these questions: What does the participant/character want? What stands in his/her way? What will he/she do to get it?

The Structural Arc of a Monologue

A storyline with a traditional beginning, middle, and end is not always necessary for a monologue, though many do follow this classic design or *structural arc*. Patterson (2008) elegantly describes one of the most well-known approaches to narrative analysis, which closely resembles classic monologic structure: the six-part Labovian model. Clauses from transcripts are classified into six elements, purported as a nearly-universal story structure when humans provide an oral narrative:

1. ABSTRACT—what is the story about?

2. ORIENTATION—who, when, where?

3. COMPLICATING ACTION—then what happened?

4. EVALUATION—so what?

5. RESULT—what finally happened?

6. CODA—a "sign off" of the narrative (p. 25)

But Patterson notes that verbatim interview narratives are not always temporally ordered, and many contain nuances, densities, and complexities that rival traditional story grammars and paradigmatic coding systems such as Labov's.

Since ethnodramatic monologues are based on the actual stories of real people, most will adhere to a fairly linear structural arc of storytelling. But there are exceptions to every rule. Some ethnodramas like *The Exonerated* (Blank & Jensen, 2004) intersperse and interweave six major participant/characters' monologic stories throughout the full-length play. Other ethnodramas such as *My Name is Rachel Corrie* (Rickman & Viner, 2006) and *Twilight: Los Angeles, 1992* (Smith, 1994, 2003), include monologues similar to reveries in which no specific action progresses forward, but the audience learns about the history, opinions, values, at-

Figure 3.2. Cheryl McLean as Dora, a Holocaust survivor, in her ethnodrama, *Remember Me for Birds.*

titudes, and beliefs of the participant/characters. Sometimes a "slice of life" monologue has no preparatory framing—we dive right into the complicating action without an abstract or orientation. If a monologue is a portrait in miniature, then the narrative styles can range from impressionism to abstraction. In other words, structural arcs are plotting devices—frameworks—that provide a sense of flow and unity to the piece.

Consider Character #6's monologue in the curtain raiser to this chapter. Compare it to Labov's six-element narrative structure to determine whether it follows that particular structural arc. Reflect on what enables the piece to stand on its own as a portrait in miniature.

Monologues from Interviews
—The Playwright as Editor

Everyday life can be quite mundane, but it is also peppered with occasional moments of excitement, tension, and conflict. An adage among theatre practitioners goes, "Theatre is life—with all the boring parts taken out." It is not just a clever saying; it is actually one way of approaching what we do with the empirical materials we collect as we transform them for theatrical presentation: take the boring parts out.

For example, following is a 310–word verbatim transcript excerpt from an interview with a high school teacher that took place in her classroom. The interviewer asked her how she deals with student discipline. The teacher's response—unedited, with all tangents, "ums," and incomplete sentences—is presented as an example of authentic data collected from fieldwork in the schools:

> I laugh because this last week has been a big discipline week for me. And, a couple of teachers on campus are talking about it. Why is it our freshmen are so unruly and disrespectful? And so I pulled out a really good book, and I'm gonna tell you this, 55 *Essentials* by—it's a teacher on the West Coast and he wrote this book and they just had a big CNN thing on him. He's great. If you want to know the name, e-mail me, and I'll get that for you. Anyways, how do I deal with discipline? I am very forward, straight, and up-front. So, I don't take crap from anybody. And I call kids on their behavior. And this happened today in class, as a kid sat there and rolled his eyes at me, again. And I just stopped him and I said, "When you roll your eyes, you are basically saying 'F.U.' to the person you're talking to and that is disrespectful and not acceptable in my room. So you either be gone and get written up for disrespect and dis-, insubordination." Here on campus it's two days suspension off campus. So, here at school, we are very, um, disciplined on the basis of respect as a number one issue. And so, I enforce that and I teach that in my classroom every day by being honest, and calling kids. Now, some kids get freaked out because that's the way they learned at home. But eventually they get used to my style and they appreciate it, and they always come back and say, "Wow. I never looked at it that way." So, it's a cool thing, but it's funny you bring it up because this week has just been a nightmare week and I don't know why. Isn't that weird? (adapted from Saldaña, 2009, pp. 103–104)

One of the goals of an ethnodramatist is to take the actual words of a participant and adapt them into an economic form that has aesthetic shape. A good actor who memorized the text above word-for-word and performed it on stage in front of an audience could possibly make it work. But the worst sin an artist can commit is to bore the audience. Theatre and performance events are bounded by time. Thus, the "boring parts" and what is sometimes called "verbal debris" need to be taken out of verbatim, unedited text, and the remainder is to be spliced together, like a film editor working with pieces of performed material captured on media. To use another metaphor, playwright Emily Mann likens her work to that of a sculptor—chiseling away at hundreds of pages of interview transcripts until a distinctive form emerges.

Below is the edited text, now 117 words—not "reduced," for that implies a negative process. Instead, the text has been *distilled* or *condensed* to capture its essence and essentials. It has also been envisioned as if it were to be performed on stage. This means that a playwright must simultaneously and reverberatively take on multiple theatrical roles—actor, designer, and director—in order to envision its mounting. Stage directions, traditionally inserted in italics throughout monologue and dialogue, become one way of transitioning research from page to stage:

> (*DIANE speaks to the audience as she cleans up her classroom after a long day*)
>
> DIANE: Why are freshmen so unruly and disrespectful? One of my students today rolled his eyes at me—*again*. I stopped him and said,
>
> (*as if talking to the student*)
>
> "When you roll your eyes at me, you are basically saying 'fuck you' to the person you're talking to. And that is disrespectful and not acceptable in my room."
>
> (*to the audience*)
>
> I don't take crap from anybody. At this school, *respect* is the number one issue. I enforce that and I teach that every day by being honest. Now, some kids get freaked out by that, but they eventually get used to my style and appreciate it. They always come back to me and say,
>
> (*as if portraying a dense student*)
>
> "Wow, I never looked at it that way."
>
> (*as herself, shakes her head, laughs*)
>
> Isn't that weird?
>
> (Saldaña, 2010b, p. 64)

Notice that the monologue adaptation pieced together only what I perceived was necessary, rearranged the order of the narrative as originally spoken by the participant, and added the full expletive for an intentional effect. These choices were made based on what I as the playwright perceived as the most effective adaptation. But they were also made to capture the overall character or personality of the teacher. Purists of verbatim theatre may object vehemently to this technique, but each artist has his or her own style and this is just one way of working. As to whether an audience member feels convinced that this is an authentic, valid, and credible rendering, that is for each individual audience member to decide. Read Cynthia M. Saunders's (2008) research-based ethnodrama on the health uninsured, *Forty Million Strong, Weak, Wrong or Right*, for an example of a monologic collage that includes only the most salient and dramatic portions of her multiple participants' stories—several as short as one to three sentences, and a few as long as three minutes in length.

On Poetic Arrangement

Anna Deavere Smith's ethnodramatic monologues in print (and a few other plays whose writers employ her style) are arranged in poetic formats. Smith feels that her participants speak in "organic poems," and thus she listens carefully for their natural pausing and parsing during transcription. The format of poetry, rather than prose, has particular effects on readers and on actors interpreting these lines during rehearsals. It's as if we are forced to pay more attention to each particular grouping of words as a single idea, and to attend to the way that the structure of free verse effects our oral reading of the poem.

The following monologues are taken from the "Overture" of *with their eyes* (Thoms, 2002), an ethnodrama by students from New York's Stuyvesant High School who witnessed the attacks on the World Trade Center, just four blocks away, on September 11, 2001. Notice how these words are not randomly but deliberately parsed into specific cadenced lines, with the end of each line suggesting the slightest hint of a pause. Anna Deavere Smith explains in the play's Introduction that a "story is more than words: the story is its rhythms and its breaths" (p. xiv). Read these monologues, paying careful attention to their punctuation and flow.

> *Kevin Zhang, sophomore*
>
> I saw this
> *huge* plane it was . . .
> it looked much bigger than the first one,
> it just,
> it looked like one of those jets, you know, in the movies,
> you know, Air Force One or something,
> one of those big jets.
> It was one of those and it just hits—
> it hit the building right there.
>
> (p. 21)

Jennifer Suri, Assistant Principal, Social Studies

There were students who came into my office to use
      the phone
to touch base with their parents
to see if they were okay . . .
and there were actually many of them crowded into my room
and the electricity went out
momentarily and the lights started flickering
and everyone screamed
and dropped to the floor, frightened.
And I just tried to comfort them.[2]

(p. 26)

Whether you write ethnodramatic scripts in standard dramatic prose or poetic arrangements is your choice. As a broad brushstroke recommendation, if the story or character is important, use dramatic prose; if the language, rhythm, or mood is important, use poetic structures. When in doubt, reexamine the oral fluency documented in a participant's interview transcript or on your audio recording of it. Read and/or listen to the text with an attunement toward their speech patterns to detect any distinct "voiceprints." An example of verbatim theatre documented in poetic structures is provided at the end of this chapter. Plus, Carolyn Lunsford Mears' (2009) *Interviewing for Education and Social Science Research: The Gateway Approach* provides intriguing methods for poetic transcription of interview texts, and her exceptional book is essential reading for those researching sensitive subjects (Mears interviewed parents of students who survived the 1999 Columbine High School massacre in Colorado).

Figure 3.3. Carlos Manuel in his one-man autoethnodrama, *La Vida Loca*. Photo courtesy of Carlos Manuel.

Ethnodramatic Exercise: Adaptation of Interview Text
—Alan Peshkin's *God's Choice*

If you do not have a set of interview transcripts with which to work, I recommend the following study as accessible ethnodramatic inspiration. The purpose of this playwriting exercise is to review extended narrative material and to make specific editorial choices that capture the essence and essentials from interviews and distill them into concise monologues for the stage.

Alan Peshkin's (1986) classic ethnography, *God's Choice: The Total World of a Fundamentalist Christian School*, is a detailed portrait of Bethany Baptist Academy (a pseudonym). Peshkin includes throughout the book extensive participant interview narratives that lend themselves to monologic formatting and adaptation. In fact, before one section of paraphrased summaries of teachers talking about their relationships with students, he advises the reader that "they should be read as the monologue of an experienced teacher talking to a newcomer" (p. 81).

1. Read Chapter 1 ("Introduction: The Setting, the Author, the Times") from *God's Choice* and condense Pastor William Muller's first-person account into a seven- to ten-minute monologue. Muller's words in Chapter 1 (pp. 1–10), if spoken, would take almost thirty minutes to read aloud at a comfortable rate of speech. Delete what you feel is unnecessary for an audience member to know about the pastor and his school's contexts. Maintain what is vital and salient. Explore the rearrangement of text for a more logical flow, through-line, and dramatic impact. (I am personally torn between starting and/or ending Muller's monologue with one of two lines he provides: either "Do you love Jesus?" or "We look around us and see Satan."). Following is an excerpt from Peshkin's account of the pastor to give you an idea of Muller's values, attitudes, and beliefs.

I believe Christian schools try to teach that in the total society of mankind, young people must abide by God's structures and God's system of order. That's why they learn to say "Yes, sir" and "Yes, ma'am" down here. We come at it from an authoritarian point of view. The very first verse in the Bible doesn't endeavor to prove that God exists; it just assumes God exists. It begins with, "In the beginning God created the heaven and the earth." So we come to these young people with a background of authority. Humanism elevates man and his reasoning. I'd put it this way: Without authority and without structure, we do a disservice to our total educational program. If there's a doubting of authority, you're going to waste a good measure of time. Our faith is *not* based upon reason, but our faith is not unreasonable. We're for structure. (pp. 8–9)

Describe or draw the best scenic pieces and hand properties (e.g., desk, chair, Bible, and so on) for the performance of this monologue on stage. Reflect on the legitimacy of the condensed monologue as a credible and trustworthy representation of Pastor Muller.

2. Other indented sections in *God's Choice* that lend themselves well to monologic adaptation are: Headmaster McGraw's address to students on the first day of school (pp. 49–53); one of the students profiled in Chapter 8, "By Their Fruits: Four Student Portraits"; and one of the students profiled in Chapter 9, "In Satan's Clutches: Bethany's Scorners." Take one of these extended interviews/narratives and set your goal of condensing Peshkin's excerpts to one-third their original length. If possible, recruit a university or professional actor to read aloud the monologues and ask him or her to assess their effectiveness from a performer's perspective. I also encourage all playwrights to not just hear their own work, but to actually speak it out loud themselves. That way, you'll get a better handle on what you're asking of actors.

On Autoethnodrama

Though I had previously written and directed four ethnodramas of other participants' stories, and conducted over one hundred interviews with children and adults about arts education, I waited until I was 53 years old to research, write, and perform one of my own life stories (Saldaña, 2008). It's not that I had nothing to say until I was that age, it's just that the impetus to do so never occurred to me, and an opportunity hadn't arisen until that time. After having done it, I highly recommend the project to every qualitative researcher and ethnodramatist, for I now advocate that you really can't learn how to tell someone else's story until you first or also learn how to tell your own.

A playwright and preferably performer of his or her own autobiographical account composes an *autoethnodrama* which, in general terms, is an autobiographical story in monologic play script format intended for performance. Autoethnodrama presents a staged portrait of a particular reflexive researcher's world and what it's like to live in it. Davis and Ellis (2008) explain that autoethnography (and thus an autoethnodrama) "is the study of a culture of which one is a part, integrated with one's relational and inward experiences. The author incorporates the 'I' into research and writing, yet analyzes him- or herself as if studying an 'other'" (p. 284).

All of the monologic playwriting principles discussed thus far apply to autoethnodramatic work, and the autoethnographic methods described by Heewon Chang (2008), Michele Crossley (2007), Carolyn Ellis (2008), and Christopher N. Poulos (2008) provide exceptional guidance for the solo writer examining his or her own life. I also discovered later that introspective *memory work* (Grbich 2007; Liamputtong, 2009; McLeod & Thomson, 2009) conducted by the individual, rather than with a group, generates not just personal stories but their motifs, connected meanings, and through-line—essentials for the structural arcs of extended monologues.

Following is an exercise I facilitate at my workshops to assist in developing initial autoethnodramatic material.

Ethnodramatic Exercise: Autoethnographic Monologue Development

The purpose of this exercise is to explore autoethnographic storytelling as a precursor to or as an extension of monologic ethnodramatic playwriting. You will develop original work based on your personal life experiences for informal presentation.

Selecting the Story Idea

Review and choose one of the following prompts as a stimulus for a personal story. This is just a recommended list, and be cautious of getting too personal (e.g., the death of a loved one). Anything told should be true as the participant experienced and remembers it.

The following story prompts are adapted from Donald Davis's (1993) *Telling Your Own Stories.* Consider:

- a time when you got into trouble for something you were told not to do
- a time you broke something that belonged to somebody else
- a night your parents never found out about
- a time when you were tricked or lied to
- the time you realized you were no longer a child
- a time you felt triumphant with an accomplishment
- the first person you ever had a crush on

Additional story prompts from Jason Rukulak's (2001) *The Writer's Block: 786 Ideas to Jump-Start Your Imagination* include:

- a secret you failed to keep
- the worst time you've ever put your foot in your mouth

- a time you defied your parents
- your most embarrassing on-the-job experience
- a time you pretended to be someone or something you're not
- "the one who got away"
- your favorite childhood toy
- meeting a celebrity

Those who wish to go deeper can talk about one of these encounters:

- your first or earliest encounter when you became aware of your race or ethnicity
- an encounter with someone of the opposite sex when you had a disagreement rooted in gender issues
- an encounter with someone you knew who came out as a gay/lesbian (or, an encounter when you, if gay/lesbian, told someone about your sexual orientation)
- an encounter with a homeless person (or, an encounter with someone when you yourself were homeless)
- an encounter with a disabled person (or, an encounter with someone else if you yourself are disabled)
- an encounter with someone whose language or speech you could not understand
- an encounter with an elderly person (or, the first time you perceived yourself as "old")
- an encounter with someone over spiritual beliefs and spiritual disagreement
- an encounter with someone who called you a name that offended you
- an encounter with a teacher who exerted his/her power over you

First Oral Draft

Each participant selects one of the prompts that stimulates a personal story. Participants select a partner and simply share their stories with each other privately. If possible, each story should last no longer than four to five minutes. Each person's story should be told uninterrupted by the partner; any questions for clarification can be asked afterward. For assessment, each partner shares what he/she enjoyed the most and what may have been unclear about the other's story. Before leaving, each partner shares with the other: "The next time you tell your story, make sure that you. . . ."

Second Oral Draft

Participants switch partners and retell their stories for each other, this time conjuring as much sense imagery as possible for the new listener (e.g., visual, aural, and olfactory details) and referring to the emotions involved with the people in the story. Participants well-versed in anthropology or ethnography can be encouraged to focus on cultural details— "those small things that are a part of the culture you're talking about that not too many people may know." Establish a time limit of five to six minutes for each story. For assessment, each partner shares whether he/she was able to get a mental picture of the environment for the story, and whether the emotions of the teller were clear. Partners then brainstorm the best beginning line and ending line for each story. (Discourage questions or "This is a story about . . ." as a beginning line, and "That's it" as an ending line.) Before leaving, each partner shares with the other: "The next time you tell your story, make sure that you. . . ."

Third Oral Draft

Participants switch partners and retell their stories for each other, this time integrating all recommended feedback received thus far and paying attention to the structure of the piece—i.e., its beginning, middle, and end, and its flow for the listener. Establish a time limit of five to six minutes for each story. For assessment, each partner shares what was most effective in the telling of the other's story, and what emotional responses may have been evoked. Partners brainstorm with each other specific titles for the stories shared (which can sometimes derive from a key line from the story).

Gestural Motif

Before the next cycle of storytelling, gather all participants and stand in a circle. Explain that just as a story has content motifs, or thematic elements that may reoccur throughout a narrative, tellers can use gestural motifs—a physical hand gesture or body action purposefully chosen to symbolize some aspect of the story. The gestural motif might accompany the beginning and ending line, and/or be repeated selectively throughout the storytelling to reinforce a thematic element. Participants simultaneously explore and practice a possible gestural motif with selected passages from their stories to incorporate into the next telling. Also have each participant share his/her opening line to the story to assess its "grab" for listeners.

First Presentation

The facilitator organizes participants into small groups of four to five, gathered with people who have not heard each other's stories, if possible. Each group assembles in a private area and shares its stories in a mock "storytelling concert." Each teller should stand in front of the seated listeners, or sit facing the others, to give the presentation a sense of occasion. Participants offer each other suggestions for the transfer of the stories into print.

From Stage to Page

Individually, each student now writes his/her personal story on paper as if it were told in the first person (i.e., a monologue). Include a title and stage directions for action. If time allows, let the story "rest" for a day, then return to it and revise it, paying attention to key details, sensory images, emotions, tension, structure, and word choices.

From Page to Stage

Have participants volunteer to share their written stories by reading the text aloud to the class. Brainstorm the type of ethnodramatic play the story might suggest. With the teller's permission, dramatize the story or a portion of it if the events lend themselves to enactment with others on stage. Have the playwright serve as director or actor.

What follows, as an example of autoethnodramatic monologue writing, is my true story of the time I realized I was no longer a child.

Becoming a Man

(JOHNNY makes a gesture that looks as if he's pushing a drawer shut with two hands)

JOHNNY: When you grow up named Johnny—not John—you always feel like you're a child. I was quite spoiled as a kid—and as a teenager. Being the youngest, the baby of the family, I was always protected by my parents, always given what I wanted, fed to the extreme and pampered.

In high school, when I was a junior, this guy moved to Texas from New Mexico and came to our school. His name was Jake Simons. And over time, because we both shared an interest in band and drama, we became best friends, but you probably wouldn't think it because we were so, so different.

I was a junior, he was a sophomore; I was Hispanic, he was white; I was short, he was tall; I was fat, he was muscular. But we became best friends, nevertheless.

(*makes the drawer pushing gesture, smiles*)

What I admired most about Jake was his confidence. He was a year younger than me, but he seemed so grown up. I didn't have to work as a teenager, but he was working part-time at McDonald's and making spare money—twenty dollar bills in his wallet, when all I had was one dollar bills stuffed in my pants pocket. He knew all that manly stuff about sports, machines, and cars. And he had a driver's license—that glorious adolescent symbol of independence—when I hadn't even taken driver's ed. Some girls confessed to me privately that they thought Jake was hot, but were reluctant to tell him so. He was tall and strong and everything I wanted to be.

But he was a year younger than me. So why wasn't I more "mature" than him?

(*makes the drawer pushing gesture, hesitantly*)

It was just an ordinary day, nothing special when I came home after school. But when I walked into my bedroom, I looked around and saw what I had become. At 16 years old, there were still stuffed animals on my dresser and toys on my bookshelves. It looked like a fourth grader lived there.

I thought of Jake and who he was and who he was becoming— then thought of me and realized I wasn't becoming anything.

(*beat*)

That was the time I realized I was no longer a "child."

(*mimes putting things in a drawer*)

So I picked up all the stuffed animals and toys and anything else that was babyish, stored them in the bottom drawer of my dresser,

(*makes the drawer pushing gesture*)

shut it, and looked around my bedroom. (*pause, smiles*) Now, this was the bedroom of an *adult.*

Jake, just by being who he was, just by being my friend, took me out of childhood and helped me grow up. He helped me to, eventually, become what I always wanted to be. He helped me become a man.

RECOMMEND READINGS

Play Scripts

You become a better playwright by reading exemplary scripts. I recommend the following plays, alphabetized by title, to expand your knowledge of monologic ethnodramas.

14 by José Casas, in *Borders On Stage: Plays Produced by Teatro Bravo*, edited by Trino Sandoval (Phoenix: The Lion & the Seagoat, 2008). The play's title refers to fourteen Mexicans who died in the desert while crossing into the United States. Casas' monologues are based on interviews with everyday citizens of Arizona and reveal their perceptions of immigration and Hispanic-White relationships. The playwright is an award-winning craftsman of the art form who demonstrates how the monologue permits poignant storytelling.

Aftershocks by Paul Brown and the Workers Cultural Action Committee (Sydney: Currency Press, 2001). Survivors' and rescuers' stories from the December 28, 1989, Newcastle earthquake in Australia are meticulously adapted and dramatized in this two-act play. Brown's Introduction to the script provides an exceptional description of the drama's evolution and reflections on verbatim theatre.

Another American: Asking and Telling by Marc Wolf, in *Political Stages: Plays That Shaped a Century*, edited by Emily Mann and David Roessel (New York: Applause Theatre & Cinema Books, 2002). Wolf's collection of interview-based monologues focuses on the destructive ramifications and consequences of the U.S. military's "Don't ask, Don't tell" policy. Gay, lesbian, and straight veterans, politicians, activists, and others provide honest and riveting accounts of the policy's effects on their lives and fellow service people.

Fires in the Mirror: Crown Heights, Brooklyn and Other Identities by Anna Deavere Smith (New York: Anchor Books, 1993). The drama profiles various perspectives about the 1991 conflict and riots in Crown Heights between African-Americans and Jews when an accidental death and retaliatory murder fueled ethnic tensions. The trade book edition of the script provides an Introduction on Smith's play development process and the chronology of the riot. A VHS (Monterey Media, 1993) and DVD (Monterey Video, 2009) of her performance are available.

I Am My Own Wife by Doug Wright (New York: Faber and Faber, 2004). Wright's Tony Award and Pulitzer Prize winning play is subtitled *Studies for a Play About the Life of Charlotte von Mahlsdorf*, an aged yet celebrated East German gay transvestite. The challenge facing the sole male actor is transforming himself into thirty-five different male and female characters, some of whom dialogue with each other in rapid succession throughout the play. Wright's Introduction in the trade book edition of the play discloses his tensions with the research and development of the work.

In Conflict by Douglas C. Wager (New York: Playscripts, Inc., 2008). Wager's docudrama is adapted from Yvonne Latty's book, *In Conflict: Iraq War Veterans Speak Out on Duty, Loss, and the Fight to Stay Alive.* Seventeen men and women's testimonies are arranged in monologic, poetic format and told with explicit honesty. Yvonne Latty also appears as a character yet transcends the narrator's role. Her emotional reactions to these soldiers' stories provide poignant journalistic commentary.

La Vida Loca: An Apolitical In-Your-Face Odyssey of a Mexican Immigrant by Carlos Manuel (Phoenix: The Lion & the Seagoat, 2010). Manuel's seriocomic authoethnotheatrical one-man play chronicles his transition from Mexico to the United States as an adolescent, coming of age and coming to terms with his ethnic, national, cultural, and gay identities. The work, primarily in English, also contains humorous Spanish language lessons for the uninitiated.

The Laramie Project by Moisés Kaufman and the Members of the Tectonic Theater Project (New York: Vintage Books, 2001). Monologues of various length are combined with brief multi-character scenes in this classic ethnodrama about a community's reactions to the murder of Matthew Shepard. The DVD adaptation (Warner Home Video, 2002) features such actors as Peter Fonda, Camryn Manheim, Steve Buscemi, and Christina Ricci. A related website about the play and its productions can be found at: http://www.laramieproject.org/

An Australian teacher's guide to the play can be accessed from: http://www.curriculumsupport.education.nsw.gov.au/secondary/creativearts/assets/drama/pdf/verbatim.pdf

Maybe Someday: Voices of HIV-Positive Women by Margarete Sandelowski, Frank Trimble, Elizabeth K. Woodard, and Julie Barroso, in "From Synthesis to Script: Transforming Qualitative Research Findings for Use in Practice," *Qualitative Health Research*, volume 16, number 10, 2006, pp. 1350–1370. This is one of the very few ethnodramas from an academic journal that has both documentary and artistic merit. The women's monologues provide a spectrum of emotional and attitudinal perspectives. Also valuable is the co-authors' account of the rigorous research that provided the empirical materials for dramatization by Trimble.

Minefields and Miniskirts adapted by Terence O'Connell (Sydney: Currency Press, 2004). The play adapts Siobhán McHugh's book of interviews with Australian women recalling their memories of the Vietnam war. A small ensemble portrays various women who served in the military, worked as journalists and entertainers, and who suffered the aftermath of veterans' post-traumatic stress disorder. Riveting monologues of atrocities and courage during and after wartime are told with stark directness.

My Left Breast by Susan Miller (New York: Playscripts, Inc., 2006). Miller's one-woman autoethnodrama about her experiences with breast cancer and a mastectomy is a comedy-drama. The poignant and startlingly honest vignettes interweave between medical tests, relationships, raising a family, and fierce resiliency. This is one of the few autoethnodramas that gets performed by other women.

My Name is Rachel Corrie, edited by Alan Rickman and Katherine Viner (New York: Theatre Communications Group, 2006). Rachel Corrie's journals, letters, and e-mail correspondence were edited by Rickman and Viner to compose the play's narrative. Corrie was a young American activist working in the Middle East and killed at age 23. The play chronicles selected writings from her adolescence to young adulthood, revealing her thoughts, values, experiences, political and social convictions, and identity.

The Permanent Way by David Hare (London: Faber and Faber, 2007). A diverse collage of voices addresses the bureaucratic chaos and tragic train wreck deaths that occurred after the privatization of the British railway system. Multiple, conflicting perspectives and individual stories of loss blend together in Hare's outstanding verbatim theatre play to create an engaging dramatic portrait told through interwoven, monologic storytelling.

ReEntry by Emily Ackerman and KJ Sanchez (New York: Playscripts, Inc., 2010). Marines and their family members present uncensored attitudes toward entering and serving in the military and adjusting to home life upon their return. The monologues are a mix of tragic and comic perspectives on wartime, post-service transition, and the culture of the United States Marine Corps.

Seven by Paula Cizmar, Catherine Filloux, Gail Kriegel, Carol K. Mack, Ruth Margraff, Anna Deavere Smith, and Susan Yankowitz (New York: Dramatists Play Service, Inc., 2009). Seven female playwrights each interviewed an international social activist member of the Vital Voices Global Partnership. Each of the participants tells harrowing stories about gender oppression and injustice in her country.

The value of this play script is in its collaborative framework. Each woman is biographically profiled in her own separate, extended monologue. Then, an adaptation integrates and interweaves portions of the seven monologues into an extended one act play. This is an excellent model that demonstrates how separately conducted interviews can be first constructed as stand-alone work, then brought together as a single ethnodramatic play script.

Spalding Gray: Stories Left to Tell, words by Spalding Gray, concept by Kathleen Russo and Lucy Sexton (Woodstock, IL: Dramatic Publishing, 2008). A five-member cast retells key excerpts from the legendary Gray's one-man autobiographical plays, also available as individual scripts by Gray and Russo: *Gray's Anatomy*; *It's a Slippery Slope*; *Monster in a Box*; *Morning, Noon and Night*; *Sex and Death to the Age 14*; *Swimming to Cambodia*; and *Terrors of Pleasure* (all available from Dramatic Publishing, 2008). Mr. Gray's performances can be seen on VHS and DVD, with excerpts accessible on YouTube.

Still Life by Emily Mann (New York: Dramatists Play Service, 1982). An ex-Marine Vietnam veteran's troubled transition to home life in the U.S. wreaks havoc on his marriage and his relationship with his mistress. Three characters with interspersed monologues (some scenes are tightly interwoven) provide honest and riveting accounts of their feelings.

subURBAN Stories by Tom Conklin (Woodstock, IL: Dramatic Publishing, 2007). Three black and three white individuals living in the same neighborhood offer their perceptions of race and urban and suburban life. Each character, ranging in age from the teens to seventies, offers his/her personal history and encounters with racism, discrimination, bias, profiling, stereotyping, and violence.

This Beautiful City by The Civilians, written by Steven Cosson and Jim Lewis, music and lyrics by Michael Friedman, from interviews by The Company (New York: Dramatists Play Service, 2010). Multiple perspectives about the religious communities of Colorado Springs are presented in this moving ethnodrama with music. The play also reveals participant opinions about the Ted Haggard scandal, which serendipitously occurred during the interview period.

Twilight: Los Angles, 1992 by Anna Deavere Smith (New York: Dramatists Play Service, 2003). Smith's verbatim interviews with an array of citizens and public figures after the riots that followed the Rodney King police assault trial are profiled in this masterwork. The acting edition of Smith's original one-woman documentary theatre play describes how the production can be staged by a company of actors. A VHS (PBS Home Video, 2000) of her performance is available.

The Vagina Monologues by Eve Ensler (New York: Villard, 2001). Ensler interviewed over 200 women about their vaginas and composed verbatim, composite, and original monologues based on their experiences. V-Day, which features the play's performance at nationwide venues, is a related grassroots movement and fundraiser to stop violence against women. Also view the DVD (HBO Home Video, 2002) of Ensler's performance with accompanying commentary and response.

What I Want to Say But Never Will by Alan Haehnel (New York, Playscripts, Inc., 2010). Haehnel appears in his drama as the playwright/narrator and constructs a few fictive dialogues between selected characters. But the majority of the play includes seventy-six brief narrative monologues written by adolescents that permitted them to voice their true and most intimate thoughts, fears, and feelings.

with their eyes, edited by Annie Thoms (New York: HarperTempest, 2002). Students of Stuyvesant High School in New York City composed these monologues after they witnessed firsthand the attacks on the World Trade Center on September 11, 2001, from only four blocks away. The monologues were based on interviews with students and school personnel and are arranged in poetic format.

Books

The following titles are recommended for autoethnodramatic playwriting.

Alterman, Glenn. *Creating Your Own Monologue* (2nd ed.). New York: Allworth Press, 2005. Alterman's approach is for theatre artists composing both fictional and nonfictional pieces, and many of his detailed recommendations deal with both the writing and performing of solo work.

Chang, Heewon. (2008). *Autoethnography as Method*. Walnut Creek, CA: Left Coast Press. The text provides a systematic approach to autoethnographic research and writing plus an excellent overview of cultural concepts. Many of Chang's exercises prepare for and transfer to the writing of autoethnodrama.

Poulos, Christopher N. (2008). *Accidental Ethnography: An Inquiry into Family Secrecy*. Walnut Creek, CA: Left Coast Press. Poulos' story examples and writing exercises stimulate deep introspection into personal memory for autoethnographic work, which can lead to autoethnodramatic solo performance.

Spry, Tami. (2011). *Body, Paper, Stage: Writing and Performing Autoethnography*. Walnut Creek, CA: Left Coast Press. Spry provides both theoretical foundations and practical exercises for the development of authoethnographic performance pieces; includes selected texts from her repertoire.

ENDNOTES

1. In Hammond & Steward (2008), *Verbatim Verbatim: Contemporary Documentary Theatre*, p. 32.
2. Text copyright 2002 by Taresh Batra, Anna Belc, Marcel Briones, Catherine Choy, Tim Drinan, Ilena George, Shaleigh Jalea, Lindsay Long-Waldor, Liz O'Callahan, Chantelle Smith, Michael Vogel, Carlos Williams, Christopher Yee & the NYC Board of Education. Used by permission of HarperCollins Publishers.

Scenes from *open heart* by Joe Salvatore

> *open heart* premiered in August 2010 at La MaMa E.T.C., New York City, as part of the 2010 New York International Fringe Festival, a production of The Present Company.

This chapter concludes with a selection of scenes from Joe Salvatore's full-length ethnodrama, *open heart*. Salvatore, a faculty member at New York University—as is Anna Deavere Smith—adopts poetic structures for his monologues and small group scenes. He also employs the verbatim theatre technique with all originally-recorded participant utterances and unique speech patterns meticulously documented in the script. *open heart* candidly yet perceptively explores nonmonogamous gay male relationships and the spectrum of attitudes from his participants about love, sex, companionship, romance, and fidelity. New York theatre critic Danny Bowes praised Salvatore's directorial and playwriting work as "unique," "compelling," and "the best possible example" of documentary art on stage.

Introduction by Joe Salvatore

The text for *open heart* comes from transcriptions of interviews I conducted in winter and spring 2009 with thirteen gay couples living in open, nonmonogamous relationships, as well as a therapist/professor who had conducted research on a similar subject. Each of the couples was interviewed as a couple and then each partner/spouse/boyfriend was interviewed separately, yielding approximately 40 hours of audio recordings. Couples were recruited through e-mail listserves, online postings, and flyers placed in businesses and community centers in New York City, and they were compensated for their participation in the interview process. At the time of the interview, each individual was asked to select an identifier—a real name or a pseudonym—that could be used as the name of the "character" in the script and the performance.

Once the interviewing was completed, I relistened to the interviews and transcribed what I believed to be compelling moments that I wanted to share with an audience. This yielded some 200 pages of typed transcriptions that included all of the "ums," "ahs," and stutters of those interviewed. In two separate workshop processes, a group of actors read the excerpts aloud, and out of those workshops, 15 of the 27 people I interviewed emerged as characters in the script: six couples and three individuals. To prepare for production, the actors used the typed transcriptions and the audio recordings of the interviews to create their verbatim performances of the 15 people.

Has to open up after 5 years

THERAPIST AND PROFESSOR
Okay
I'm glad you brought that up because
McWhirter and Mattison
wrote a book called *The Gay Male Couple*.

PROJECTION
Therapist and Professor

THERAPIST AND PROFESSOR
It ah
is considered seminal
ah they looked at uhff
I need my notes in front of me to remember
but they looked a whole bunch of gay couples
in the San Diego area
um and wrote a book.
And it was in the popular gay press for a while
and any time you look at the issue of non-monogamy in the
    academic literature
you come across that book like
that's what people
and always people who
like you
were more scholarly.
There are other people who've written about monogamy
or mentioned it like guess what gay people are not monogamous
as an aside and they quote McWhirter and Mattison.
And McWhirter and Mattison were the ones they found
they found that any couple who was together more than five years
    was not monogamous
and so um
now
their research has come under
it was like 129 couples
in San Diego
all of the reas- data was collected before the HIV
crisis
um
and um they
ah it was a lot
of their their research is come under criticism.

Anyway it was an important study
and it was a a landmark study in many ways.
But my own
but it's an old study
and a flawed study in my
you know all studies are flawed.
But my what my research showed was that
I mean they were basically saying you have to be you know the
    relationship has to open
up
after five years.

Does that mean I cheated on the pancakes?

TYLER
But I believe you can be totally in love with someone
but also infatuated with another person
and what's wrong with that?

PROJECTION
Tyler, 25

TYLER
We're diverse creatures we like diversity.
I love pancakes.
That doesn't mean I want them every day I could have them every
    day for while if I had eggs once does that mean I cheated on
    the pancakes?
I mean with all of our powerful primal feelings
hunger you know
sex why is sex any different?
We're creatures of diversity we like diverse things.
Habitat.
You know people didn't just plop down in one area
that you know in if if you if you don't
have these diverse things people feel unsatisfied
you feel dissatisfied.
Ummm
you live in the same
you know
you never travel you feel unsa- unsatisfied.
You only hook up with one person, well don't tell me

that you're not—you're thinking about
other people and a part of you feels like you never you sowed your
    oats
and you know or you know let's pretend you who wants to eat
    pancakes for the rest of your life and never have eggs.
That doesn't mean you don't love pancakes.
I don't know.
I think we're diverse creatures I don't think we're built for
    monogamy apparently though there is one creature that is
    all monogamous 90% of them are monogamous and they
    are called
the uh
it's a one word
uh
it's not skeet.
Uh they're very small I'll think of it
uhh
but uh
they're they're monogamous 90% of them. I don't know.

He doesn't give me a raging hard on

TOM
Well

PROJECTION
Tom, 44

TOM
as uhm
one other
point I should make
is just that
my partner is not actually my sexual
my most sexually exciting
person.
It's not like "oh he's my dream
erotic person."

So
I suppose I would prefer a partner who
is that super sexually exciting person,
so I seek that sexual excitement some in some sense in my fantasy
    life in
if I go out to a sex
space or something like that.
But then I come home to this
wonderful person
who just
happens to be not my
he doesn't give me a raging hard on he doesn't like
that's not just a matter of time
he never was that
person.
It's just a person I happened to meet and I woke up really
    comfortable in his arms and there was some kind of
connection of
at the level of comfort
and sexual
compatibility but not
not dream lover kind of thing.

Maybe you wanted to be caught

JOEY
And so
while I was at my sister's house
decorating for Christmas on a Sunday afternoon
with my

JOHN
He doesn't believe in Jesus so that doesn't even matter.

JOEY
It doesn't but it was a Norman Rockwell painting.
With my sister and brother-in-law and two children

    (clears throat)

I get a cell cell phone call with someone I don't know and I answer
    it in front of them
With garland in hand as I'm wrapping a banister.
And
Tsshh
quickly figured out what was happening,
pretty quickly,
and managed to get
out
side of the house to confirm
what I was
suspecting.
And

JOHN

And it wasn't just that da- I it wasn't just that I gave anybody you
    know his cell number I gave like the craziest fuck in the world
    his phone number,
you know?
It wasn't just like he was some uhm
you know some guy who was like normal but was just trying to get
    hooked you know hook up.
It was like some weird psychopath *(laugh)* strange asswipe
who called repeatedly after that.
After he knew he had the wrong number.

JOEY *(overlapping)*
Yes.

JOHN

And then when I finally got a hold of him
and tried to to tell him to stop calling he continued to call Joey.
After that
it was it was uhm
evil.

JOEY

Well our cell phone numbers are identical except for two digits.

JOHN
Right.

JOEY
So it's it's not a difficult thing for one of us to accidentally
  transpose and of course he dials my number all the time and
  not his own so

JOHN *(overlapping)*
Well and I
and I
yeah.
And I just didn't,
so it was

JOEY
And then again I guess we could get all
psychological about it and say that maybe you wanted to be caught
  but

JOHN
I did, I did.

JOEY
I know you did.

JOHN
Trust me. *(laughter)*

JOEY
Uhm,
I know you did.
It worked.

Rules

THERAPIST AND PROFESSOR
The open couples
in my research
each seem to have rules and agreement,
rules, guidelines, whatever you want to call them,
that preserve the primacy of their relationship.

PAUL

For us it's like, you know
if you're hungry
you know
and one of
you know somebody's not going to cook
then it's okay to go eat.

THERAPIST AND PROFESSOR

Number one is a rule that came out in the non-monogamous
    couples
was safer sex.
Ah it was really important to protect
they might have unsafe sex with each other
but they were going to have safer sex outside the relationship.

PAUL

Uh we're not like Fire Island gay people.
We don't have anonymous sex.
Whoever we're having
whoever the other person might be is strictly
you know
also a friend
but a a fuck buddy.

MATTHEW

It used to be no one in our bed
so we'd just fuck them on the couch and then send them home.
Or in the guest room.
But then we got a really small apartment so the no boys in our bed
    rule didn't really work
anymore cause we didn't have a guest room
and our sofa became a love seat so it was hard to work three boys
    onto that.

THERAPIST AND PROFESSOR

There were some couples where it was
as soon as you come home you tell everything.
And as a matter of fact
for many of those couples it was a sexual turn on
and it got them all horned up and all of this.

MATTHEW

So our sex is consistent.
If anything the boys are just
fun and it's
and it's another way for me to appreciate
him like I love watching him have sex
both with me and with other people. It's very exciting.

THERAPIST AND PROFESSOR

Then there were couples
where it was like
do not talk about it.
Uh if you do it I don't wanna hear about it
and they were the don't ask don't tell kind of couples.
And I found for those couples
there was a more of a concern about jealousy and competition.

PAUL

If you have to talk about it you shouldn't be doing it.

THERAPIST AND PROFESSOR

So that was another
you know frequency.
How often they saw someone outside.
Ah many of the couples I saw a limited to
one you can only see them one, maybe two times
and then you have to cut it off.

PAUL

Uhm I would never sleep with a stupid person
because they
could potentially destroy what David and I have.
They wouldn't understand what we have.
They might
call at the wrong time, do the wrong thing,
make have a confrontation scene.

THERAPIST AND PROFESSOR

My guys were very careful like
you don't get emotionally involved.
You see them once.
Maybe you don't kiss them.

Maybe you don't do certain sex acts with them that you only do
   with me.
Uhm
we only have sex with each other when we're I mean we only have
   outside s- we're only
we're monogamous unless we're not in the same zip code.

MATTHEW

International waters were obviously fine.
Overseas if we were traveling cause you know it's overseas.
It's only so often you get cute British uncut cock.

THERAPIST AND PROFESSOR

But um you get a sense of of the nature of these these uhm rules
   and guidelines.

It's something that we grow into

SHAUN

I think masculinity
and male bodied-ness
brings a lot with it.
Some very real things about needing to be ourselves.
Alone. *(laughter)*
To be strong
to be
who we are independent.
And uh
if we don't honor that and be real with that
I think we battle for supremacy.
And I don't think there's a need for that.
I think we can have caring and intimacy
and connection and vulnerability
uhm
with another person another man
as long as we honor and acknowledge that we both must retain a
   sense of strength
and power
and
individualness individuality
within the context of that relationship.

If we don't then we supplant each other and
we very quickly I think need to
move away from each other
to find ourselves.
If we don't know
who we are
within the context
of the relationship
I think that's why most relationships last
not very long.
Because it's all fun and new and then it's not fun and new and
    then I can't figure out who I am.
I only know myself through
the fact that I'm in a partnership.
Uh if I lose myself
then yeah
I probably need to not be in a partnership I need to know who I
    am.
So that's what I look for is someone that
doesn't complete me
but someone who
uhm
we can create something new with
and that
whatever that new thing is
that it's something that we grow into.

Writing Ethnodramatic Dialogue

Recording actual dialogue rather than interviews can simply be
a more immediate and therefore more powerful way of telling the
story, but it is also about giving the characters more realism and
depth. The audience gets to know a person far better by seeing them
interact with their colleagues and friends rather than just with
[an interviewer].

—Alecky Blythe[1]

Dialogue, consisting of two or more participant/characters in verbal action, reaction, and interaction, is a slippery modality in ethnodrama. Some dialogic exchanges can be gathered from fieldwork participant observation and two- or three-person or focus group interviews, transcripts of court proceedings, and even from a dialogic interview exchange between the researcher and a participant. In one-person plays, the solo actor may transform and reverberate back and forth between one participant/character and another to simulate dialogue within a single scene.

But most ethnodramatic dialogue is a *plausible construction* or *creative nonfiction* (or "faction"—a blended word from fact and fiction). Not every ethnography or empirical source provides the necessary detail for authentic dialogic replication on stage. There are times when we have to rely on the evocative power of the writer's imagination and language to reconstruct the culture and events portrayed on stage. David Hare's (2004) play, *Stuff Happens*, dramatizes political motivations of the Iraq war entry by former American President George W. Bush. The drama includes "characters" such as Bush, Dick Cheney, Colin Powell, Condolezza Rice, Tony Blair, Saddam Hussein, and other central figures in conversational exchanges. Hare accessed multiple sources, both public and private, to authenticate the contents, and relies on verbatim text for portions of monologue and dialogue. But he also notes that his playwright's imagination was employed when he speculated on what may have been discussed by these leaders behind closed doors. Radio documentary producer Natalie Kestecher

(2010) takes it a step further by blurring fact and fiction to create "un-reality"—plausible yet sometimes overtly theatrical text based on her original interviews: "I just often found that it was easier for me to create characters than to find them. They told listeners things that I was sure the real interviewees believed or felt but wouldn't talk about" (p. 109).

In this chapter, playwriting strategies for dialogic writing are outlined with an emphasis on avoiding the static "talking heads" plays all too common in academic ethnodramas. An exemplar of monologic and dialogic exchange is included at the end—Jo Carson's oral history adaptation, *Voodoo*.

Functions of Ethnodramatic Dialogue

Dialogue between characters can first consist of *an exchange of ideas, everyday conversation* that flows about a topic of mutual interest or concern. However, natural dialogue can sometimes be quite mundane or so contextual that its unedited transfer to the stage can seem quite purposeless for an audience. When participant/characters simply "talk about" something, its primary purpose most often is to inform listeners about a particular cultural world and what it's like to live in it.

As an example, I include an excerpt from *Street Rat* (Saldaña, Finley, & Finley, 2005), an ethnodrama about homeless youth in pre-Hurricane Katrina New Orleans. Dialogue in this play was both constructed and reconstructed from several sources: the original ethnographic-based short story by the Finleys (1999), an earlier unpublished reader's theatre script adaptation of field notes, and published poetic constructions by the fieldworkers. Monologic and dialogic snippets were pooled together according to their common topic, then strategically arranged or "spliced" together into a plausible conversational order of traditional turn-taking. These snippets sometimes originated from multiple participants who were interviewed individually, but for the ethnodrama the lines were assigned to two primary characters for a fictional dialogic exchange between them as they killed time on the street waiting for passers-by in order to ask for spare change.

In this scene from *Street Rat*, Roach and Tigger are two homeless young men and best friends talking about male hustling in their subculture. Their status with each other suggests they can be open about what they proclaim as their respective values, attitudes, and beliefs. The characters' use of profanity and ease with discussing sexual subjects are authentic to their natures, and enhance most audience members' attention due to the explicit content.

> ROACH: People try and trick with me for money all the time. I just say, "Fuck off, I'm not a whore." People figure that if you're in the gay district, you *are*. I'm not gonna sell my ass.

> TIGGER: I know plenty of fucking straight up prostitutes. They're cool as hell, but that's not something I'm going to do.

> ROACH: It makes you compromise yourself. People who do it have to be comfortable with doing it. Sometimes people get caught up in it, when they aren't comfortable doing it, but they do it anyway. That causes so many problems.

> TIGGER: That, and the simple fact that people who hustle—not the people who hustle, but the people who hustle them—it's like, the only reason why these rich fuckin' guys are doing this shit, lots of times, the simple fact is they know they can grab a guy off the street and just say, "Come home and fuck me!", "Come home, do this with me," and just take control. I don't know, it's just fucked up.

> ROACH: And then they act all disgusted when you tell them, "No." Like you're nothing if you don't do something like that to earn money.

> TIGGER: Like you don't have any choice in the matter. (p. 146)

Notice that the dialogic exchange above builds on what each participant/character says to the other. In other words, stage dialogue becomes more purposeful when each character actively listens to what the other says and reacts appropriately, thus creating plausible interaction between them.

Further, ethnodramatic dialogue can also emerge when characters *"play" their objectives* which *initiate action*, and when they *display their various attitudes toward one another*. In the excerpt that follows, note how the two young men play their objectives: for both, to collect spare change, and for Tigger, reaching for the leftover beer, to quench his thirst or to feed his alcohol addiction. The Waitress and Gay Tourist each react differently, exhibit different attitudes toward the two boys, and take different actions.

> (*a WAITRESS on her way to work passes by*)

> ROACH: Spare change?

> TIGGER: Spare change?

WAITRESS: (*smiles at them, pulls a coin from her apron pocket, and puts it in ROACH's outstretched hand*) There you go. (*looks back at ROACH as she exits*)

ROACH: Thanks.

TIGGER: Thanks.

(*ROACH and TIGGER leer at the WAITRESS as she leaves*)

ROACH: Now, if a woman wanted to pay me to have sex with her, I would.

TIGGER: Well, depends on the woman.

ROACH: Yeah. If it's some Nancy Reagan-looking woman, then no.

(*a GAY TOURIST enters, wearing Mardi Gras necklaces and with a clear plastic cup of beer in hand, walks past the boys*)

ROACH AND TIGGER: Spare change?

(*the TOURIST glances quickly at ROACH, shakes his head "no," and sets his half-empty cup on the sidewalk by a trash can; exits; TIGGER goes for the beer*)

ROACH: Fuck him. Sneakin' peeks at my facial tat. (*as TIGGER gets the beer, ROACH smiles and starts a private joke between them*) Just say "No!"

TIGGER: No! (*he drinks from the cup, offers ROACH the last swig*) (pp. 146–147)

Dialogue reaches its most impacting moments in a play when *tension* or *conflict* emerges between characters. When their objectives oppose each other, obstacles arise and tactics are employed, often resulting in strong emotional and attitudinal actions, reactions, and interactions. As the street scene between Roach and Tigger continues, Roach's plans to meet a drug dealer meet with Tigger's disapproval. Also note the use of particular subcultural terms.

TIGGER: (*rooting through the trash can for food*) We better make quick work of the schwillies, man. We gotta sp'ange enough for all weekend today; it's gonna rain tomorrow.

ROACH: How do you know that? Are you a weather man now?

TIGGER: I read it in the paper. Town is gonna be packed and we can make bank. The Clover has a sign welcoming some conference, so there's plenty of green around. We just gotta get it while the weather holds.

ROACH: *(looks down the street)* I've gotta meet that guy in a couple hours. *(pulls out some partially-smoked cigarettes from his pocket, gives one to TIGGER; they both light up)*

TIGGER: *(worriedly)* Right. I don't buy it. I don't trust him, Roach.

ROACH: *(tries to reassure TIGGER but sounds doubtful)* I'm not going to have anything on me. The guy holds the stuff. I just go find customers. I take them to him and he gives me a runner's fee. I'm not going to have the stuff on me.

TIGGER: Never in my life have I fucked with the needle.

ROACH: *(insistent)* I'm not using it, Tigger. I'm just running it.

TIGGER: You've done it before, now you'll want to do it again.

ROACH: No! It's only a job. I'm going to get money so we can get a place and we can eat. *(TIGGER does not look at him; impatiently as he sits)* I'm a fuckin' slinger, man. I sell drugs on occasion.

TIGGER: Being around the needle, talking about the needle, makes me very uncomfortable. Fucks with my head. But if someone's gonna do it, they're gonna do it. I've seen it—friends dead.

ROACH: You snort coke with me, but if I try heroin with the guy I'm going to sell it for, that makes it wrong? You're such a fucking hypocrite!

TIGGER: No I'm not! You know what I think's going to happen? You're going to start slammin' it again.

ROACH: *(singing the end of Neil Young's song to TIGGER)* "I've seen the needle and the damage done, a little part of it in everyone, but every junkie's like a setting sun." *(laughs; pulls TIGGER by the arm)* C'mon, let's get outta here.

TIGGER: *(yanks his arm away from ROACH's grip)* You do what you gotta do, I'll catch ya later.

ROACH: Tigger, . . .

TIGGER: *(as he exits)* I'll be on the Square. Hook up with me when you're through.

ROACH: Tigger! Damn. *(shouts after TIGGER)* I hate it when we fight! We fight just like a couple of fucking married people! (pp. 147–148)

Not every fieldwork project we conduct and the associated data collection methods generate opportunities for dialogic exchanges between participant/characters on stage. But if you actively search for and document these interactions from natural social life, you're more likely to generate material for possible dialogic adaptation. Nilaja Sun's (2008) *No Child . . .* was originally performed as a one-woman show about her experiences as a teaching artist in an inner city high school. Ms. Sun displayed not only her writing but performance prowess as she physically and vocally transformed herself instantaneously into a variety of characters with rapid-fire precision. The excerpt that follows consists of nine different characters exchanging dialogue in a span of approximately one minute.

COCA: Miss, did you hear? Someone stole Ms. Tam's bag and she quit for good. We got some Russian teacher now.

MRS. PROJENSKY: Quiet Quiet Quiet Quiet Quiet Quiet Quiet. Quiet!

MS. SUN: Miss, Miss, Miss. I'm the teaching artist for . . .

MRS. PROJENSKY: Sit down, you.

SHONDRIKA: Aw, snap, she told her.

MRS. PROJENSKY: Sit down, quiet. Quiet, sit down.

MS. SUN: No, I'm the teaching artist for this period. Maybe Miss Tam or Mrs. Kennedy told you something about me?

JEROME: *(shadowboxes)* Ah, hah, you being replaced, Russian lady.

MS. SUN: Jerome, you're not helping right now.

JEROME: What?! You don't gotta tell me jack. We ain't got a teacher no more or haven't you heard? *(he flings a chair)* We are the worst class in the school.

MRS. PROJENSKY: Sit down! Sit down!

MS. SUN: Guys, quiet down and focus. We have a show to do in a few weeks.

COCA: Ooee, I don't wanna do this no more. It's stupid.

CHRIS: I still want to do it.

JEROME: Shut the fuck up, Chris.

JOSE: Yo man, she's right. This shit is mad fucking boring yo.

COCA: Yeah!

XIOMARA: Yeah!

BRIAN: Yeah!

SHONDRIKA: Yeah!

COCA: Mad boring.

JEROME: Fuckin' stupid.

MRS. PROJENSKY: Quiet! Quiet! Quiet![2] (pp. 18–19)

Excerpts from Ms. Sun's performances can be accessed on YouTube; one possible link is: http://www.youtube.com/watch?v=vbx5MNj0a-A

Ethnodramatic Exercise: Cross-Cutting Dialogue

A few ethnodramas include scenes that are taken from interviews with couples or groups of people (e.g., Robin Soans' *Life After Scandal* and *The Arab-Israeli Cookbook*), and thus in the dramatization we hear two or more characters jointly telling a tale. But other ethnodramas fictively construct dialogue between two or more people who were interviewed individually.

Figure 4.1. From *Athabasca's Going Unmanned*, an ethnodrama by Dr. Diane Conrad, University of Alberta. Actors from left to right: Sarain Waskewitch and Cole Humeny (appears with permission from Canadian Actor's Equity Association). Photo by Michael Coulis.

Paul Brown and the Workers Cultural Action Committee (2001) developed *Aftershocks*, a documentary theatre production of survivors' and rescuers' stories from the December 28, 1989 Newcastle earthquake in Australia. Most of the participant interviews were conducted individually, but similar and contrasting stories from various individuals were interconnected in the play script. Brown explains that once the transcripts were reduced by half, each interview was segmented into what was called a *grab*, "each grab constituting a discreet [*sic*] story fragment. These were trimmed if necessary to enhance the dramatic effect, without changing the intent or mood of the story, and certainly without altering the unique grammatical constructions that belonged to each speaker" (p. xiv). In the drama, grabs that were thematically related are juxtaposed and interwoven with each other to create a *node*, as in this excerpt from a scene titled "First Aid".

KERRY: We're just lining people up, like you see in a war zone, you know . . . all on the median strip. In sections, as to who is hurt more than others.

MARG: We know an awful lot of the people that we're getting out, and the people that are so badly hurt, we just know them.

KERRY: One of them is out to it. Get her on her side, coma position, can't get her teeth out . . . and this other chappy comes up and he says, "Look, I'm an ex-ambulance man." So he gets her bottom teeth out.

MARG: The girls from the kitchen are hurt, 'cause everything just flew off the stove all over them. A few of them are covered in boiling water, and whatever. And traffic is still on King Street. Traffic is still flowing and we're carrying people across the streets, dodging cars . . . *(Laughing)* It's incredible. They don't even know there's been an earthquake . . . they just don't know what's happened.

KERRY: There's no ambulance, and we're flagging down cars on the street . . . to take people to hospital. . . .

MARG: We're just trying to stop bleeding with our bare hands, type of thing . . . which is, you know, friggin' difficult.[3] (p. 14)

As an ethnodramatic exercise, interview two people separately about the same event or topic. After the separate interviews have been transcribed, review them to explore how the two participants' versions can be interwoven or cross-cut into a single three to five minute scene or node that cuts back and forth from one to another. Find moments of interview text that parallel, juxtapose, and comment on each other when strategically placed together. Performance ethnographer Yolanda Nieves recommends interviewing people with opposing perspectives on a topic separately, then adapting and interweaving their responses to the issue for a plausible, conflict-laden dialogic exchange.

Examples of topics for the interviews might include:
- occupations (each one describes a typical day at work)
- a former teacher (ask one participant to describe his best teacher, the second participant to describe his worst teacher)
- The September 11 terrorist attacks or some other tragic event or news story (if you and the participants feel comfortable discussing it)— memories, perceptions, and feelings about the event
- a favorite singer, musician, or type of music (if possible, encourage the participants to sing or hum on the audio recording for adaptation into the script and a possible staged reading)

Ethnodramatic Exercise: Purposeful Bantering —*The Managed Heart*

The purpose of this improvisational and playwriting exercise is to explore plausible dialogic construction and exchange between characters based on an ethnographic excerpt.

Arlie Russell Hochschild's (2003) classic sociological study, *The Managed Heart: Commercialization of Human Feeling*, examined airline flight attendants and the "emotional labor" that pervades virtually all facets of their training and work routines. Aside from the obvious need to maintain civility and emotional restraint when dealing with difficult passengers, flight attendants also engage in emotional labor between themselves:

> As trainers well know, flight attendants typically work in teams of two and must work on fairly intimate terms with all others on the crew. In fact, workers commonly say the work simply cannot be done well unless they work well together. The reason for this is that the job is partly an "emotional tone" road show, and the proper tone is kept up in large part by friendly conversation, banter, and joking, as ice cubes, trays, and plastic cups are passed from aisle to aisle to the galley, down to the kitchen, and up again. Indeed, starting with the bus ride to the plane, by bantering back and forth the flight attendant does important relational work: she checks on people's moods, relaxes tension, and warms up ties so that each

pair of individuals becomes a team. She also banters to keep herself in the right frame of mind. As one worker put it, "Oh, we banter a lot. It keeps you going. You last longer." (p. 115)

Writing a tension-filled exchange between two people has its challenges, but it is much more difficult to compose an interesting scene between two people who simply banter. There is much more to "small talk" than meets the ear when you consider that each character has the following present within him or her:

- *objectives* or motives in the form of action verbs such as "to persuade," "to reassure," "to maintain calm";
- *conflicts* or *obstacles* confronted by the character which prevent her from achieving her objectives;
- *tactics* or *strategies* to deal with conflicts or obstacles and to achieve her objectives;
- *attitudes* toward the setting, others, and the conflict;
- *emotions* experienced by the character; and
- *subtexts* or the character's unspoken thoughts, underlying moods, or impression management.

1. Write or verbally improvise with a partner and document plausible dialogue that may occur between two flight attendants for one minute, as profiled by Hochschild in the previous excerpt. Explore the types of dialogue that may get exchanged as two people simply sit as if they are in a van or bus on their way to the airport. The goal is not to develop idle chatter but *purposeful bantering*. Remember that these flight attendants' objectives consist of the following:
   - to check on a person's mood
   - to relax any tension
   - to warm up ties for teamwork
   - to keep one's self in the right frame of mind

   Explore how the bantering may change and even become more active by working with some rehearsal props such as plastic cups and water as two flight attendants work together in a simulated compact galley or kitchen space of an airplane.

2. After purposeful bantering ("talking about") has been explored, develop plausible dialogue that emerges from two other forms of stage dialogic exchange:

- playing objectives and displaying attitudes: two flight attendants talking about particular passengers on the plane as they work in the galley or kitchen
- tension and conflict: one flight attendant in an uncomfortable exchange with an unruly or drunk passenger; or, one flight attendant supervisor criticizing a crew member for unsatisfactory performance

Choral Exchanges

It is rare to find ethnodramas with more than two characters that dialogue and interact with each other at any given time in the play. But sometimes there is a *choral exchange*, a nonrealistic, presentational mode in which multiple actors/characters speak both individually and collectively, sometimes in overlapping ways. The effect is a cascade of multiple thoughts and impressions, used most often to highlight the diversity of possible perspectives about an issue. At other times, the technique can be used purposefully for dramatic effect when the rapidity of utterances creates a sense of ironic juxtaposition, comic cacophony, or surrealistic chaos. Think of choral exchange as a form of *vocal collage* that provides a heightened sense of omniscient insight about the characters or issues for audiences.

Following is an excerpt from *Handle with Care?*, an ethnodrama about metastatic breast cancer (Gray & Sinding, 2002). In this scene called "Diagnosis," a male doctor is seated with his female patient while a chorus of three women (A, B, and C) stand behind her. During the exchange, the doctor speaks continuously as he explains to the patient her test results while the chorus voices aloud the dizzying array of thoughts going through the patient's mind.

> DOCTOR: Good morning, Mrs. Martineau. I have the results of your tests and I'm afraid the news isn't good.
>
> *(PATIENT & CHORUS ABC look up and take quick breath in)*
>
> DOCTOR: We now know that the hot spots that showed up on the bone scan are metastatic lesions.
>
> CHORUS ABC: I don't want to be here. *(they look away)*
>
> DOCTOR: I think we should go ahead and start you on treatment and see how things progress. I need to tell you that when breast cancer spreads to the bone, it is no longer curable . . .

CHORUS C: *(face front)* Oh, no.

CHORUS A: *(face front)* I'm dying!

CHORUS B: *(face front)* My kids!

DOCTOR: . . . but there are treatments that we can give you.

CHORUS ABC: How's Joe going to cope?

DOCTOR: Many women do well for a long time, many years in fact.

CHORUS ABC: *(to DOCTOR)* How long do I have?

DOCTOR: The usual course of treatment is to begin hormone therapy.

CHORUS ABC: There's so much I haven't done.

CHORUS C: *(face front)* Hawaii.

CHORUS A: *(face front)* My book.

CHORUS B: *(face front)* The garden.

DOCTOR: So I would recommend that we start you on tamoxifen . . .

CHORUS ABC: Who's going to look after Mum?

DOCTOR: . . . which is an anti-estrogen hormone that comes in a pill form.

CHORUS ABC: Maybe they're wrong.

DOCTOR: It's effective for many women. And if it stops working . . .

CHORUS ABC: *(turn away and protect self)* I can't cope with this.

DOCTOR: . . . there are other hormone therapies . . .

CHORUS C: *(face front)* Update my will . . .

DOCTOR: . . . and chemotherapy available . . .

CHORUS A: *(face front)* Music at my funeral . . .

DOCTOR: . . . and sometimes radiation treatment is used.

CHORUS B: *(face front)* I'm going to die . . .

CHORUS C: My kids.

CHORUS A: Joe.

CHORUS B: Pain.

DOCTOR: There may also be some new clinical . . .

CHORUS A: *(to PATIENT)* Breathe.

DOCTOR: . . . trials available here that we might consider. So down the road . . .

CHORUS A: Breathe.

DOCTOR: . . . we may want to discuss that in more detail.

CHORUS AC: *(not in unison)* Don't faint. Breathe . . . *etc.*

DOCTOR: The important thing for you to know is that although your cancer has spread . . .

CHORUS ABC: Breathe, don't faint! *(keep doing intermittently, building throughout DOCTOR's speech)*

DOCTOR: . . . there are things we can do to keep the disease from progressing. And we'll also deal with any symptoms that might occur. Our focus is to provide you with the best quality of life possible.

(PATIENT collapses, wails; CHORUS becomes silent)

DOCTOR: Now I realize that this must be difficult for you and I'm going to ask my nurse to come in and spend a few minutes with you. I'm sure you'll have a lot of questions later. Do you have any questions now?

CHORUS ABC: Pull yourself together!

PATIENT: *(to DOCTOR)* No.

(adapted from Gray & Sinding, 2002, pp. 42–44)

The Researcher as Character

One decision most ethnodramatists must make is whether to represent and present one's self on stage with other participant/characters. A key question to consider is, "Whose story is it?"

A few theatrical adaptations have been made of remote ethnographic fieldwork, such as Allen & Garner's (1997) dramatization of Andean society in *Condor Qatay*, and Peter Brook's production of *The Ik*, based on Colin Turnbull's African field study with *The Mountain People* (Higgins, Cannan, & Turnbull, 1984). But the anthropologist is present as a character in *The Ik*, while deliberately excluded from *Condor Qatay*. Turnbull's interactions with and reactions to the Ik tribe played a pivotal role in its original write-up, and thus his inclusion in the ethnodramatic adaptation is justified. But the fieldworkers for *Condor Qatay* chose to prioritize the people they studied and focused on one Chilean family as the principal characters for their dramatization. The family members' dialogic interactions tell the particular story the playwrights wanted told.

A few researchers/ethnodramatists incorporate themselves into their own plays as narrators. My very first ethnodrama, *"Maybe someday, if I'm famous. . ."* (Saldaña, 1998b) included myself as a researcher/narrator who asked participants questions replicated from interviews, spoke verbatim from my field notes as actors played out the action, and talked directly to the audience to provide exposition and the study's context. As a first-time venture into ethnodramatic writing for a targeted audience of educational theatre researchers, it was probably considered good scholarship but shaky dramatic writing. In retrospect, I noticed myself falling into the trap I often see in newcomers to ethnodrama: thinking like a social scientist and not like an artist. I mistakenly assumed that my artistic venture somehow lost credibility without traditional academic discourse woven into it. To reinforce a principle I stated in Chapter One: A play is not a journal article. A reader of a juried article may want to know what your study's conceptual framework is, but it has no place whatsoever in an ethnodrama's monologue or dialogue.

I discourage the use of the researcher as narrator, in the traditional sense, to fulfill such mechanical elements as delivery of exposition, setting the context, and transitioning from one scene to the next in ethnodramatic work. When your experiences as a fieldworker played a *pivotal* role in the consequent research story, such as journalist Yvonne Latty in Douglas C. Wager's adaptation of her book on Iraq war veterans, *In Conflict*, your presence on stage as a character may be justified. But if your participants can speak for themselves (and indeed they most often can), then let *them* tell the story. Use the narrator function sparingly and strategically in ethnodramatic work. Sometimes the best place for the researcher during the play is offstage.

Ethnodramatic Exercise: Writing Creative Nonfiction—Jennifer Toth's *The Mole People*

The purpose of this exercise is to adapt a chapter narrative into a multiple-character dialogic scene portrayed by several actors for the stage. Jennifer Toth's (1993) journalistic account of *The Mole People: Life in the Tunnels Beneath New York City* provides intriguing material for dramatization. Ms. Toth investigated firsthand the dangerous, subterranean, subcultural world of New York City's homeless. Her account sometimes replicates dialogue and sometimes narrates what was spoken by or to her and others.

1. Select a chapter from Toth's book with multiple character-participants in narrative dialogue (e.g., "Hell's Kitchen," "Harlem Gang," "J.C.'s Community"). Adapt and dramatize an excerpt from the chapter into a seven- to ten-minute scene for the stage. Create original dialogue for the character-participants when Toth describes, rather than quotes, what they told her. For example, from the opening to "Harlem Gang":

    Blade [Toth's informant], who says he was once a tunnel dweller and now still frequents the tunnels as a graffiti writer, is walking the underground with me when we stumble across the gang. . . . Blade says I look pale, and begins to lead me on a "shortcut" to the surface.

    We climb a few levels higher, but the air thickens with fumes and, feeling nauseated, I ask Blade for a quick exit to air. He knows of none. "Besides," he smiles, "we're in the middle of Harlem. You're safer down here" (p. 183).

    In this brief excerpt, the only full line of dialogue in quotes is Blade's "Besides, we're in the middle of Harlem. You're safer down here." This is a line that can be inserted directly into the adapted scene, but as a playwright, the goal is to create plausible dialogue based on what Toth narrates and what is appropriate for the characters' ways of acting, reacting, and interacting (based on what has been and will be learned about them in the remainder of the book). A sample exchange of dialogue with stage directions might read thusly:

    (BLADE and JENNIFER walk in near darkness; JENNIFER coughs, almost gags)

    BLADE: You ain't lookin' so good.

    JENNIFER: Oh, God, the stink.

    BLADE: Sewer gas, girl.

    JENNIFER: Oh, God. *(covers her mouth with her hand)* I think I'm going to be sick.

    BLADE: Aw, Jesus fuckin' Christ.

    JENNIFER: *(getting panicked)* Blade, I've got to get out of here *now*. I need some air. Where's the way out?

    BLADE: Aw, Jesus. *(looks around)* There's . . . No. . . . Well, I ain't sure there *is* a way out near here. *(chuckling)* Besides, we're in the middle of Harlem. You're safer down here. *(JENNIFER makes a sound as if she's holding back vomit)* Come on, girl. Keep up. *(they continue walking, BLADE leading the way)*

Blade and Jennifer continue through the tunnels until they encounter a hostile gunman in the dark. As you read this excerpt from "Harlem Gang" in *The Mole People*, visualize the action and hear the characters speaking in your mind:

"You got someone down there with you?" demands the gunman.

"Yeah," I answer, trembling. "I'm a reporter."

Blade shakes his head again, exasperated. He twists his hands at his thighs as though wishing he had snapped my neck like a chicken. The two of us move back toward the light.

We must look cowed and helpless because the gunman laughs in relief. I introduce myself, explaining that I'm collecting material on tunnel people.

"Good thing," he says importantly. "Don' want to waste no lead. Don' have lead to waste."

His fear and hostility have largely disappeared. "How about me interviewing you?" I ask.

"Don' see it as no problem," he replies, "long as we know where to find you."

You won't know, I tell him, but soften it by offering to withhold names and descriptions. "I'm writing a book, and in a book you'll live forever," I say.

That seems persuasive. "I'll have to clear it with Doc," he says.

I can see him more clearly now as we move forward—a tall, slim man, perhaps in his twenties, but looking much older. We turn a sharp corner that seems flooded with grate lights to find Doc, their leader, a short, heavyset man with dark glasses.

He likes the idea of being part of a book. He also trusts my guide.

"She's with Blade," he says. "It's cool."

Surprised, I look questioningly at Blade. He just nods to Doc and ignores me.[4] (pp. 185–186)

The chapter continues with Toth learning about subterranean gang culture among the men. After you've read the full chapter (indeed, the entire book to put the chapter in context), explore how Toth as a character can be woven into the scene without narrating directly to the audience. If we were to stage *The Mole People*, we should consider how dialogue exchanged between characters, rather than one-person monologic narration, can carry the plot, storyline, and scene changes forward.

2. Recruit university or professional actors to read aloud the scene composed and ask them to assess its effectiveness from a performer's perspective. Reflect on the challenges of dramatizing a scene with multiple character/participants. Also reflect on the challenges of dramatizing an ethnographic account as a secondary source for an ethnodramatic adaptation, and the legitimacy (i.e., credibility, trustworthiness, and ethics) of creating dialogue that was not documented in the original account.

Storylining and Plotting the Ethnodrama

Now that the very basics of monologue and dialogue construction have been covered, the next step is to address the larger scheme of their placement within a longer play. Think of the individual monologues and scenes of dialogue you've written as separate pearls; what strings them together is the storyline and plot.

In traditional dramatic literature parlance, a *plot* is the overall structure of the play (linear, episodic, revue, prologue, epilogue, one act, full length, and so on). The *storyline* is the sequence of events or character actions that occur within the plot (what happens first, second, third, climax, denouement, and so on). In qualitative research terms, the plot of a study is its conceptual or theoretical framework, while the storyline is the fieldwork's investigation, analysis, and write-up stages. I differentiate between plot and storyline because each one plays an important role in the structural design of a play script, though we may not always attend to them in our beginning playwriting ventures. Storylines will be discussed first since they are intricately related to characters and are usually constructed first by a playwright.

Storylining

Verbatim theatre playwright Robin Soans cautions:

> I maintain that it is just as important for the audience at a verbatim play to want to know what happens next as it is in any other play. No matter how compelling the speeches are in terms of truthfulness and revelation in their own right, the verbatim play must be more than a random collection of monologues if it is to sustain interest over a whole evening. . . . [It] must still set up conflicts and attempt to resolve them. Characters should be shown to undertake journeys of discovery of some kind, even if these journeys take place while the character is sat in a chair, talking. (Hammond & Steward, 2008, p. 26)

Traditional playwriting storylines include primary characters who *change* in some way from the beginning to the end of the play. This is the "journey of discovery" Soans refers to. For example, in Elissa Foster's *Storm Tracking*, the ethnodrama begins with Deborah, the female protagonist, in the early stages of a troubled marriage, which then escalates in tension toward an inevitable divorce, yet ends with a sense of a new beginning to her life. In Anne Nelson's *The Guys*, the drama begins with a distraught fire captain trying to make sense of the tragic losses of his men from the September 11 terrorist attacks, then progresses toward his healing by the end of the play through cathartic writing of eulogies with a sympathetic journalist. Roach's tragic journey in *Street Rat* starts with his everyday struggle to survive as a homeless youth through tough bravado and street smarts, only for him to painfully realize by the end of the play how much he desperately wants to go home but probably never can.

"What happens next?" is an almost universal question that drives our interest in reading and listening to stories. Once we as audience members become engaged with a character and his or her conflicts, we sustain our curiosity and attention by wondering what happens next to the character as the storyline progresses forward and new revelations unfold. Just as a monologue has a structural arc, so does a play—usually referred to as its *spine*. A litmus test dramatists apply to discern a play's spine is to describe in one sentence what a play is about in terms of its central character's conflict, journey, and change. Thus, the spine of *Storm Tracking* is an academic wife's painful realization that the only way to heal her broken marriage is to initiate the end of it so she can move on with her personal and professional life. Before or as your own ethnodrama develops, explore how you can, in a single sentence, describe what your play is about. In qualitative research terms, this is comparable to stating the purpose of the study.

Most playwrights will construct a narrative treatment—a prose or bullet-pointed outline—that simply tells the story of the play in discrete units of action. In qualitative research terms, this is comparable to the traditional methods section before the findings of the study are presented. The treatment is a road map of sorts for the script's developmental journey. A few playwrights will not compose a treatment but instead get right to the dialogue and literally discover in what direction the characters take them as the text is written. But this is most often a tactic for fictional works. Ethnodramatic plays rely on a corpus of interview transcripts, field notes, and/or documents for dramatization. In a sense, we don't really "write" ethnodramas, we *adapt* the stories told to us.

Figure 4.2. A hospital attendant subdues an elderly woman with dementia in Oma Morey's ethnodrama, *The Long Journey Home*. Actors: Frank Petronella and Shirley Wettling. Director: Oma Morey.

As the empirical materials are collected and reviewed, some ethnodramatists will code or make margin notes on hard copy about potential monologue excerpts, possible scenes, expendable passages, theatrical images on stage, and other preliminary matters. But remember my cautionary mantra: Stop thinking like a social scientist and start thinking like an artist. Don't code your empirical materials as you would for a traditional qualitative study. Some ethnodramatists have reported lackluster play scripts when they employed this method; categories of transcript excerpts don't always suggest units of action or scenes (Robinson, 2010; Saldaña, 1998a).

Each ethnodrama's database is different, so it is quite difficult to prescribe how to storyline and plot a play script. That is why I am a strong proponent of reading lots of quality ethnodramatic play scripts. It is from these case study examples that you accumulate a repertoire of dramatization ideas. My personal way of working is admittedly a holistic, heuristic process. I cut and paste interview transcript and field note excerpts in a word processor file into an initial skeletal structure. It is literally like painting a blank canvas improvisationally with words, thinking theatrically as I experiment with arrangement and flow. I reverberate quickly back and forth between the roles of playwright, actor, director, designer, and audience member as I explore how the text might be performed and perceived on stage. If I know specifics ahead of time such as performance venue, size of cast, and possible scenographic elements available, those parameters help shape what I can and cannot initially put on the page and thus on the stage. The script eventually takes shape as creative ideas emerge for how the work progresses in units and as a unified whole. And through workshop readings and the rehearsal process, the play becomes *re*written to better tell the story.

I hope you don't feel that all I can offer is a "just do it" charge for writing an ethnodrama. But I *have* provided more specific recommendations and advice for monologue and scene development. These are cornerstone methods and what dramatic literature consists of. Storyline and plot, however, are more difficult to provide specific guidance for because each story is different and each original production is site-specific. You must think of your ethnodrama as a case study, artistically rendered and customized in its structural design with the unique empirical materials you've collected.

Plotting

Ethnodramas such as *Storm Tracking*, *The Guys*, and *Street Rat* are longer one-act plays with both monologic and dialogic structures. Their storylines and spines involve characters in conflict with themselves and others because they involve two or more characters in action, reaction, and interaction. But what of exclusively monologic structured plays, the kind most frequently written for ethnotheatrical production?

A monologic play also has a spine, but it is expressed in terms of the multiple characters' collective journey through the drama's central topic or idea. For example, the spine of Alan Haehnel's *What I Want to Say But Never Will* is about adolescents voicing their private and secret concerns about their personal lives that peers and adults must hear, no matter how trivial or painful these important concerns may be perceived to be.

Soans cautions playwrights that "a random collection of monologues" will fatigue an audience. Therefore, some sense of unity and direction must be evident in the plot because multiple storylines from multiple characters are coming at spectators in relatively quick succession. Several monologic scripts like *The Exonerated* employ a *rotation plot* in which we hear different characters' presentations or journeys interspersed throughout the play as it progresses; for example:

- Character A's Monologue, Part 1
- Character B's Monologue, Part 1
- Character C's Monologue, Part 1

- Character A's Monologue, Part 2
- Character C's Monologue, Part 2
- Character B's Monologue, Part 2
- Character C's Monologue, Part 3
- Character A's Monologue, Part 3
- Character B's Monologue, Part 3
- Characters A, B, and C's Choral Monologue Finale

But other ethnodramas with multiple and unique characters present only one monologue apiece, such as the plays of Anna Deavere Smith. I once worked with a playwright on the plotting of his monologic ethnodrama and advised him to carefully consider the sequential order of the pieces. Most of the monologues, in and of themselves, were very well composed. Yet I advised him that the linear arrangement of his twenty-five or so monologues seemed not random but without a sense of build. Each monologue addressed the same topic, yet the overall play still lacked unity and a sense of journey. As I read the play, I noticed that virtually each monologue had its own emotional perspective: Some of the pieces were very humorous, some contained bitter feelings, a few were very angry, some were hopeful, and others were poignant and bittersweet. But the overall erratic sequencing of emotional rhythms felt chaotic. I advised him to reclassify his monologues according to their overall tone, and to *thematically plot* them into phases or categories for the characters' and audience's emotional journeys:

- begin with one or two very humorous monologues to engage the audience from the beginning;
- progress toward the bitter monologues;
- progress toward the angry monologues;
- divert us with a humorous monologue;
- steer us toward the poignant and bittersweet monologues;
- ease us with a humorous monologue;
- the most humorous or the most emotionally gripping story/monologue is the climax; and
- end with the hopeful monologues; the most inspiring or peacefully gentle monologue in this category is placed last to provide a sense of closure.

If your monologic ethnodrama has a variety of emotional tones, consider how their strategic grouping and ordering can be plotted to provide the audience with a sense of journey from one place through another then through another then toward the end.

Other common structures in drama include the *chronological plot*, in which time is maintained as a linear construct—the story's events unfold on stage in the order they happened in real life (e.g., Saldaña, Finley, & Finley's *Street Rat*). Some plays explore *"time travel" plots* in which the sequencing of events is purposefully out of chronological order, such as the one-person play whose characters' stories iterate from present to past to present to past to present to past and so on (e.g., Doug Wright's *I Am My Own Wife*). A *braided plot* (rare in ethnodrama but quite common in teleplays for dramas and situation comedies) interweaves three different storylines whose scenes alternate and progress from first story scene, to second story scene, to third story scene, to first story scene, second story scene, third story scene, and so on. Finally, the *revue plot* is a series of stylistically different yet topically related pieces strategically organized and ordered to provide overall dramatic variety in tones, tempos, and rhythms to the play, such as an opening group song followed by a monologue followed by a three-person scene followed by a solo song followed by a dance followed by a two-person scene followed by another monologue, and so on (e.g., The Civilians' *Gone Missing*).

Like a storyline, the plot or overall structure for your ethnodrama depends on your unique database plus your creative vision for the play.

Figure 4.3. Burundian refugee Nagwida Ntibagirigwa, Haitian immigrant Myken Milsette, and Johnson & Wales University student Jasmine Randolph in *Three Purple Plums*, an ethnodrama about HIV/AIDS and child-headed households in Africa. Photo by Dorothy Abram.

On Themes, Lines, and Moments

We've been taught by teachers to look for the theme or moral in a selection of literature, including plays. I always had an aversion to this—and I was trained as an English teacher myself! As a student, I usually guessed what the theme was and most often I was wrong. Usually a theme in dramatic literature never came to me, yet when a play was didactic or instructional, the theme was so blatantly present that it was embarrassingly obvious.

As a playwright, should you somehow insure that a theme of some sort is woven into your play? My answer is no. If you write with a message, moral, or lesson in mind, the result is most often a heavy-handed, theme-driven fable rather than a character-inspired and story-driven drama. You may have a particular social agenda or specific perspective in mind as your project develops, and there is certainly nothing wrong with that. Indeed, some of the best ethnodramas take sides or take a stand on their issues. But they generally do so by letting their participant/characters speak for themselves. It is the individual audience member who then reflects on what messages to take from their stories. In traditional qualitative research studies in article or book format, I am a vehement proponent of presenting answers rather than reflective questions toward the end of the report. But in ethnodramas, sometimes no direct answers to the problems posed by or toward the characters work best to stimulate audience thought and possible post-performance reflection and dialogue.

Instead of a central theme, strive to include or create individual lines of monologue or dialogue and specific moments of stage action that hold significant insight and may make a memorable impact on audience members. From fictional dramatic literature, for example, I am always moved by the storyteller's line in Bertolt Brecht's *The Caucasian Chalk Circle* when he proclaims after we witness a humane act during a war, "Even in the worst of times, there are still good people." I was also taken aback when I saw a performance of the ethnodrama, *The Laramie Project: Ten Years Later*, and heard a citizen who resented the exploitation by the theatre company's work in their town say in the play, "We are not a 'project'; we are a *community*." And from the autoethnotheatrical production of *shots: a love story*, the nightmarish addiction of alcohol gone out of control was staged by a three-minute movement sequence of characters drinking one shot after another in rapid and robotic succession over loud, pulsating dance club music. These are performance moments that have been burned into my memory because they made a personal and powerful impact. Whether other audience members experienced the same "wow" factor (or "aesthetic arrest," as it is also called) that I did is unknown. But this is just one way ethnodrama and ethnotheatre can leave a legacy: make the performance memorable—always through quality work, and particularly through moments of dramatic and theatrical awe.

RECOMMENDED READINGS

Play Scripts

You become a better playwright by reading exemplary scripts. I recommend the following plays, alphabetized by title, to expand your knowledge of dialogic ethnodramas.

Betrayed by George Packer (New York: Faber and Faber, 2008). Packer's investigative journalism and interviews with Iraqi citizens assisting U.S. military forces in the Middle East formed the basis for his drama. The major characters are composites, and dialogue was constructed from interview transcripts and what Packer created as plausible conversations and action.

The Guys by Anne Nelson (New York: Random House, 2004). Based on Nelson's actual experiences, a journalist helps a New York City fire captain write eulogies for fire fighters who lost their lives during the September 11 terrorist attacks. The script features several poignant monologues by the journalist reflecting on the tragedy. Also view the DVD film version of the play (Universal Studios, 2003). The acting edition of this script is available from Dramatists Play Service, but the Random House trade publication includes excellent background material by the playwright.

Having Our Say: The Delany Sisters' First 100 Years by Emily Mann (New York: Dramatists Play Service, 1996). This two-person play, based on Delany, Delany, and Hearth's (1993) oral history, chronicles the true stories of growing up as African-American women in the U.S. Mann's adaptation creates joint storytelling between the two figures, addressing the audience as if we are invited guests to their home.

The Investigation by Peter Weiss, English version by Jon Swan and Ulu Grosbard (Woodstock, IL: Dramatic Publishing, 1966). Weiss creates a documentary drama from testimony derived from the Frankfurt war crime trials. The dialogue is formatted in question-answer structures exchanged between a judge, prosecuting attorney, counsel for the defense, nine witnesses, and eighteen accused. The lengthy but gripping tribunal play contains graphic descriptions of concentration camp atrocities at Auschwitz.

Kind of Blue by Martin Glynn (Birmingham, UK: Sankofa Associates, 2011). This one–act play is an intergenerational drama about two black Britons struggling with advanced glaucoma and its effects on their lives and outlooks. Playwright Glynn states that his play "is less of a story about loss of sight but more about the transcending of difficulties in the face of adversity."

Nickel and Dimed by Joan Holden (New York: Dramatists Play Service, 2005). Holden freely adapts Barbara Ehrenreich's classic investigative journalist account of trying to make a living on minimum wage jobs. Constructed dialogue between co-workers and significant others in Barbara's life illustrates how narrative transforms into dramatic action. Barbara functions as both a character and direct address narrator.

No Child . . . by Nilaja Sun (New York: Dramatists Play Service, 2008). Nilaja Sun performs sixteen different characters in her serio-comic one-woman show, many of whom dialogue with each other in rapid-fire succession. Sun is a visiting theatre artist who stages a play with socially challenged and disenfranchised youth at a Bronx high school. The play is based on Sun's own teaching experiences and can also be performed by a larger ensemble of actors.

Storm Tracking by Elissa Foster, in *Ethnodrama: An Anthology of Reality Theatre*, edited by Johnny Saldaña (Walnut Creek, CA: AltaMira Press, 2005). Foster's gripping autoethnodrama is an honest yet painful account of the disintegration of her troubled marriage. The dialogue exchanged between husband and wife is starkly confrontational.

Street Rat by Johnny Saldaña, Susan Finley, and Macklin Finley, in *Ethnodrama: An Anthology of Reality Theatre*, edited by Johnny Saldaña (Walnut Creek, CA: AltaMira Press, 2005). Dialogue between the homeless characters was constructed from various interview sources, and adapted from unpublished and published fieldwork accounts by the Finleys. The play also features the original work of Macklin Finley, who appears in the drama as a poetic narrator.

Comparative Readings

1. Read Barbara Ehrenreich's (2002) investigative journalistic account, *Nickel and Dimed: On (Not) Getting By in America,* then read the play script adaptation of her work by Joan Holden (2005). Reflect on the theatrical adaptation's choices and the effectiveness of what the playwright included, excluded, and adapted from Ehrenreich's book. Pay particular attention to the dialogic constructions in the play, such as the conversations between the women as Merry Maids.

2. Read Sarah A. Delany, A. Elizabeth Delany, and Amy Hill Hearth's (1993) *Having Our Say: The Delany Sisters' First 100 Years*, then read the play script with the same title adapted by Emily Mann (1996). Reflect on the theatrical adaptation's choices and effectiveness of what the playwright included, excluded, and adapted from the book. If you can gain access to the 2001 VHS recording of the made-for-television film adaptation of *Having Our Say* (starring Diahann Carroll and Ruby Dee as the Delany sisters; Columbia Tristar Home Video, 2000), view it and compare the teleplay to the original book and stage play adaptation.

3. Read Lisa M. Tillman-Healy's (1996) autoethnography, "A Secret Life in a Culture of Thinness: Reflections on Body, Food, and Bulimia." Explore the multiple ways possible for dramatizing Tillman-Healy's story as either a one-woman play or with multiple characters on stage; consider monologic, dialogic, and/or choral exchanges. What potentially significant lines and visual moments exist in the adaptation and production?

Endnotes

1   In Hammond & Steward (2008), *Verbatim Verbatim: Contemporary Documentary Theatre*, p. 93.

2. *No Child . . .* received its World Premiere by Epic Theatre Center, New York, NY in May 2006. Originally produced off-Broadway in New York at the Barrow Street Theatre by Scott Morfee and Tom Wirtshafter.

   Permission for use of *Our Country's Good* by Timberlake Wertenbaker in *No Child . . .* was granted by the Estate of Thomas Keneally and Timberlake Wertenbaker. First presented at the Royal Court Theatre, London, on September 10, 1988.

   Information: All rights for *No Child . . .* are reserved. Production scripts and rights are available through Dramatists Play Service (http://www.dramatists.com/).

3. Copyright 1993, 2001 The Workers Cultural Action Committee, Paul Brown; courtesy of Currency Press Pty Ltd, PO Box 2287, Strawberry Hills NSW 2012, Australia, http://www.currency.com.au

4. From *The Mole People: Life in the Tunnels Beneath New York City* by Jennifer Toth. Copyright © 1993 by Jennifer Toth. Used with permission of Chicago Review Press.

Voodoo by Jo Carson

Voodoo demonstrates monologic and dialogic forms of realistic writing. *Voodoo* also provides an example of how an oral historian both adapts and transforms her interviews into a finely crafted story for the stage. Ms. Carson is an exceptional researcher-playwright who relies on the elegant language of her participants and the essential elements of the well-told tale to compose works that exemplify theatrical storytelling at its best. After the play script, Jo Carson offers her comments and reflections on the development and universal meanings of the piece.

Chicago, Illinois

A Man and three women: the Man's Mother, the Mother's Sister Bissa and the Voodoo Woman. All are on stage in different places from the beginning of the story. Use the stage as a tour of events in the story. The Man is the one who moves. He must travel with his Mother to get to Bissa, travel with Bissa to get to the Voodoo Woman; then, he must pass Bissa and his Mother again on his way back out with new understanding. It is a formal version of the classic hero's journey.

MAN: I was not an easy kid. I was a liar and a thief and I didn't do my homework and didn't like school and I hung out with a bad group. I was a half-assed juvenile delinquent. But my mother was no charmer either. She was a controlling woman, and her punishments were sometimes close to torture. She'd of been in trouble with the Geneva Convention folks and I've got the scars to prove it. She was a professing Christian, and she spent a lot of time at church, so for a long time I spent a lot of time at church, but it didn't make any less a sinner out of either of us, it just made us feel guilty about what we did do, which made us even meaner to one another. My mother came from the South, Deep South, backwoods people, and she'd worked hard to get to Chicago, and then to make something of herself when she got here. And she had made something of herself, she was a nurse, and from all reports, a good one. I never knew her as a nurse. If I was sick, I got locked in my room with a pot to shit in, a pitcher of water and some crackers, while she went and did her eight-hour shift. I'm not making that up. This was junior high, somewhere about seventh grade, and I was sick for almost a month. It was right after that I started getting into real trouble, and she sent me to the voodoo woman.

(A car made of two chairs. The Man's Mother is in the driver's seat.)

MOTHER: Get in here.

(He enters his Mother's sphere.)

MAN: She picked me up after school in a car. We didn't have a car, and I didn't even know she knew how to drive, but she did. And she drove me out to O'Hare Airport, drove like a bat out of hell, and it turned out she had an airplane ticket, and she was trying to make the connection. The ticket was for me. *(To his Mother.)* Where am I going?

MOTHER: You'll find out. Bissa's gonna pick you up when you get there.

MAN *(To the audience)*: Bissa. Her big sister. Bissa was short for "Big Sister." I was scared sometimes of my mother, but Bissa struck terror in my heart. I mean Bissa could pick you up by the scruff of the neck and sling you like a cat against the wall. And Bissa didn't mind doing it. I mean, I had been partway through one wall already, the wall between the kitchen and the bathroom in our house, thanks to Bissa, when she came to Chicago for Thanksgiving, and I hadn't really done anything that bad. I'd talk back to mother in her presence. And then we had to get through Thanksgiving dinner, my collarbone was cracked, and my manners weren't all Bissa thought they ought to be. She had my mother in tears all through dinner and I was afraid to eat anything. May have been the only time in my life I was ever afraid to eat. I mean, I've been in jail, and I've been in some tight situations, but I've not since been so scared to sit at a table and eat. Bissa. But at least I knew where I was going. Back South. Bissa still lived back where Mother started. *(to his Mother)* Do I have to stay with Bissa?

MOTHER: While you're there, you get to.

MAN *(To the audience)*: "Get to," you hear that, "get to" . . . *(To his Mother)* How long am I going to be there? *(To the audience)* But she didn't answer that. She popped me on the airplane—no luggage— just barely in time to take off. It's my only airplane trip so far.

(He leaves his Mother and passes to Bissa's sphere.)

Well, Bissa met me at the other end. Bissa was not as big as she had been. Truth was, Bissa was dying. This was the last thing she knew to do for her sister, try to help her with me. Truth was, Bissa had bought me the airplane ticket. But I didn't know all this then. Bissa put me in her car and we drove through the town where she lived. We drove for a long time, out into swamp country. I've never seen anything like it. *(To Bissa)* Where are we going?

BISSA: You know when we get there.

MAN *(to the audience)*: We must have driven forty, fifty miles, and we come onto cars parked by the side of the road out in the middle of nowhere, and Bissa pulls up behind the last one and parks.

BISSA: You got an appointment, all these others just waiting in line.

MAN *(To Bissa)*: "In line" for what?

BISSA: To see the Sister. She's gonna put some starch in you, straighten you right up.

MAN *(to the audience)*: And we walked down a path that led into the woods, and we came to a clearing and a little one-room cinder-block building that didn't seem to have any windows. There were people seated around outside on benches, maybe eight or nine men and women, and there was a woman beside the door to the house. Bissa told her who we were and that we had an appointment, and she told us to take a seat. We sat. No one spoke. We all just looked at one another. A man came out of the house, and then the woman by the door called my name . . .

(He leaves Bissa's sphere and enters the Voodoo Woman's.)

. . . and motioned me into the little house. There was no light inside the house except what came in the door, and, as I had thought, no windows. It didn't smell dirty, anything like that, but it was damp, you know, concrete damp. A tiny woman lay on a little bed and watched me come in. At first I didn't see her, my eyes weren't adjusted to the dark.

(Voodoo Woman, VDW, looks at him for an uncomfortably long time.)

VDW: So you're the bad boy, are you? I don't see nothing so bad about you. What do you do that's so bad?

MAN *(to VDW)*: I don't like school.

VDW: I asked you what you do that's bad. I didn't ask what you thought about school. You lie, son?

MAN: Sometimes.

VDW: Um-hum. You take things?

MAN: Only if . . .

VDW: Do you take things don't belong to you?

MAN: Sometimes.

VDW: Sometimes ain't no answer. Have you taken things that don't belong to you?

MAN: Yes.

VDW: Ma'am!

MAN: Yes, ma'am.

VDW: Um-hum. You a liar and a thief. You ever murdered anybody?

MAN: No. *(He remembers)* Ma'am.

VDW: You ever cut up on dogs or cats or other living things just for the fun of it?

MAN: No . . . I wouldn't.

VDW: You ever set fire to things or pee your bed?

MAN: NO! Ma'am.

VDW: So you're the kind of boy does little bad things.

MAN: I guess so.

VDW: You guess so?

MAN: Yes, ma'am, I do. But, Mama, well, Mama . . .

VDW: You fixing to tell me your mama whips on you?

MAN: Yes . . .

VDW: Sounds like she should, boy, you a liar and a thief.

MAN: She gets madder than that.

VDW: Oh.

MAN: It's like she stays mad and it doesn't matter what . . .

VDW: Oh. So you're telling me your mama whips and whips and whips on you, and it don't do no good anymore 'cause she already whipped on you for everything she can think of. And, now, you just waiting to get old enough to leave home.

(No response.)

Am I right?

MAN: They don't try to find you after you're sixteen. I mean you're supposed to be eighteen, but nobody looks for you if you're sixteen already. Not in Chicago. I don't know about here. And I'm fourteen almost and—

VDW: Here. *(Hands him a plastic baggie of something)* This be a kind of memory powder. Every morning, you take a pinch and you put it on your tongue, and as it melts, you remember that easy days go faster than hard ones, and if you don't do something to make her mad, the days will go faster for you. Now, go and take your powder and think about getting through high school before you're so anxious to leave home. Go.

(He enters Bissa's sphere again.)

BISSA: What she say to you? She tell you to behave like you're supposed to? What she say?

MAN *(To Bissa)*: She gave me this.

BISSA: What is this?

MAN: It is powder to make me do the right thing.

BISSA: Aw, hell, she supposed to put a spell on you, just her powder don't work no better than what you get at the drugstore.

(He leaves Bissa's sphere.)

MAN: *(To the audience)*: I wondered, for years, how that old woman could have looked at me and seen so much. Bissa drove me right straight back to the airport, she didn't even feed me supper. I got on another plane and got into Chicago about midnight. Mother was there to meet me.

(He enters his Mother's sphere again.)

MOTHER: You learn anything this afternoon?

MAN *(To his Mother)*: Yeah.

MOTHER: What she tell you?

MAN: To behave.

MOTHER: She put a spell on you?

MAN: I think so.

MOTHER: You feel any different?

MAN: I think so.

MOTHER: Let me see the powders.

MAN: How do you know about the powders.

MOTHER: Bissa called and told me. *(She tastes them)* This is just baking soda. Hell. All that money for a damn bag of baking soda.

(He leaves his Mother's sphere and is by himself.)

MAN: *(To the audience)*: It did taste like baking soda. Memory powder evidently does. I took those powders a pinch at a time, the bag lasted about six months, and the old woman was right, the easy days did go faster. After that, my memory was better, I didn't need the powder anymore. I won't claim I was any better in school for my visit to the voodoo lady or that I quit lying or that I quit taking things sometimes. I didn't. I did quit throwing things so much in my mother's face, I tried harder to stay out of her way, and it did make what was left of our life together easier. I left home at sixteen.

• • •

This was a journey that was even more mystic than it looked as I wrote it, but you saw some of that if you saw it on stage. The oral history itself was not nearly so coherent as it seems in the story I wrote. It was about forty pages of difficult stuff, and the first difficulty was that it was difficult to read at all. My job was to glean something useful. An abusive mother was there, fearsome Bissa was there, and the trip to a voodoo woman kept coming up as maybe the most important thing that had ever happened to him. I basically ignored everything else but these things. This man had pulled his act together sufficiently to move from homeless to a single-room occupancy hotel, an SRO, in Chicago. The play was made of stories from people who lived in the new SRO; all of them had recently been homeless. This man played himself on stage. What he said of this piece was that he hadn't understood how important this story was to him until I wrote it like I did. I think about that. I'm writing this paragraph more than ten years after I wrote that play, and I still think about his remark. All of us have these mythic constructs in our experience. You can make a version of the hero's journey out of almost anybody's life; we are a hero unto ourselves if to nobody else. Almost everybody has some version of Sisyphus' endless labor, too, and if we're smart, we've already done Camus's turn on it for ourselves. Do I not sit at this computer seemingly endless hours? And when something is done, do I not start back at the bottom again with something else? And haven't I come to love the work? Well, yes. I think many of us never find or understand how these old myths might apply to our lives, and seeing such an application is sometimes a terrific revelation. I do love this stuff, and sometimes, writing these stories, I get to play with it.

Part of this man's deal for getting into the SRO was that he would get a GED and a job. I hope he did it. He's already faced the voodoo woman, the GED (with some study) should be a piece of cake.

Envisioning Ethnotheatricality

*Performance creates fictions to depict reality. . . . Ethnodramatists
have the task of presenting real stories in performance in whichever
way they feel will best tell their stories. Not being life-like may be
the most effective way to depict life.*

—Judith Ackroyd & John O'Toole[1]

Ethnodramas are rooted in reality but their playwriting and productions need to consider, if not exploit, the multiple possibilities available on the page and on the stage. Chapters Three and Four focus primarily on realistic writing, while this chapter explores nonnatural, "theatrical" approaches to text, staging, and performance. I call these approaches *reality*[2]—reality squared— suggesting the exponential attributes of ethnotheatricality.

I cannot possibly cover everything about scenography (i.e., theatrical design), acting, and directing in just one chapter. Instead, I focus on a few key elements that relate specifically to ethnotheatrical production. If you are not involved in theatre or performance as your primary discipline, consult with a director or theatre educator for guidance. As always, when it comes to creative vision for a play or media production, stop thinking like a social scientist and start thinking like an artist. A stunning example of this is included at the end of the chapter—the complete script of John Caswell, Jr.'s autoethnodrama, *shots: a love story.*

The Performance Venue and Space

An actual theater building provides a sense of occasion to ethnodramatic performance. The formality of the setting literally and metaphorically frames the event for spectators. But there are generally expectations of higher quality and richer aesthetics from the production company in such a space, especially if payment for admission has been made. Smaller studios or laboratory theaters suggest an event of less magnitude and a more intimate and experimental approach— tones perhaps more in harmony with ethnotheatrical aesthetics (see

Chapter Six). Community-based devised works are generally held in more publicly accessible and embedded spaces such as recreation centers, museums, and school auditoriums. Ethnodramatic performances at conferences most often occur in whatever room has been assigned for the session by conference organizers. Most academic audience members acknowledge the performance limitations of a hotel or university campus breakout room, yet depending on the association or conference theme, they may also expect a more scholarly approach to the creative work.

If an actual theater is not possible for your performance, this does not mean you're limited in your production concept. In fact, some of the most exciting and emotionally moving theatre I've ever seen has been performed in small spaces, not large theaters. Brainstorm the possible and accessible venues in your area, thinking about what is required and suggested by the action of the ethnodrama. For example, an ethnodrama about health care performed in a hospital is a compatible choice. Selecting the specific space for your project should accommodate the production's physical and technical needs, plus provide audience-friendly comfort, audibility, and accessibility. Regardless of performance venue, the ethnotheatrical product should be the best that it can be. Smaller spaces should never suggest lesser quality.

A current trend in contemporary theatre production is to break away from the notion of traditional picture-framed spaces in auditoriumlike buildings in order to create evocative environments in found spaces for the action of the play. Interiors not traditionally associated with performance are transformed through visual means to create not just a setting but a *cultural world* in which new and more intimate actor-audience relationships are formed. Jonathan Holmes' (2009) ethnotheatrical production, *Katrina: A Play of New Orleans*, took place in an abandoned five-story warehouse. Each audience member was given a black disposable rain poncho to wear, and they moved from one floor to the next throughout the performance. Stairwells were scenically designed with graffiti symbols and slogans reminiscent of the disaster, and even a destroyed Mardi Gras float awaited the audience on one level.

I originally wanted to set my ethnodramatic production about homeless youth outdoors in a city alleyway but I could not muster the technical resources and permits necessary to make it happen. I instead used a "black box" or multipurpose studio space that was converted to simulate an alleyway complete with trash-strewn floors. *Street Rat* employed a traverse stage: a narrow rectangular performance area that ran through the center of the studio with audience members seated on one of two sides facing each other. The effect allowed the audience to witness naturalistic action with actors performing literally one foot away from the front rows.

Scenic Elements

I know of virtually no "real time" ethnodramas in which the complete action of the play progresses in a single place at the same rate as the events unfolded in real life. Many ethnodramas include multiple characters with action occurring in multiple settings across multiple time periods. Even one-person autoethnodramas suspend the traditional conventions of linear storytelling by jumping back and forth from one period or site to another. Time and space are fluid in theatre, changing tempos and shifting in locations as seems necessary for the story or stories to be told. With this structure comes the necessity to accommodate the action of the play in physical ways on stage that enable performative malleability.

The *unit set* is a method of theatre production for this type of malleability to occur. A neutral, versatile, and flexible arrangement of everyday pieces such as stools, chairs, benches, tables, boxes, and so forth on a flat or multilevel platform stage floor can be shifted and placed as needed within a few seconds to suggest a transformed setting for the play's action. This protean variety also maintains visual novelty and interest for audiences. On unit sets, primacy is placed on the actors and their characters, not on scenographic trappings. Plus, media technology (discussed later) is being used more and more in contemporary theatre production to supplement minimalist scenery.

Ethnodramas can take advantage of their ethnographic fieldwork transferred to the bare stage through strategically chosen artifacts as set decorations and hand properties. Think of what few select items participants handled or were observed in key spaces that might suggest the cultural world of the play. For example, before my rehearsal period for *Street Rat*, I conducted quick ethnography in New Orleans to capture the visual spirit of the French Quarter. I noticed that Bourbon Street was littered with various kinds of trash. I also interviewed homeless youth in the city and asked them what I might see inside if I were to visit a squat. This fieldwork generated an idea to literally "trash" the acting and audience seating areas with debris. Since the production was to premiere in Arizona, I contacted my friends in New Orleans to send me authentic trash from the area that could be scattered on the stage floor.

It was an unnecessary detail, for Arizona trash would have sufficed. But I was in search of authenticity with this production, and Louisiana artifacts that had regional brand names (e.g., Deep South Peanut Butter, Piggly Wiggly plastic grocery bags) provided more local color to the ethnotheatrical event.

My personal recommendation is to keep the physical set as simple and as streamlined as possible for ethnotheatre. Place more emphasis on the immediate design elements around the actor: hand properties and costumes.

Hand Properties as Artifacts

Properties most often refer to physical objects handled by actors during the play. They are the things in everyday life we work with and manipulate to conduct routines, and they inform someone looking at us of our immediate cultural worlds and values. On stage, properties serve the necessary action of the play, suggest character, and maintain visual interest for spectators. In Robin Soans' (2004) ethnodrama, *The Arab-Israeli Cookbook*, all participants interviewed are cooking, preparing, or eating meals as they speak to the interviewer (implied by direct address to the audience). Kitchen tools and food items are necessary properties to serve the action of the play. Similarly, the anthropologist character Harry F. Wolcott in *Finding My Place: The Brad Trilogy* (Saldaña, 2002) is seen handling throughout the play his tools of the trade: a tape recorder, index cards for notes, writing pads, and pens. I was also a stickler for period accuracy in this production. Since the play was set in the early 1980s (but produced in the early 2000s), I placed on Wolcott's desk several first editions of classic qualitative research books that were published during the 1980s.

As for hand properties suggesting character, focus on items that we tend to associate with particular occupations or personalities. I occasionally but briefly played the role of a high school band director in my one-man autoethnodrama, *Second Chair*. Whenever the character was portrayed, I held and used a key artifact that suggested his occupational status and identity: a conductor's baton. Doug Wright's central character in *I Am My Own Wife* displays antiques from his massive collection throughout the ethnodrama which not only generate particular stories from Charlotte von Mahlsdorf, but also serve as a small-scale visual spectacle for the audience.

Even if a script does not suggest or include in its stage directions any specific properties, as a director I always try to think of items that are appropriate for the characters to work with occasionally during their monologue and dialogue. I have found that properties in an actor's hands for accompanying and appropriate stage business make him more comfortable with the world of the character, give him a sense of performative purpose, and in many cases generate more realistic monologue and dialogue because of the actor's heightened belief.

Some ethnodramatic productions employ a reader's theatre approach with binders containing the script in the actors' hands or on music stands throughout the play. If this is the case, directors should compensate for fewer hand properties with more whole body movement throughout the performance.

Costuming and Makeup

Very few period plays exist in the ethnodramatic literature; most titles are set in contemporary time frames. One exception is William Gibson's (1999) *American Primitive (John & Abigail): The Words of John and Abigail Adams*, which may use early American costume pieces from the 1700s as the actors take turns reading letters written by these two historic figures. Culturally specific plays and participants/characters will benefit from appropriate attire, such as the international figures portrayed in Cizmar et al.'s (2009) *Seven*. The stage directions recommend costuming performers in the cultural dress of the women's home countries: Mu Sochua from Cambodia "dressed elegantly in a traditional silk skirt and blouse"; Congresswoman Anabella De Leon in "Guatemalan native dress"; Afghan Women's Network member Farida Aziza in a burqa; and so on. Plays with characters in occupational or work roles such as Joan Holden's *Nickel and Dimed* would require accessories such as aprons and cleaning gloves. Several ethnodramas about the Iraq war require its soldier characters to wear appropriate military uniforms.

Just because an ethnodrama's action takes place in the present day with everyday citizens, this doesn't mean that the actors can wear whatever they want from their personal wardrobes. Most people make associations and inferences about a person based on the way he or she is dressed. The clothing's colors, patterns, textures, fit, brand labels, and other design elements combine together to create or connote a sense of character. That same everyday life principle can be transferred into the costuming choices we make for an ethnodrama's stage production. Reflect on each character's overall personality and select appropriate pieces that reveal such aspects as age, occupation, socioeconomic status, presentation of self to others, and so on.

In my ethnodramas based on actual people I interviewed, I made note of their general clothing styles so they could be replicated on stage. For example, one man wore long-sleeved shirts buttoned at the cuff, not rolled up. So, the actor who portrayed the character on stage was asked to do likewise. In my ethnodrama about homeless teens, we selected clothing that was appropriate for the characters' ages and personalities, but we also made sure the clothes were distressed: wrinkled, dirty, and not well maintained, as might be the case with street youth.

I also rely on selected stage costuming principles to add an aesthetic dimension to the designs. For example, impulsive or erratic personalities are costumed in busy prints; stuffy, formal, or hard characters are dressed in well-ironed, crisp fabrics; protagonists and antagonists are costumed in complementary colors to heighten their opposition (e.g., the hero in a palette of solid blues and the villain in a palette of dark browns). In productions in which an actor plays multiple roles, some companies utilize a basic outfit common to all the characters, with carefully selected accessories such as scarves, hats, or glasses to suggest particular characters.

Special makeup is rarely needed for ethnotheatrical productions. There are exceptions to every rule, however; one that comes to mind is David Hare's *Stuff Happens*, in which actors must be made up to look like political figures such as George W. Bush and Dick Cheney. I have not used makeup very often since most of the characters on stage are inspired by real people, and I believe that little to no makeup reinforces this concept by helping the actors to appear natural. In larger theatres, basic or "straight" makeup is used to accentuate the actor's natural features so they are not washed out under bright stage lighting. Smaller studio spaces usually employ basic street makeup for women actors. Only once have I used makeup for special effects: in *Street Rat*, in which the homeless youths' faces were made up to look unwashed and worn. The character Roach also received a special effects tattoo: a spider web inked across his face. Selected ethnotheatrical productions about illness will sometimes make up the actors to look pale if this suits their physical ailment. Generally, the closer the actors are to the audience, the less makeup is needed.

Media Technology

Mainstream theatre is integrating media technology into productions on a more frequent basis. Many professionals currently specialize in media design and entertainment technology for the stage. PowerPoint and specialized software have the ability to project everything from text to stills to animated visuals on screens and scenery. Ethnotheatri-

Figure 5.1. Patrick Santoro in his multimedia autoethnodramatic solo performance, *At the Mercy of Ruin*. Photo by Jonathan Gray.

cal productions can incorporate this technology not just for aesthetic effects but also for media's ability to establish place, evoke mood, and reinforce ideas (see Figure 5.1).

Authentic pictures and video clips from fieldwork provide the audience a sense of "being there" as if in a documentary film. My production of *Finding My Place: The Brad Trilogy* employed photos of the drifter's actual makeshift cabin constructed on Harry F. Wolcott's property in Oregon and assorted photos to accompany changes in the action's setting (the woods, a mental health clinic, a courtroom, and so on). Also in that production and in *"Maybe someday, if I'm famous . . ."*, I used slides to project significant words and phrases from dialogue throughout the performance to supplement and highlight the spoken text. This technique tends to give audiences a more research-oriented framework for the production. Projections can also be used as ironic commentary on the stage action, particularly when it juxtaposes—for example, scenes of war's atrocities and destruction projected during a pro-war military officer's monologue.

Now and then, "technology happens"—meaning that technical glitches interfere with the smooth-running plans for the show. Media is the one production element that seems to trip up most ethnodramatic productions I've seen, from initial bad feeds to late cues. If you incorporate this technology, designate a highly qualified person to set up and run the equipment.

Lighting

The primary function of stage lighting is a common sense principle: the audience needs to see the action on stage. Once that basic need has been met, lighting can explore additional design elements for ethnotheatrical production.

I have attended ethnodramatic performances at professional academic conferences in which minimal control was possible regarding room lighting levels and focus. You perform where you can and under

Figure 5.2. Stage lighting creates a powerful visual effect in John Caswell, Jr.'s ethnodramatic production about gay men and homophobia, *Closet Drama*. Photo by Leslie M. Rugg.

the conditions available. But if you have the ability to perform in a venue in which you can control the intensity, direction, and color of lighting, you can evoke some powerful moods to accompany the ethnodramatic performance. In fact, the more theatrical you can be with lighting through vivid background colors, intense spots, and symbolic gobos (template patterns projected through a lighting instrument onto a screen), the more evocatively you intensify the action and mood of the scene (see Figure 5.2).

Consider the audience seating area. Keeping it as brightly lit as the stage suggests that spectators are witnesses to the reality unfolding before them, much like jurors in a courtroom listening to testimony and arguments. Such lighting can bring the audience closer to the action and make them feel more integral to the performance, but at the same time it may violate an expected sense of comfort in darkness and dispel private reflection on the event. As a side effect, however, stage lighting effects are diminished since bright audience lighting washes out most illumination in the performers' area.

Sound and Music

Many beginning theatre artists are so concerned with how a production looks that they neglect to work on how it *sounds*. Much of this is accomplished with an actor's dynamic voice, but it also refers to the use of live and/or recorded sound effects and music.

Good ethnographers pay particular attention to the ambient and background sounds generated within their field sites, for that rich aural soundscape says much about the activities and social conditions of the setting. If you've never done so, conduct participant observation fieldwork while seated with your eyes closed for a few minutes and truly listen to the environment. If I am in an elementary school classroom primarily observing a teacher and her twenty students interacting dialogically, I can also hear through the walls other teachers lecturing to their students, children's purposeful footsteps as they walk through the hallways, the occasional loud cranking of pencil sharpeners in other classrooms, children yelling in high-pitched voices on the playground, and so on. *Sound* as well as place suggests a particular microculture in aural motion.

If I were to stage an ethnodrama whose setting or environment contains culturally rich and indicative sounds, I would consider playing a recording of these softly in the background during appropriate action in the play. It could also be used purposefully before a scene begins to establish the setting or mood, then fade out as actors begin to speak. These recordings could also be used before the production itself as audiences wait for the play to begin, in order to suggest the cultural world of the ethnodrama. Sound effects CDs are readily available if you are unable to record environmental sounds yourself, but the length of the tracks may be shorter than needed. Good quality yet inexpensive recording and playback equipment are available, so strive for well-produced sound amplified through medium to large speakers rather than the "tinny" effect of a laptop computer.

Well-selected music is one of the most powerful and suggestive production elements in theatre. Contemporary production practice seems to be adopting soundtracking with musical scores more often these days, following the style of feature films. For example, the time period of my production of *Finding My Place: The Brad Trilogy* was established using pop songs from the 1980s. These songs also served as effective filler and transitions from one scene to the next. In Vanover and Saldaña's (2005) *Chalkboard Concerto*, the protagonist attends the symphony as an escape from his high-pressure teaching job. Classical music by Verdi, Mozart, and other composers plays softly in the background during the character's reflective monologues. In my autoethnodrama *Second Chair*, fifteen minutes of preshow music by a key composer referenced in the play greets the audience as they enter the theater for the performance. For *Street Rat*, a play set in New Orleans, Cajun and zydeco music were featured prominently throughout to establish both locale and mood. And *Minefields and Miniskirts*, an ethnodrama about the Vietnam war, features occasional interludes of period songs sung by the ensemble, such as "One Tin Soldier" and "Saigon Bride."

Another vital aural element is the actors' voices. If the audience cannot hear them, then the performance event is all for naught. Microphone the actors if necessary for comfortable audibility.

The Ethnodramatic Actor

The character/participants are the soul of ethnodrama. All of the design elements discussed thus far contribute nothing to ethnotheatrical production without good actors. You may have an outstanding script with emotionally gripping monologue and dialogue, but without rich interpretations and solid performances, audiences will be less likely to care about the play and its issues. When you cast, try to secure the best actors available. A folkloric notion in theatre purports that 80 percent of the director's job is casting the right people for the show.

Actors portraying real people in ethnodramas should exhibit an ethic of respect for the characters they're representing since it may be possible those very people will be in the audience during the performance. Stereotypes and caricatures should be avoided (unless the stylistic demands of the ethnodrama veer toward satire, parody, or expressionism). The challenge to create realistic and natural talk must be carefully balanced with performative expectations of a respectable level of energy and interpretive finesse. Ackroyd and O'Toole (2010) posit, "It has been suggested that dialogue accounts for only 35 per cent of communication in theatre, as in real-life interactions. The remaining 65 per cent is through other aspects of the semiotic process, such as facial expression, gesture, the space between performers, and costume" (p. 47). An ethnodramatic actor's body becomes a critical component of the performance. Rather than simply sitting or standing on stage, subtle and overt movements communicate rich subtext and inferences about the character's psychological states. Some ethnotheatrical performances I've seen have even incorporated dance as the actors spoke verbatim text. But I am also a stickler for how a play *sounds*, and I pay particular attention to coaching the actor's voice to exhibit a melodic range and a variety of appropriate rates and rhythms of speech.

The actors with whom I've worked in ethnodramas were fascinated that they were portraying real people and not fictional characters. Some took the initiative to speak with the actual person I interviewed, when possible, to learn more about him or her. The actors portraying homeless youth in *Street Rat* observed and conversed with homeless teens in the streets of our city, asked passersby for spare change, and even spent a night sleeping outdoors to capture the experience of homelessness to portray it more faithfully and believably on stage.

I've found documentary and instructional films (if available) an excellent way to acquaint actors with the topic or culture they're portraying in performance. The actor portraying Brad in *Finding My Place: The Brad Trilogy* had to simulate paranoid schizophrenia as the play progressed. Watching a few psychology videos of people with this mental illness helped the performer understand how individuals with this condition move, talk, and perceive the world. Anna Deavere Smith recommends that actors research the news and watch video footage of the events portrayed in her 1990s plays. But playwrights Jessica Blank and Erik Jensen respectfully request that actors do *not* contact the actual people they interviewed for *The Exonerated* out of respect for their privacy.

Many ethnodrama company members testify that their social consciousness was heightened through performing in an ethnotheatrical experience, particularly if they themselves conducted the interviews with participants and helped devise the staged work. Embodying the words and feelings of actual people transforms their awareness of the issues in the play. Some feel that the performers may get more out of the production than the audiences because actors take deep cognitive and physical ownership of their roles and empathize with the participants' lives throughout rehearsals and performances.

Some ethnotheatrical projects opt to incorporate the actual research participants themselves, rather than experienced actors, into the production. This is commonly seen in community-based ventures, some devised works, participatory action research studies, and drama therapy programs. The rationale is that the participants are the ones best suited to voice their own stories, and the positive outcomes from the rehearsal and performance processes, under an expert facilitator/director's guidance, can enhance the self-esteem of its presenters. I caution, however, that some people without theatrical experience may not be ready for the self-discipline necessary for rehearsals and the stress that accompanies performance in front of a live audience. In some cases, the practice can also be perceived as one that exploits rather than honors the participants if not handled with their best interests in mind. And depending on the leadership and natural talent of the group, the performance product itself may be perceived as one that was executed in good faith, but nevertheless is of lesser quality. Your research goals determine whether you incorporate actors or research participants (or both) as performers of the ethnodramatic project. Keep in mind that casting—deciding which person portrays which role—becomes not just an artistic but an ethical matter if you use research participants as performers.

The Ethnotheatrical Director

All of the production elements discussed thus far are facilitated by a director who plans and guides the production company to the play's realization on stage. Ideally, theatre is a collaborative venture in which multiple talented artists with their individual specialties come together to coordinate and execute a total work of art. But the realities of available human resources for production sometime necessitate that the playwright of an ethnodrama also serve as the director and designer of the project. There is nothing wrong with that, for one-person production programs are quite common in educational theatre settings such as secondary schools. But it does make the project more labor- and time-intensive. If this is the case, keep your artistic vision realistic yet find creative solutions to mount the play economically and elegantly. Less is more, as the famous design saying goes.

To me, the most important pre-production role of the ethnotheatrical director is to function as a creative visionary. This is the capacity to imagine in your mind's eye and ear the way in which all the visual and aural elements come together in the performance space. It also includes the capacity to explore all the creative possibilities for realizing its staging in an engaging manner for its audience. These ideas should be documented in some way so that as rehearsals get underway, the vision becomes clearly articulated. Obviously, available human, financial, and physical resources dictate what you can and cannot do on stage. But don't think of these as limitations to your vision. In fact, focus more on the actor as a form of living scenography. Ethnodramas are primarily about people, not about theatrical machinery.

The second most important directorial function is to communicate effectively with actors to generate the best performances possible. This requires the ability to guide artists in discovering how to interpret and take ownership of their characters. It also requires instantaneous problem-solving when they ask questions about their roles or the play script. If the ethnodramatic work is a devised or cast-created construction, the director's job exponentially increases as a facilitator and arbiter of improvised exploration. Overall, the director must help the actors feel secure in their character development and push them toward self-disciplined artistic excellence. A production company needs a sense of security from a confident and collegial leader.

The third most important function of a director in ethnotheatre is to work closely with the playwright to develop the best script possible during the pre-production and rehearsal periods. The director and playwright should work collaboratively and collegially and keep personal ego out of their working relationship. The goal is for the director to function as a dramaturg to advise and guide the playwright toward constructive rewrites. In some cases, the playwright may also function as the director of his/her own ethnodrama. Though it is not advised, sometimes it cannot be helped.

I emphasize throughout this text that if you want to become a better playwright, you should read a lot of plays. If you want to become a good director, see a range of good theatrical productions, from classical to contemporary, from realistic to experimental, and from professional to community, and reflect on the techniques that made them effective artworks.

Reality² (Reality Squared) Writing and Staging

Sometimes the production principles of naturalism and realism are the most effective ways to stage ethnodramatic work. But if we assume that sometimes "not being lifelike may be the most effective way to depict life," that suggests we may find intriguing staging ideas for ethnodrama through some creative approaches to text and production. But be cautious of taking a different slant just to appear trendy, clever, or novel. Any deviation from naturalism should seem justified as part of the overall production style and feel comfortable to the actors. Plus, the more the text deviates from reality, the potentially less ethnodramatic it seems to audiences.

Ethnodrama is a *genre* of writing, yet there is a range of *styles* within that genre. Most ethnodramas are realist but a few exceptions are known. Chapter One introduced you to choral approaches to ethnodramatic text (*What's the Fine Line?*) and even musical ethnotheatre as a possible variant (*Gone Missing*). Another approach is not a single storyline or plot but a performance collage or *revue*, comparable to the television variety show format. Victor Ukaegbu and Jumai Ewu (2010) facilitated a community-based project in Australia that showcased the local artists, history, and voices of a black rural population: "The [ethnotheatrical] performance was in parts biographical, epic, naturalistic, and occasionally expressionistic, all contained in a flexible episodic storytelling framework. It accommodated other expressive forms such as music, dance, poetry, re-enactment and multi-media" (p. 178).

A few ethnodramatic titles deliberately take a comic slant to their representations; some of these even veer into biting social commentary in the guise of slapstick. Academic Christopher N. Poulos (2010) dramatizes his rocky and controversial journey toward tenure and promotion in his one-act autoethnodrama, *Transgressions*. A chorus of positivist and quantitatively-driven faculty peers blusters at the creative scholarship of his autoethnography in the following scene titled, "The Meeting."

> *The spotlight clicks on, revealing THE PROFESSOR slumped on the stool, then quickly clicks off. A softer, almost ethereally dim light shines on the round table, where the CHORUS, still hooded, is seated. A mist rises around their feet. Looking closely, you can see that a black cauldron, sitting under the center of the table, is the source. Music blasts loudly—the opening of Guns 'n Roses' "Welcome to the Jungle"—then stops abruptly after the line "we got fun and games.").*

NARRATOR: *(in a deep, serious voice)*: The tenure meeting.

ONE *(whispering)*: Double, double, toil and trouble.

TWO AND THREE *(whispering, slightly louder)*: Fire burn and cauldron bubble.

CHORUS *(chanting loudly)*: Double, double, toil and trouble. Fire burn and cauldron bubble!

TWELVE: Let's call this meeting to order.

ONE: Right, let's start.

SIX: The first case.

THREE: Red flag!

TWO: A vote against!

ONE: Look at *that*, will you?

SEVEN: What's this guy doing?

ONE: I don't like this.

TWO: His work is not . . . right. It's too—

THREE: —*emotional*!

FOUR: Right. He can write, but—

FIVE: —his writing—

SIX: Isn't mainstream!

SEVEN: It's downright *therapeutic*.

EIGHT: It's *dangerous*.

TWELVE: I kind of *like* danger.

NINE: Emotional!

TWELVE: But—

TEN: What's his *agenda*, anyway?

CHORUS: *Pathos*!

TWELVE: So?

ELEVEN: Dangerous!

CHORUS *(except for TWELVE, whispering)*: Crucify him!

TWELVE: But—

CHORUS *(except for TWELVE, chanting loudly)*: Crucify him! Crucify him! Crucify him!

TWELVE: But—

ONE *(pausing for a moment, then intoning in a deep, booming voice)*: PROFESSOR! What is it that you do? *(the spotlight shines on THE*

PROFESSOR, blinding him).

CHORUS *(rising from the table, encircling the PROFESSOR, and moving in a circular clockwise direction, just outside the circle of light, bodies swaying, voices overlapping)*: Who are you? What are you doing here? Why do you do this? What's the *point*? Where's the generalized knowledge? What is the nature of your research agenda? Where's your data? What are your hypotheses? What are your predictions? What, exactly, do you *explain*? What have you discovered?

THE PROFESSOR *(stammering)*: I—

CHORUS *(voices overlapping)*: This is *research*? How? Knowledge? What? Wait. Generalize, man, generalize! Predict! Control!

NARRATOR *(voice booming)*: Just what are you trying to *prove*?

(the lights go down; the PROFESSOR walks offstage; the CHORUS returns to the table)

ONE: Time to vote.

TWO: No.

THREE: No.

FOUR: No.

FIVE: No.

SIX: No.

SEVEN: No.

EIGHT: No.

NINE: No.

TEN: No.

ELEVEN: No.

TWELVE: Yes.

ONE: No!

NARRATOR: The vote is 11 against, one in favor.

(the stage goes dark)

(pp. 77–78)

Some ethnodramas can incorporate fantasy juxtaposed with stark realism. Mulcahy, Parry, and Glover (2009) researched cancer patients and co-created the ethnodrama, *Between Diagnosis and Death*. In this play, the

Father is a composite character whose words were adapted from multiple interviewees' transcripts. Caitlin M. Mulcahy, one of the play's co-authors, served as the basis for the role of the Daughter. In the scene that follows, Father and Daughter are seated on a park bench on a cold day. The Daughter is "haunted by a ghost she cannot escape" (p. 30). Notice how the fantasy character appears onstage and interacts with her.

(*Her father coughs into his gloves*)

FATHER: I was in bad shape when I was diagnosed.

DAUGHTER: Oh god. It's starting.

GHOST: What's starting?

FATHER: And I was not given a good diagnosis. I was told I may have two to three years to live. (*shakes his head*) There was no explanation. None. (*long pause*)

DAUGHTER: (*to Ghost*) Oh he's pausing, but he won't stop there. The story never ends. It's on loop. I don't know what he's looking for, but he never finds it.

FATHER: You're not prepared. When you get that diagnosis . . . the whole world goes out of whack! (*gestures wildly*) Everything goes crazy! Your mind goes through the worst scenario. . . . It's just awful . . . we just deal with these horrible diagnoses and we don't have anything to help with something like that.

GHOST: (*circling downstage right*) It's hard to write about this stuff when you have a parent who has cancer. Your co-authors know that. They've both gone through cancer with their own parents. They'll understand.

DAUGHTER: (*snorts*) If you think the writing's hard, you should try listening to this stuff all the time. It's the listening that's driving me crazy. (*checking pockets*) Where's my iPod? Did I leave it at home? (*fumbles through pockets for iPod while Father continues*)

FATHER: (*sniffs*) When you're in treatment, cancer's in your face every day. It's impossible to be getting on with your life. Your life is on hold. And then, you finish treatment and then what, you know? (*wipes a glove across his nose*)

DAUGHTER: (*exasperated*) Where is it, for god's sakes?!

(*He pulls out a fistful of Kleenex and blows his nose. She finds her iPod.*)

Yes! (*puts headphones in ears*)

FATHER: I found it to be extremely isolating going through the treatments. And when you go to a clinic, nobody talks to anyone. They're in their own space. You know it's as if they were all on iPods, cancer iPods, or something.

(She sighs and tucks her iPod back into her pocket.)

DAUGHTER: I guess that's the end of that.

(pp. 32–33)

Another juxtaposed approach in ethnotheatrical events is realistic monologue and dialogue accompanied by or interpreted with stylized actor movement and/or theatrical spectacle. Chapman, Swedberg, and Sykes (2005) collaborated on *Wearing the Secret Out*, a one-act ethno-drama about nonheterosexual physical education teachers. The script consists of verbatim extracts from interviews with lesbian participants, but Jennifer Chapman and Anne Swedberg, as the actors, deliver their lines with abstract and symbolic movements throughout the performance. The excerpt that follows provides detailed stage directions that physically and visually highlight the "tug-of-war" tensions between hiding and disclosing one's sexual orientation to students.

(JENNIFER crosses upstage to grab a sheet, which she drops over ANNE's head, encircling her body as ANNE reaches center; ANNE picks up the megaphone and crosses to center, speaking the following line into the megaphone)

ANNE: Of course there are lesbians on our basketball team and our coach was lesbian, but of course people didn't talk about it publicly but everyone knew. *(at the end of the line, ANNE freezes as the sheet comes around her; she bends slowly to set the megaphone down and rises in slow motion as the tug-of-war begins and JENNIFER begins speaking)*

JENNIFER: I guess I don't think it would be good for my students to know—it's like, what more of a role model could they have, if they've already decided they like me. They make statements like, "I've never met a gay person," and I make statements like, "Yes you have, you just don't know it." *(raises sheet to shoulder, then high above head, pulling in opposite directions, ANNE facing downstage and JENNIFER facing upstage)*

ANNE: *(twists her end of the sheet around her body, turns upstage to face JENNIFER, turns JENNIFER to face out and supports her weight as she goes all the way down to the floor, face down, and then ANNE pulls JENNIFER back up to standing again)* I'm as out as somebody who supports all marginalized groups of people, so basically I don't tell everybody, "Hello, here I am, I'm gay." But I'm out to them as somebody who celebrates diversity in all ways.

(pp. 110–111)

Mediated Resources

At the time of this writing, a few scholars (e.g., Park, 2009) have experimented with the *screenplay* as a format for ethnodrama. I am admittedly inexperienced in this form of writing, but I have seen promise in the ways their research has been rendered in print including such filmic conventions as camera angles, cuts, voice-overs, and subtitles. This genre overlaps with the practices of documentary filmmaking, and we enter muddy waters, if not an entirely new book, about the ethnodramatic screenplay and its film version as artistic renderings of field research (including commercial films such as *Quitting, Howl,* and *United 93*). The innovative mediated work of Kip Jones' visual ethnography and performative social science has created unique hybrids of dramatic representation and presentation (these can be viewed at http://www.kipworld.net/ and http://kipworldblog.blogspot.com/). Individuals with technological and filmmaking expertise are the ones to better address these artistic methods for colleagues.

Several ethnodramatic performances available on YouTube or theatre company Internet sites showcase the dynamic and theatrical approaches to their work. One of the most celebrated internationally was The National Theatre of Scotland's *Black Watch* (Burke, 2007). The play, based on interviews with Scottish soldiers stationed in the Iraq war, incorporates monologue and dialogue (with the strong and coarse language of soldiers) plus folk songs and dance from the country. Stunning visual images and sequences are set to haunting music, lighting, and sound effects that capture the poignant loneliness and violent horror of war. The YouTube clip found at http://www.youtube.com/watch?v=UyPhBLfROuI&feature=related provides a sample of *Black Watch*'s production dynamics with a fascinating costume change and movement sequence about the history of the Scottish military uniform.

One of the most intriguing "underground" ethnodramatic productions was Ken Davenport's (2009) *My First Time.* The Internet site www.myfirsttime.com collected people's stories about their first sexual experiences. The play is based on these contributions and even collects information from audiences (e.g., the age of your first sexual experience, the place where you lost your virginity) before the performance

Figure 5.3. The acting ensemble of John Caswell, Jr.'s autoethnodrama, *shots: a love story*. Photo by Leslie M. Rugg.

begins, which is incorporated into the play. Slides are used extensively throughout the production to highlight famous people's quotes about sex, data and statistics on sexual activity, and title slides with case numbers of the original story contributors. Two men and two women provide mostly monologues and rapid-fire choral exchanges in a reader's theatre presentation that graphically, comically, and seriously describes everyday people's first sexual experiences. To learn more about the production, access www.myfirsttimetheplay.com.

Sometimes the subject or content of the ethnodrama may suggest a particular stylistic approach. One trend I have noticed is that plays dealing with substance abuse and addiction tend to be explicit and raw in their tone and action, with most titles venturing into a surrealistic style with overt theatrical devices. The skewed, nightmarish reality that results from substance abuse and addiction seems to transfer into the script and staging of the issue. One example is the abstract, expressionistic, dance-drama staging of alcoholism in the Progressive Theatre Workshop production of John Caswell, Jr.'s autoethnodrama, *shots: a love story*. Alcohol is symbolized by a street-savvy male, simply named He, controlling and manipulating the destructive behavior of a character represented by a chorus of three women: Her, (her again), and (her once more) (see Figure 5.3). The stark and painful true stories they tell and the seemingly random snippets of talk, such as a verbatim litany of motivational phrases from an Alcoholics Anonymous manual, are accompanied by both athletic and disjointed movements.

The full text of the play can be found at the end of this chapter. A trailer or collage of scenes from the production that gives viewers a sense of the performance style can be accessed at http://www.youtube.com/watch?v=JFfR2Pw-ojw&feature=related.

Ethnotheatrical Exercise: Envisioning Reality on Stage

Following is an eyewitness account of a natural disaster. Read the selection a few times to get acquainted with the story, then brainstorm the possible ethnodramatic adaptations and ethnotheatrical staging ideas suggested by this brief narrative text.

> When Mount St. Helens erupted in 1980, we were hundreds of miles away in Pullman, Washington. We heard on the news that the volcano's force was tremendous, and a huge cloud of ash was coming our way. In the early afternoon we could see it far off in the sky, and the smell of sulfur was getting stronger and stronger.
>
> Pullman is a small college town where nothing much happens, so the students were quickly and excitedly organizing "Volcano Parties" with their friends. It was one of those freakish, act-of-God events that made everyone look up toward the sky with awe and cheer "Woo-Hoo!" Because no one had ever been through something like this. No one knew what to do.
>
> At two in the afternoon, the black ash cloud covered the city completely, and it became as dark as midnight—*at two in the afternoon*. The whole town became dead silent as people stayed indoors to protect themselves from the falling ash. It sounded like fine grains of sand raining gently on our roofs, and it smelled like strong, burnt matches. We turned on our TVs and radios to get the latest news, and all the officials could tell us was to stay indoors and wear protective covering around our noses and mouths. No one could drive because the ash would clog the engines and bring cars to a complete standstill within minutes. All we could do was wait it out. Some of us, like fools, went outdoors to witness the ashfall. And it was an indescribable experience: Eerie. Mystic. Like Hell was just quietly and indifferently passing through our town.
>
> After a few hours it began to get brighter outside, and people started slowly coming out of their homes wearing handkerchiefs and bandanas wrapped around their lower faces to see what had been left behind by the massive ash cloud.
>
> It was unbelievable. Everything—everything—was grey. Sidewalks, parked cars, trees, flowers—all around. It was like thick, nonradioactive fallout. It looked like grey death.
>
> No one had ever been through something like this. No one knew what to do next. But a lot of us did collect volcanic ash in jars and bags as a memento of this day.

Though staging ideas may have emerged concurrently with adaptation ideas, focus first on the written adaptation (yet jot down the staging ideas and/or sketches for later reference).

Ethnodramatic Adaptation

Consider how the play script will differ if one actor is alone on stage presenting the story, or if a cast of several actors share the stage to represent the people suggested in the tale. Explore how monologue, dialogue, choral forms, and/or movement could be used to tell this particular story. Consider whether the vignette should maintain its elegant length, or whether expanded monologue and dialogue should be imaginatively constructed to flesh out the story for the stage. Would the scene work better with one ethnodramatist adapting the story as a script, or with a company of actors under a director's guidance experimenting to improvisationally and collectively devise the adaptation? Also consider the "bottom line": Is this story worth telling theatrically? Does it lend itself to ethnodramatic adaptation at all?

Ethnotheatrical Possibilities

Assuming the story is moving forward as an adaptation, what possibilities exist for its realization on stage? Jot down or make thumbnail sketches of the visual look of the production and its aural qualities. Go through each scenographic element and write or draw what may be the most effective choices for:

- the performance venue and space
- scenic elements
- hand properties
- costuming and makeup
- media technology
- lighting
- sound and music

The Logistics of Producing and Publishing

As much as some would like to deny it, art is also a business and industry with financial concerns and legal parameters. This section addresses a few logistical matters to consider regarding the production and publication of ethnodramatic work.

Production Rights for Published Ethnodramas

If you wish to mount a performance of a previously published ethno-drama (such as *The Laramie Project* or *The Vagina Monologues*), you must work through a *play leaser* or the playwright's agent or legal representation for formal contracted permission at least three months before rehearsals begin. Depending on the play script, you will be required to purchase a minimum number of copies of the *acting edition* of the work. Acting editions are scripts formatted for company use during pre-production matters and rehearsals. For example, Anne Nelson's play, *The Guys*, first appeared in print for the general reading public as a trade book published by Random House (Nelson, 2002). But Random House is not the play leaser. Playwrights will work through companies whose business is to publish and market acting editions of scripts, negotiate with production companies for performance rights, authorize productions of their represented works, and manage all business and financial matters such as script sales and royalty payments. The acting edition (Nelson, 2003) and production rights for *The Guys*, for example, are handled by Dramatists Play Service, Inc., one of the largest play leasers in the U.S. and one that manages most of the well-known ethnodramas in print. Four major leasers can be found on the Internet at the addresses that follow:

- Dramatists Play Service: www.dramatists.com
- Dramatic Publishing: www.dramaticpublishing.com
- Playscripts, Inc.: www.playscripts.com (visitors to the site will be able to access the beginning 90 percent of all play scripts for preview reading)
- Samuel French, Inc.: www.samuelfrench.com

The leaser will charge a nominal *royalty* for each performance. The price varies from script to script and from leaser to leaser and whether the production company is an amateur or professional group. Script sales and royalties allow playwrights as artists to make their living. If special conditions apply to your production, such as using excerpts from the play rather than the full work, or performing for an invited audience rather than the general public, each leaser has its own policies for special circumstances. Contact the company directly for any answers and negotiations.

Reprint Permissions of Dramatic Works

Every play script excerpt in this book—from the shortest monologue to the longest complete play—required a permission clearance of one kind or another, with approximately half of the publishers and/or playwrights charging a nominal fee. Copyright and permissions processes for dramatic works, poetry, and song lyrics are much different than those from scholarly and general nondramatic literary sources.

I strongly caution you to set aside at least three to six months for any permissions clearances you may need to obtain to reprint an excerpt—regardless of length—from a dramatic work in one of your own publications. Some agents and publishing house permissions departments can be notoriously slow or even ignore your initial request. (I wanted to include some wonderful ethnodramatic excerpts in this book, but I never heard back from a few agents regarding my follow-up inquiries.)

Application processes vary in complexity, with some publishers willing to handle matters through simple e-mail exchanges, while others require online Internet site requests or hard copy correspondence only. And some clearances may apply only to selected world territories, necessitating additional permissions requests to different agencies for the same material. Some publishers and agents may grant permission to include an excerpt from a play script in another publication at no charge. Others may request an average fee of about fifty dollars, depending on the length of the excerpt, the print run of your publication, and other details. If you feel a fee is too high, negotiate with the representative for a lesser charge—a few were quite willing and gracious to lower their initial price for me and this particular book project.

Copyright Registration

Always copyright your unpublished ethnodrama to protect your creative product. For U.S. authors, access www.copyright.gov and register to copyright your play as a Performing Arts Work—Script/Play/Screenplay (or, the Motion Picture/Audiovisual Work category if you're copyrighting a DVD recording of an original ethnotheatrical performance). There are specific instructions to follow, forms to complete, materials to submit, and a small fee that accompanies the application.

Copyrighting your work before publication does not mean that journals or play leasers cannot carry your play. It is simply a way to guarantee the security of intellectual property. Also, if you have collaborated closely with a few key participants to create your ethnodrama, consider whether joint copyright ownership should be negotiated. This is both a legal and ethical matter that should be considered between the primary playwright and his or her participants.

Publishing Your Ethnodrama

As a playwright, you obviously have a deep investment in and take committed ownership of your original creative work. But it is a journal editor, book publisher, or commercial play script leaser who determines whether your script has publication and/or production merit. Academic-oriented ethnodramatists may find journals such as *Qualitative Inquiry* (Sage Publications), *Text and Performance Quarterly* (Routledge), or the *International Review of Qualitative Research* (Left Coast Press, Inc.) receptive to publishing shorter works or excerpts from full-length play scripts. Discipline-specific journals in such fields as health care, psychology, and anthropology may also be receptive to reviewing and publishing ethnodramatic works whose topics relate to their readerships' interests. Academic book-length works may include research-based play scripts in chapter collections. And the new online journal and e-book trends may also be receptive to digital publication of downloadable full-length scripts. When in doubt, contact an editor or academic publisher to assess his or her receptiveness to arts-based research.

Getting your ethnodrama accepted by a commercial publisher or managed by a play leaser is just as, if not more, difficult. The bottom line, regrettably yet understandably, is their willingness to invest in your work's potential marketability. Will other individuals, programs, or production companies find your play worth mounting as part of their artistic seasons? Arguably, the most recent commercially successful and frequently produced ethnodrama worldwide is *The Laramie Project*. Its appeal lies not only in its artistic quality and socially-conscious merit, but also in its compatibility for the needs and goals of educational and regional theatre companies: a medium-size cast that's gender balanced, minimal technical requirements (thus relatively inexpensive to design and build), and title recognition for audience draw and box office sales. Perhaps the second most-produced ethnodramatic title is *The Vagina Monologues* for many of the same reasons and for its grassroots feminist popularity.

Most ethnodramas are signature works, meaning that they are produced once by a particular individual or company and will more than likely not be produced by others. This is not intended to downplay or denigrate the merit of those works. All dramatic literature, regardless of genre, includes only a relatively few titles that receive multiple productions and achieve popularity or canonized status. Dreams of exorbitant financial profit should not be the driving force behind the creation of new ethnotheatrical work, otherwise the social goals of the art form may be seriously compromised. Producers and audiences, not you, determine whether the play you've written has transferability beyond the one-shot production or a publication's first printing. As I was told by one of my playwriting mentors years ago, "Just write the play you need to write, and let the play find its own audience."

Whenever possible, include production photographs, shot at a high resolution of your ethnotheatrical work, to accompany the published script. Readers can get a better sense of the play's style with a few visual prompts. If permissions and releases have been obtained, consider posting video excerpts or a video of the entire performance online through such sites as YouTube. If you are unable to get your written play script published, consider making your copyrighted text available online as well. The ethnodramatic community gains much from Internet accessibility to these texts to see how fellow artists approach topical material.

Recommend Readings and Viewings

Play Scripts and DVDs

You become a better playwright by reading exemplary scripts and viewing exemplary productions. I recommend the following plays, books, and media, alphabetized by title, to expand your knowledge of ethnodrama's ethnotheatrical possibilities.

And Then They Came for Me: Remembering the World of Anne Frank by James Still (Woodstock, IL: Dramatic Publishing, 1999). The playwright interviewed two Holocaust survivors, Eva Schloss and Ed Silverberg, as primary source material for this dramatic adaptation of their stories and the times. Excerpts from their videotaped interviews (which can be secured from the play leaser) are played throughout the performance. These interviews, plus additional video images, music, sound effects, voice-overs, and live stage action, are carefully interwoven in the script.

The National Theatre of Scotland's *Black Watch* by Gregory Burke (London: Faber and Faber, 2007). The drama includes stories and perspectives of Scottish soldiers in Iraq, based on Burke's research and interviews with veterans. The script and company's staging ranges from coarse realism to powerful visual storytelling. A DVD of the landmark and award-winning production is available in Region 2/PAL format (John Williams Productions Ltd., 2008). At the time of this writing, the production is also available in eleven parts on YouTube: http://www. youtube.com/watch?v=A4cIV-e1wcU.

columbinus by the United States Theatre Project, written by Stephen Karam and PJ Paparelli, dramaturgy by Patricia Hersch (Woodstock, IL: Dramatic Publishing, 2007). Fact and fiction merge in this documentary drama about the Columbine High School shooting massacre, based on interviews and forums with students, teachers, parents, and community members of Littleton, Colorado. Act I focuses on high school and adolescent culture through a barrage of choral litanies, while Act II both documents and speculates on the motives and actions of Eric Harris and Dylan Klebold.

The Exonerated by Jessica Blank and Erik Jensen (New York: Faber and Faber, 2004). The trade book of the play offers a behind-the-scenes introduction by Blank and Jensen. The drama is an adaptation in both monologic and dialogic formats of interview transcripts, court proceedings, police case files, and other documents related to six exonerated individuals. The DVD (Courtroom Television Network, 2005) features such actors as Susan Sarandon, Brian Dennehy, and Danny Glover.

Gone Missing, written by Steven Cosson from interviews by the company, music and lyrics by Michael Friedman, in *The Civilians: An Anthology of Six Plays*, edited by Steven Cosson (New York: Playscripts, Inc., 2009). This charming one-act musical ethnodrama is a monologic and dialogic revue with overlapping and interweaving stories about the things people lose and find—literally and metaphorically.

Katrina: A Play of New Orleans by Jonathan Holmes (London: Methuen, 2009). The play consists primarily of verbatim and gripping monologic survivor testimony and national news broadcast texts, but the staging and stage directions suggest the production as an installation in various found spaces that the audience moves into throughout the performance. Environment, music, sound effects, lighting, and technology play key roles in this ethnotheatrical event that utilizes unique facets of New Orleans culture.

The Katrina Project: Hell and High Water by Michael Marks and Mackenzie Westmoreland. (New York: Playscripts, Inc., 2006). Various sources such as televised news conferences, interviews, and other found texts were used to create an account of Hurricane Katrina's wrath in Louisiana and Mississippi. The play includes everyday citizens as well as public figures such as former Governor Kathleen Blanco, former Mayor Ray Nagin, rapper Kanye West, and filmmaker Michael Moore. Stage directions encourage the use of choreographed movement, special lighting and fog effects, music, media projections, and actual video footage of the disaster.

Liars, Thieves and Other Sinners on the Bench by Jo Carson (New York: Theatre Communications Group, 2009). Carson's outstanding collection of short, dramatized oral histories and folk wisdom showcases a variety of monologic, dialogic, jointly-told, and choral forms. The participant/characters are uniquely rural American, and her elegant playwriting blurs the boundaries between traditional storytelling and dramatic narrative. Most scenes are accompanied with Carson's background notes on the stories' origins from fieldwork. One of her plays, *Voodoo*, is included in this book in Chapter Four.

Life After Scandal by Robin Soans (London: Oberon Books, 2007). The play is an eclectic blend of interwoven monologue, dialogue, and jointly-told storytelling of actual U.K. figures publicly tarnished by scandals such as fraud and sexual deviance. Not only are the people's stories explicitly told, but the media are critically examined for their tabloid journalism, social influence, and abuse of power.

My First Time by Ken Davenport (New York: Samuel French, Inc., 2009). Davenport's script adapted first sexual experience stories submitted anonymously to www.myfirsttime.com. The production incorporates media projections throughout the play, and solicits preshow information from the audience that is used in performance. The structure of the script is an intricate blend of monologue, dialogue, jointly-told storytelling, and choral forms. Access information about the production at www.myfirsttimetheplay.com.

sista docta by Joni L. Jones, in L. C. Miller, J. Taylor, & M. H. Carver (Eds.), *Voices Made Flesh: Performing Women's Autobiography* (Madison, WI: University of Wisconsin Press, 2003). Jones' serio-comic one-woman autobiographical show profiles her perceptions as an African-American professor in predominantly European-American academia through monologue, poetry, improvisation, dance, audio-recorded voice-overs, media projections, drumming, and audience participation.

Standing Ovation: Performing Social Science Research About Cancer by Ross Gray and Christina Sinding (Walnut Creek, CA: AltaMira Press, 2002). The paperback book includes an accompanying studio-quality VHS tape with two ethnodramatic productions. The book does not include the full play scripts, but the video of *Handle with Care?* and *No Big Deal?* demonstrates how the topics of women's breast cancer and men's prostate cancer can be dramatized using presentational monologic, dialogic, and choral forms with movement.

United 93: A Newmarket Shooting Script Series Book by Paul Greengrass (New York: Newmarket Press, 2006). This book contains the director's final shooting script and commentary about the making of this ethnodramatic film. Most intriguing and relevant are the sections describing how the production company meticulously and ethically researched documents and people to create a plausible account of what may have happened on the doomed September 11 flight. Also view the DVD of the film (Universal Pictures, 2006) and listen to the director's commentary with the soundtrack for background information on sources and rationale.

Voices in Conflict by Bonnie Dickinson and the Theatre Students of Wilton High School in Wilton, Connecticut (New York: Playscripts, Inc., 2008). Various sources were used for the play's monologues, rap, poetry, and song including documentary films, essays, books, newspaper and magazine articles, televised interviews, Internet sites, and personal letters. The play also includes reference to its own censorship controversy.

Comparative Readings

1. Read and compare these two one-woman autoethnodramas, both of which focus on breast cancer. Examine how each playwright chose to tell her story; reflect on whether one or both plays maintain your interest as a reader and why, and whether one or both plays stimulate your imagination for visualizing a performance of it on stage.

- *A Clean Breast of It* by Linda Park-Fuller (2003)
- *My Left Breast* by Susan Miller (2006)

2. Read and compare two or more of the following ethnodramas, all of which focus on the war in Iraq and/or military service. Note how the same general topic is approached from different artistic and participant/character perspectives, ranging from civilians to military personnel to national political leaders. Reflect on which plays maintain your interest as a reader and why, and which ones stimulate your imagination for visualizing performances of them on stage.

- *Aftermath* by Jessica Blank and Erik Jensen (2010)
- *Betrayed* by George Packer (2008)
- The National Theatre of Scotland's *Black Watch* by Gregory Burke (2007)
- *In Conflict* by Douglas C. Wager (2008), based on the book by Yvonne Latty
- *ReEntry* by Emily Ackerman and KJ Sanchez (2010)
- *Stuff Happens* by David Hare (2004)
- *Voices in Conflict* by Bonnie Dickinson and the Theatre Students of Wilton High School in Wilton, Connecticut (2008)

Theatre Companies and Artists

Photographs and video excerpts from ethnotheatrical productions can be viewed at the following sites.

The Albany Park Theatre Project: http://www.aptpchicago.org/. Chicago's celebrated and award-winning youth theatre ensemble creates devised work from interviews with local community members. The company's productions exhibit a strong and unique visual style.

Banner Theatre: http://www.bannertheatre.co.uk/. This politically and socially conscious company uses "theatre, music and song, digital imagery and 'actuality' (recorded voices captured by video or audio)" to create "issue-led productions based on people's real-life experiences and in support of disenfranchised sections of society."

The Civilians: http://www.thecivilians.org/. New York City's professional company conducts "investigative theatre" with actors interviewing everyday citizens and transforming their words into plays with original songs. Their most well-known ethnodramatic works are *This Beautiful City* and *Gone Missing*.

Kimberly Dark: http://kimberlydark.com/. Ms. Dark is a sociologist and an autoethnographic spoken word performer with vibrant energy and haunting poetry. Her website states, "Often times, I'm asked whether my performance work is autobiographical. 'Yes and no,' I explain. All of the stories are about me, but I'm not the subject of the stories. I'm using my own life—very personal aspects of my own life— in order to open dialogue about themes that are hard to discuss—gender, sexuality, poverty, race and privilege."

The Laramie Project: http://www.laramieproject.org/. Information on *The Laramie Project* productions, photos, video excerpts, blogs, and other related pages, including *The Laramie Project: Ten Years Later*, can be accessed from this website. An online community site is also available at: http://community.laramieproject.org/.

Recorded Delivery: http://www.recordeddelivery.net. Alecky Blythe's verbatim theatre company utilizes actors wearing earphones during rehearsals and performances to replicate participants' audio-recorded interviews exactly as spoken.

Sojourn Theatre: http://sojourntheatre.org/. Portland, Oregon's award-winning company develops community-engaged, site-specific productions. Artistic Director Michael Rohd holds an international reputation as an outstanding drama/theatre workshop facilitator.

Tempest Productions: http://www.bodyandsold.org/. This organization helps producers coordinate local performances of *Body & Sold*, a documentary play about the sex trafficking of American children and adolescents. The event is used as an awareness campaign and fundraiser.

ENDNOTE

1. In Ackroyd & O'Toole (2010), *Performing Research: Tensions, Triumphs and Trade-Offs of Ethnodrama*, p. 51.

shots: a love story

written by John Caswell, Jr.

shots: a love story demonstrates reality² (reality squared) autoethnodramatic writing. I was fortunate to see a production of this work, also directed by Caswell, which was a stunning theatrical tour de force. The poetic stage directions in his uniquely formatted script provide readers not just the visual and aural, but the mental and emotional representation of alcoholism and recovery. Caswell insightfully renders spoken and written verbatim texts into expressionistic and surrealistic choral forms to portray the nightmarish character of addiction. His introduction to the play provides readers the candid origins of and artistic approach to his work.

Introduction by John Caswell, Jr.

Writing and producing shots: a love story was a necessary step as a person and artist to reconcile my relationship with alcohol as it pertained to myself as well as to my father. The material is a culmination of my own experiences with illness caused by excessive drinking, memories of my father's own disease, and medical and psychological literature related to the subject of alcoholism. By bringing these elements together, I sought to devise a theatrical piece that abstracted the psyche of an addict.

While learning to articulate the purpose and overall feel of the project, I soon settled on a description: Imagine we were inside an addict's subconscious. We are sitting in a screening room watching the random thoughts, images, negotiations, small victories, and eventual defeats that come with addiction and recovery. What might that look like on stage? How can I display real information, data, texts, and memories pertaining to the subject of alcoholism without the end product being didactic and a simple staged speech about my own experience?

The thought of a one-man, whining, crying, confessional play did cross my mind. I believe strongly that such a production would have done nothing for me. I was already accustomed to discussing my issues in front of strangers. I wasn't about to do it again. I wasn't willing to rehearse the same Alcoholics Anonymous speech for four weeks.

The initial production was staged in an extremely collaborative environment. The emotions were still raw and I found it necessary to create a family of artists that made me feel secure and comfortable. The end product, while somewhat effective, was nothing more than a carnal scream of pain and fear. It became evident that future productions would require myself to act solely as director rather than collaborator and cast member. Because this piece was about my own experiences, it was only appropriate that I reshape it to be exactly what I felt it needed to be—for me. It was time for me to take the scream and turn it into a self-meditation that was more emotionally accessible. Subsequent productions, which included a performance at The New York International Fringe Festival in 2008, were demonstrations of contained chaos. I decided to stage chaotic disease via an aesthetic that was angular, highly stylized, controlled, militaristic, and oppressive.

This text is open and from the fiber of my being, but I don't know exactly how to tell you what this is.

• • •

A—Pre-Show

audience comes in.
they hear/see/feel the following:
a soundscape. it says that things are about to explode. it clicks. it ticks. it
scats. pianos riff. radios tune. most importantly, there is a rhythm to it all. a
rhythm of darkness that feels
wonderful one moment and horrifying the next.
and guns cock. but they don't fire. not yet.
HE is on stage along with HER, (her again), and (her once more).
HER starts getting ready. (her again) and (her once more) watch closely, knowing what is to come and eventually walk to where they are supposed to be and sit. they read a book. a big book. a giant book. it says nothing.
they read the nothingness out loud. it sounds empty.
HE moves to HER. HE watches HER get ready. HE attaches himself to HER and moves toward his seat center. she feels his pull.
between HE and HER are shot glasses lined up neatly.

the pull is stronger now.
HER stands and moves to HE via the shots gulping each as she moves closer and
closer.
a gun shot each time the liquid is thrown back.
she settles in next to him.
they begin.

B—Sucked In

(her again) and (her once more) speak looped text until end of scene.
she looks at him. HE looks at HER. she looks away.
she looks at him. HE looks at HER. she looks away.
HE feels HER thigh. she sees his hand. she looks away.
HE grabs HER chin. HE turns HER face toward his. she pulls away. she turns
HER face away from his.
HE grabs HER cheeks. HE turns HER face toward his. she pulls away.
she turns HER face away from his.
HE grabs HER head. HE turns HER face toward his. she pulls away.
she turns HER face away from his.
they stare into each other's eyes.
she stands to leave.
HE grabs HER shoulder.
HE pulls HER down.
she stands again.
she walks away.
HE pulls HER in.
repeat everything five times.
things pick up pace each time.
it all explodes. the soundscape, the movement, the vocalizations, the audience.
boom.
the last time HE pulls HER in, she lands in his arms.
everything goes silent and still.
catastrophe. love.
HE gives HER a bottle. HE gives HER a glass. HE gives HER a kiss. HE leaves.

C—Alone 1

she stares at what HE left behind.
she prepares herself a drink calmly and neatly.
vodka is poured gingerly into a glass. she sips. it's gone.
she continues serving herself drinks.
one after another.
each time she becomes increasingly shaky, unstable, and on edge.
each time HER arms and hands begin to move as if possessed.
each time she loses agency of the action.
it is happening . . . eventually . . . without HER physical permission.
(her again) and (her once more) approach from behind.
they take over.
they take the bottle and glass to a service station where an array of pre-prepared
drinks sit.
all drinks are in a shot glass. the shot glasses should vary in size from standard
to giant.
there should be many of them. but not too many.

D—Ring of Fire

there is music now.
perhaps Ring of Fire?
(her again) and (her once more) bring HER shot
after shot
after shot
starting first with the smaller sized drinks
increasing to larger glasses
the pace becomes frenetic
quicker
more liquid
it spills all over HER
there is too much to swallow
they keep coming
more and more until she is soaked and there aren't any left
she gasps for air

HE enters with a tray of shots.
HE tapes HER mouth shut.
HE kisses her gently and hands them to HER one at a time.
she stares at the first drink.
HE snaps. she drinks. the liquid can't enter HER mouth. the tape. HE serves her
the rest, one by one and then leaves.

E—Alone 2

silence. she stands. gathers herself a bit. removes the tape. stumbles to another
place on stage. she sits.
HER
quietly. self affirmation.
I'm fine. We're fine.
silence
I said I'm fine.
silence
speaks to herself for a while under her breath. we can't hear what she is saying.

F—Diagnosis Robot

elevator music starts to play. clinical. sterile. robotic. diagnostic.
enter (her once more) as a doctor. a shrink. not quite human. not quite
machine. mechanical. programmed. but there is a glimmer of hope that perhaps
she might be real.
a small glimmer.
doctor has a bell, a notepad, and a pen.
(her once more)
You have a maladaptive pattern of substance use.
HER isn't biting
You have a maladaptive pattern of substance use.
still nothing from HER
You have a maladaptive pattern of substance use.
long silence
You have a maladapt—

HER

I have a maladaptive pattern of substance use.

(her once more)

pause

Good.

HER

beat

I have a maladaptive pattern of substance use leading to clinically significant impairment or distress, as manifested by one or more of the following, occurring within a twelve month period.

lists

Recurrent substance use resulting in a failure to fulfill major role obligations at work, school, home.

ding

Recurrent substance use in situations in which it is physically hazardous like driving an automobile or operating a machine when impaired by substance use.

ding

Recurrent substance-related legal problems such as arrests for substance-related disorderly conduct

ding

Continued substance use despite having persistent or recurrent social or interpersonal problems caused or exacerbated by the effects of the substance

ding

Arguments with spouse about consequences of intoxication, physical fights

ding

(her once more)

Abuse is long gone. Dependence.

HER

No.

pause

No.

pause.

Dependence

(her once more)

Dependence

pause

Dependence is?

HER

during the following, the doctor becomes increasingly less connected to the patient and much more robotic.

A maladaptive pattern of substance use, leading to clinically significant impairment or distress, as manifested by three (or more) of the following, occurring at any time in the same 12-month period:

lists

tolerance, as defined by either of the following:

a need for markedly increased amounts of the substance to achieve intoxication or desired effect

ding

markedly diminished effect with continued use of the same amount of substance

ding

withdrawal, as manifested by either of the following:

the characteristic withdrawal syndrome for the substance

ding

the same (or a closely related) substance is taken to relieve or avoid withdrawal symptoms

ding

the substance is often taken in larger amounts or over a longer period than was intended

ding

there is a persistent desire or unsuccessful efforts to cut down or control substance use

ding

a great deal of time is spent in activities to obtain the substance, use the substance, or recover from its effects

ding

important social, occupational or recreational activities are given up or reduced because of substance use

ding

the substance use is continued despite knowledge of having a persistent or recurrent physical or psychological problem that is likely to have been caused or exacerbated by the substance like continued drinking despite recognition that your pancreas was dying and was made worse by alcohol consumption

I like abuse better.

(her once more)

now in full-on mechanics and autopilot.

To diagnose properly, our questions focus on two things. First, the consequences

gun cocks. shot to the head, HER dies. it all rewinds. is alive again. elevator music resumes. it never happened.

And the perceptions of drinking behavior.

HER

I'm fine. We're fine.

(her once more)

C.A.G.E. Cage.

C. Have you ever felt that you should Cut down on your drinking?

HER

I'm okay, really.

(her once more)

A. Have people Annoyed you by criticizing your drinking?

HER

I think I'm okay now.

(her once more)

G. Have you ever felt bad or Guilty about your drinking?

HER

I just need some time to think. So thank you.

HER is about to leave but decides to play along.

(her once more)

E. Have you ever had an Eye opener? A drink first thing in the morning to get rid of a hangover?

HER

All the time. Everyday. Never ends. And. Every morning.

(her once more)

Breath indicated recent drinking. Looked for mean corpuscular volume, high density lipoprotein cholesterol and triglyceride levels, serum glutamic oxaoacetic transaminase level, alkaline phosphate level, alanine aminotransferase *(and then about 15 seconds of gibberish that should be scripted, rehearsed, and repeatable so it sounds as convincing as the medical terms that precede it)*

HER

I absolutely and completely agree.

(her once more)

How often do you drink alcohol? Never. 2 to 3 times a week. Monthly. 4
or more times a week. Or 2 to 4 times a month?

HER

All day. Monday through Friday. *pause* Plus the weekend.

(her once more)

How many drinks containing alcohol do you have on a typical day when
you are drinking? 1 or 2. 3 or 4. 5 or 6. 7 to 9. 10 or more?

HER

One . . . . . . gallon.

no reaction from doctor

It was a joke.

(her once more)

How often do you have 6 or more drinks on one occasion?

HER

34 hours a day. 10 days a week. 365,000 days a year.

(her once more)

How often during the past year have you found that you were not able to
stop drinking when you started?

HER

The past year.

(her once more)

How often during the past year have you failed to do what was normally
expected from you because of drinking?

HER

I don't remember.

(her once more)

How often during the past year have you needed a first drink in the
morning to get yourself going after a heavy drinking session?

HER

I'm fine. We're fine. I love him.

(her once more)

How often during the past year have you had a feeling of guilt or remorse
when drinking?

HER

Even though he beats me senseless.

HE is now standing at HER side

(her once more)

How often during the past year have you been unable to remember what happened the night before because you had been drinking?

HER

HE kisses HER neck. she dissolves

I don't remember. I don't remember. I don't remember.

HE leaves. she follows.

(her once more)

to no one

Have you or someone else been injured as a result of your drinking?

Has a relative or a friend or a doctor or other health worker been concerned about your drinking and suggest you cut down?

Are you still with me?

Are you still with me?

Are you still with me?

Are you still with me?

Are you still with me?

Are you still with me?

Are you still with me?

things dissolve

G—Alone 3

she enters with giant vodka bottle and several small bottles. she fills the small bottles up with liquid from the large. she hides them one by one. she sits center.

H—Drinking Machine

HE enters and sits next to HER, connected once again. a knock at the door.

she gets up.

HE

I'll answer it.

HER

I don't mind.

HE forces HER to the chair without touching. HE detaches.

HE

I'll answer it.

HE leaves.

this is HER chance. (her again) and (her once more) rush on and pull HER up.
his music begins. they all search for a way out. they appear to be bungee-corded
to the center. they move in various directions and levels but each time reach a
point of tautness that snaps them back to their seats.

finally they are pulled center, locked down, and become the machine.
(her again) stands upright. HER sits with arms bent at elbows, hands in front
of HER ready to be handed something, they are like claws. clamps. (her once
more) is to the other side of HER sitting on the floor facing HER, hands cupped
like a bowl. she is the receptacle.

HE enters with cart holding shots. escape is no longer an option.
music. machine music. German techno machine-like music. no one is human
any longer. they are all possessed and move to the will of someone else.

the following should be performed with intent, precision, and identically each
time. arms are the main focus of machine but movement of body is fine as long
as it is sharp and mechanical.

with left hand, (her again) picks up shot, holds it eye level, looks through it, and
delivers it to the right hand of HER. at the same time that HER brings shot glass
to HER lips, (her again)'s left hand returns to tray for next shot. after HER drinks
shot, she places glass in left hand while (her again) holds up next shot at eye level.
when (her again) hands HER the next shot the same way as the first, HER places
empty shot glass into (her once more)'s bowled hands. as soon as second shot hits
HER lips, (her once more) launches shot glass over head into preset trash can
marked "Put shot glasses here." this entire process repeats until music breaks.

music stops. machine sits still in silence for a moment. then the words hit like a
lawnmower trying to get itself started again, a chugging sound leading to near
ignition and then descent into silence again.

(her again)

Binge

HER

Drink

(her once more)

Sleep

(her again)

Binge

HER

Drink

(her once more)

Sleep

(her again)

Vomit

HER

Shower

(her once more)

Repeat

(her again)

Vomit

HER

Shower

(her once more)

Repeat

(her again)

Vomit

HER

Shower

(her once more)

Repeat

(her again)

Vomit

HER

Shower

(her once more)

Repeat

silence for a while

repeat above text faster. at the end, it catches. the machine starts back up as the
music resumes.

music resumes. for a little while. they drink more.

music stops again. record scratch. they stand together, looking up. silence so lengthy the audience should wonder what's wrong. then.

ALL

move toward god
God grant me the serenity to accept the things I cannot change
The courage to change the things I can
And the wisdom to know the difference

rewind. serenity prayer plays on sound system backwards. it's their voices but not live

group moves backward away from god to their previous positions
machine resumes. music resumes. for a while they drink. stop. music ends

ALL

Binge?

silence

ALL

Binge?

silence, then collapse to floor.

ALL

Binge?

HE enters. takes cart away.

I—Aquafina or Talking to Yourself

all three women sit center. they are the same person. throughout, they carry out a conversation with themselves via the deconstruction of the psyche of HER. take great care to establish one voice. physical unison and simultaneous moments of gesture throughout.

ALL

overlapping. each woman starting at different times.
Drinking daily. Shot after shot after shot. My body simply couldn't take it anymore.

their bodies receive a blow. they take a moment to recover.
the rest in unison.
These feelings are normal. You are feeling again.
Curled up like a child. An infant. Looking desperately for a moment of relief.

(her again)

I haven't felt in a long while. It's magnified. It feels larger than it is.

HER

I needed another drink. I could barely stand.

(her again)

Why?

(her)

Because I knew it would dull the pain.

(her again)

Silence the feelings. So now I feel what I should have felt all along.

HER

I was looking for a quick fix in the emergency room.

(her once more)

I smelled like death and tried to hide it with Altoids and cheap perfume.

HER

I smelled ok. They probably didn't notice. I was admitted. My pancreas.

ALL

varied starting points, overlapping

Forced rehabilitation. Sometimes the body

knows it's time for help and shuts itself down.

If I wasn't going to a detox,

it was going to get me help somehow.

(her once more)

Acute alcohol withdrawals. Shakes. Sweat. Dreams.

(her again)

My sheets were always wet.

HER

I'm sure I smelled ok. They gave me drugs.

ALL

Do you drink alcohol?

HER

No.

(her again)

No.

(her once more)

No.

ALL

No.

they all laugh

HER

I don't drink. Only a little.

(her again)

The body must know when enough is enough and tries to end it all. The mind. The soul directed the body to stop short of death.

HER

I make no sense.

ALL

in the round. row row row your boat style

I can't feel the left chair outside of the fence. Get the matches! Leave the food behind! Get the matches and bring them over. We can get over the wall. Bring the matches!

(her once more)

Delirium tremens. You make no sense. You lose your mind. Shake. Shake. Shake. Seeing images in the mind's eye. When the alcohol leaves the body, nightmares are often spoken out in horror.

ALL

row row row the boat

What kind of training camp is this?! So I'm starting today. What is the name of my superhero? I'm the yellow one I think. I can't breathe. No one believes me. I can't breathe. It's not asthma. They are sitting on my chest.

silence

I was unable to walk. I fell to the floor.

HER

I shit myself. When I fell.

(her again)

The addict is its own person. It gets into the very makeup of that which we normally refer to when living our daily lives. To make decisions, choices. This all makes sense to me.

HER

It didn't look good.

(her again) and (her once more)

It doesn't look very good.

(her again)

they walk, examining themselves

We begin to watch ourselves through the eyes of the other. We begin to see our existence in a haze. It becomes a bizarre film with us as the star who would win an award if only it were a performance.

HER

(her again) and (her once more) hit certain words as (her again) speaks

I lose myself. And every now and again I see glimpses of the insanity that is my addiction and look for something to grab hold of to pull me out of the pit

lighting shift . . . .

ALL

And then we snap back.

lights shift

HER

Doctors came in and out always waking me the fuck up

(her once more)

More. Demerol. Intravenous. Intramuscular not strong. IV. Central line. I need. More.

(her again)

More.

HER

Always more.

They pierced my side and drained a pocket of infection the size of a walnut.

(her once more)

Staph infection

(her again)

I watched it on a screen as they drained it completely dry.

HER

Internal masses

(her again)

What if that pocket of pus was where the entire problem could be found?

(her once more)

They were draining it out of me. Thank you. Take it out.

(her again)

When you lay in bed for weeks at a time, you start to stink. My feet are peeling.

HER

I smelled ok. You can dump it into an Aquafina water bottle and leave the house for the day.

On your way. Always feeling warm. Aquafina water bottle.

Good place to hide. How did I get here?

(her once more)

Where am I?

(her again)

Who are you?

silence, the sounds of medical disaster.

ALL

Am I going to die here? Am I going to die here? Am I going to die here?
Am I going to die here? Am I going to die here? Am I going to die here?
Am I going to die here? Am I going to die here? Am I going to die here?
Am I going to die here?

flat line. for a long time. then revived.

(her again)

Are you ready this time? Are you really ready to stop?

ALL

Hello my name is

(her again)

Why did it take so long to stop?

(her once more)

We admitted we were powerless

HER

Because I was powerless.

(her again)

Okay.

HER

Because I was shaking when I stopped.

(her again)

Of course.

HER

Because I had to go to work.

(her again)

I was fired.

HER

This was before.

(her again)

It would have made more sense to quit before being fired and go into treatment?

HER

Anything would have made more sense.

(her once more)

How did I get to work?

HER

I drank in the morning. I stopped shaking. I went to work late.

(her again)

How late?

HER

Two weeks.

(her once more)

I picked up my things in the front office.

(her again)

So I didn't have a job. Why not treatment?

HER

I started applying for new jobs. I interviewed drunk. I impressed them with my . . . Bravado.

(her once more)

They hired me.

(her again)

How long between the firing and the hiring?

HER

Three weeks.

(her again)

Detox only takes a few days.

(her once more)

Training was four weeks long. I couldn't focus on the orientation paperwork.

HER

Everything was blurred. It had been a few hours.

(her once more)

We broke for lunch.

HER

The store was only a few blocks away. I drove sober. More difficult than driving drunk.

(her again)

The things I'd do for a paycheck.

HER

I needed money. I spent all that I had.

(her again)

I needed money to spend more money to get more money to spend more money.

ALL

To get more money to spend more money to get more money to spend more money to get more money to spend more money to get more money to spend more money to get more money to spend more money to get more money

HER

I get it. I get it.

(her once more)

I get it

(her again)

I get it

HER

Let's do the math. A bottle of vodka . . .

ALL

Vodka

HER

A bottle of vodka a day.

10 bucks a bottle.

(her again)

Only ten?

HER

Popov.

(her again)

Ah. The good stuff.

HER

$70 a week. No say $100. Some days I drank more.

$100 a week. $400 a month.

$4800 a year

Times three years.

$14400 dollars of vodka.

ALL

Vodka

HER

Vodka.

(her again)

How much did I make last year?

HER

Taxable wages: $9200. 10 grand.

(her once more)

Minus $4800

HER

Equals $5200. But I wasn't eating. So what I was spending on

ALL

Vodka

(her again)

I was saving on food. *pause* I still think like an addict. I am still an addict.
I will always be an addict. I will never not be an addict. But I can be a
non-practicing addict. *pause* I'm Catholic. Our Father, Hail Mary, and all
of the guilt that goes along with it. But I don't go to church. I don't read
my bible. I don't go to confession. I don't take the sacrament. But I'm
Catholic. May the Lord be with you.

HER and (her once more)

And also with you.

HER

So I'm a Catholic.

(her again)

Catholic

(her once more)

Catholic

(her again)

Addict.

HER

Addict?

(her once more)

Addict

(her again)

Addict

HER

And?

(her again)

And I should stop practicing. Be an addict from a distance. Don't take of the body and blood. Throw out your rosary. And whatever you do, don't fucking go to mass.

HER

Not even on Easter and Christmas. Never.

(her again)

Listen to me.

(her once more)

Listen to me.

HER

Listen to me.

pause

ALL

Listen to me.

Listen to me.

Listen to me.

Listen to me.

music. (her again) and (her once more) exit and continue chanting through next transition.

HE enters. attaches himself to HER. she gets up and moves somewhere further away from him. she fights against his pull. she picks up a bottle and chugs. she picks up a suitcase and garden shears.

J—Leaving You One

she enters meekly.
end chanting of "listen to me"
she stands with shears in one hand, suitcase in other.
quiet. like riding an elevator. then . . .
a prerecorded war cry plays. it's her voice 100 times over. layered. it says, "I'm
leaving you."

HER

I'm leaving you

HE doesn't respond

HER and (her again)

I'm. Leaving. You.

still doesn't respond

HER, (her again), and (her once more)

I'm leaving you!

HER

I packed. *holds up suitcase*

HE

You don't have anything.

HER

I have clothes.

HE

You have rags.

HER, (her again), and (her once more)

I'm leaving you

HE

Okay

she pauses. sets down the suitcase.

Back so soon?

HER

I thought I knew you.

HE

I haven't changed. Since the day we met. I've never changed.
Not an ounce.

HER

You were different.

HE

I haven't changed.

HER

You. Were. Different.

HE

I haven't changed.

HER

You were warm. You made me laugh. I could be myself with you. I could
be anything I wanted to be with you. You'd hold me in your arms and
whenever I thought I might be losing you, I just looked in your eyes one
more time and I was warm all over. Warm. But you've changed.

HE

I haven't changed.

HER

You never used to beat me. In the beginning.

HE

I beat you the day I met you.

HER

I think I'd remember being beat.

HE

What did you eat for dinner last night?

HER

Chicken.

HE

Beef.

HER

I forgot.

HE

I've always beaten you. To a pulp.

HER

Fine. Fine. You've always beaten me.

HE

And that is why you're leaving me.

HER

No. Because you've changed.

HE

I haven't changed.

HER, (her again), and (her once more)

Stop saying that! Stop. Why do you lie to yourself?

HE

What I was on day one is what I am now. Warm, transparent, predictable, charming, always ready to listen, and a wife beater.

HER

You have really lost your mind. You don't know how bad off you are.

HE

What was I wearing the day we met?

HER

What?

HE

When we first met. What clothing did I have on?

HER

as she says this she realizes he is STILL wearing the clothing she is about to describe.

Black pants. Button up . . . shirt.

HE

I haven't changed.

And you aren't leaving me.

HER

No. I AM leaving. You.

HE

Sit down.

HER, (her again), and (her once more)

No!

HE

Sit . . .

she sits as if someone has pushed her down. an invisible hand of steel. she is pinned to the chair.

Down.

I love you more than I could ever begin to express.

HER
You've said this before. Same words.
HE
I love you more than I could ever begin to express.
HER
I'm not sure if I believe you.
HE
I. Love. You. More. Than. I. Could. Ever. Begin. To. Express.
HER
How do I know it will be different this time?
HE
It won't be different. It will be the same. You'll stay with me. I'll keep
slapping you silly. Things will be predictably disastrous. Don't you like
stability? I like stability.
HER
The same? The same. The same.
HE
The same. I'll be there when you need me.
HER
And you won't beat me again?
HE
I will beat you again. I will beat you. Nothing will change.
HER
Okay.
HE
HE grabs suitcase. begins to open it.
Let's unpack.
HE opens it. it is empty.
Nothing.
You have nothing.
You have me.
HE leaves.
HER, (her again), and (her once more)
He loves me.
I love him. I love him. I love him. I love him. I love him. I love him.
music turns out the lights as they chant.

K—God

HE enters and attaches himself to HER with a kiss. blindfolds her. HE retreats
still keeping the physical attachment in place. GOD enters as two people
played by (her again) and (her once more). GOD is knitting. while the two
are both GOD, they are completely different from one another. HER is very
close to GOD. So close she can almost reach her physically. But she is just out
of arm's reach. she tries though. GOD isn't interested.

HER

God? God? God?

(her again)

What is it?

(her once more)

I'm knitting.

(her again)

Can it wait?

HER

Grant me the serenity to accept the things I cannot change

(her once more)

Jesus Christ, that again?

thinks

Fine.

(her again)

There.

(her once more)

Poof. Done.

(her again) and (her once more)

Now shut the fuck up.

as a unit, GOD scoots a little further away from HER. When GOD speaks
next, she is quieter. further away. longish pause

HER

And the courage to change the things I can

(her again)

Excuse me?

(her once more)

Pardon?

HER

Courage. To change things.

(her again)

Sorry. Can't hear you.

(her once more)

Speak up. I'm knitting.

HER

Courage? COURAGE

(her again)

Don't shout.

(her once more)

Courage. Here you go.

again, GOD moves further away and gets quieter.

HER

And the wisdom to know the difference.

(her again)

I hear the birds.

HER

Wisdom.

(her once more)

It's her again.

(her again)

What's she saying?

(her once more)

I don't know. *to HER.* What???

HER

Wisdom!

(her once more)

No thank you.

HER

Wisdom!

(her again)

We don't play tennis.

HER

Wisdom! Wisdom! Wisdom!

(her once more)

Yes, that's fine with me! Go right ahead!

to (her again)

She wants to know if she should buy a horse.

HER

GOD!!!!

(her again)

Who's Bob?

(her once more)

Who isn't?

they scoot further away

HER

God.

God.

God.

God.

God.

(her again)

Do you ever get the feeling that someone needs something from you?

(her once more)

All the time.

(her again)

Like you feel responsible for the entire world?

(her once more)

Everyday.

they scoot further away. they slowly transform into HER.

HER

God?

(her again)

God?

(her once more)

God?

HER

God?

(her again)

God?

(her once more)

God?

long silence waiting for a reply. clock ticking. sound stops.

ALL

No answer.

L—Leaving You Two

same as Leaving You One. faster, more familiar, more routine.

M—Power In Numbers

music plays. in darkness they look for answers. they emit lights from within themselves. the lights pass over the faces of the audience. at times, we see the light shine on the face of HIM who can see everything. as music fades, the image settles into three beams of light held by the women shining either on their own faces or down upon full shot glasses placed on the floor.

the following is a chant, read in unison

Easy does it.

First things first.

Live and let live.

But for the grace of God.

Think think think.

One day a at time.

Let go and let God.

K.I.S.S.—Keep It Simple Stupid.

Act as if.

This, too, shall pass.

Expect miracles.

I can't, He can, I think I'll let Him.

If it works, don't fix it.

Keep coming back, it works if you work it.

Keep coming back, it works if you work it.

Keep coming back, it works if you work it.

Stick with the winners.

Keep on trudgin'.
Sobriety is a journey, not a destination.
Faith without works is dead.
Poor me, poor me, pour me another drink.
To thine own self be true.
I came; I came to; I came to believe.
Live in the NOW.
If God seems far away, who moved?
Turn it over.
A.A.= Altered Attitudes.
Nothing is so bad, a drink won't make it worse.
We are only as sick as our secrets.
There are no coincidences in A.A.
Be part of the solution, not the problem.
Sponsors: have one use one be one.
I can't handle it God; you take over.
Keep an open mind.
It works it really does!
It works it really does!
It works it really does!
Willingness is the key.
More will be revealed.
You will intuitively know.
You will be amazed.
No pain, no gain.
Go for it.
Keep the plug in the jug.
Do it sober.
Let it begin with me.
Just for today.
Sober 'n' crazy.
Pass it on.
It's in the book.
You either are or you aren't.
Before you say I can't, say I'll try.
Don't quit before the miracle happens.

Some of us are sicker than others.

We're all here because we're not all there.

Alcoholism is an equal opportunity destroyer.

Practice an attitude of gratitude.

The road to sobriety is a simple journey for confused people with a complicated disease.

Another friend of Bill W.'s.

God is never late.

Have a good day, unless of course you have made other plans.

Decisions aren't forever.

It takes time.

90 meetings in 90 days.

90 meetings in 90 days.

90 meetings in 90 days.

You are not alone.

Where you go, there you are.

Don't drink, read the Big Book, and go to meetings.

Use the 24-hour plan.

Make use of the telephone therapy.

Stay sober for yourself.

Look for the similarities rather than differences.

Remember your last drunk.

Remember that alcoholism is incurable

progressive

fatal.

Try not to place conditions on your sobriety.

When all else fails, follow directions.

Count your blessings.

Share your happiness.

Respect the anonymity of others.

Share your pain.

Let go of old ideas.

Try to replace guilt with gratitude.

What goes around, comes around.

Change is a process, not an event.

Take the cotton out of your ears and put it in your mouth.

Call your sponsor before, not after, you take the first drink.

Sick and tired of being sick and tired.

It's the first drink that gets you drunk.

To keep it, you have to give it away.

Man's extremity is God's opportunity.

The price for serenity and sanity is self-sacrifice.

One alcoholic talking to another one equals one.

Take what you can use and leave the rest.

What if . . . .

Yeah but . . . .

If only . . . .

Help is only a phone call away.

Around A.A. or in A.A.?

You can't give away what you don't have.

One drink is too many and a thousand not enough.

Half measures availed us nothing.

Anger is but one letter away from danger.

Courage to change.

Easy does it, but DO it.

Bring the body and the mind will follow.

There are 12 steps in the ladder of complete sobriety.

Fear is the darkroom where negatives are developed.

Before engaging your mouth, put your mind in gear.

I want what I want when I want it.

There is no chemical solution to a spiritual problem.

We can be positive that our drinking was negative.

Spirituality is the ability to get our minds off ourselves.

Faith is spelled a-c-t-i-o-n.

If I think, I won't drink. If I drink, I can't think.

Stay in the main tent, and out of the sideshow.

circus music, lights shine on HIM, lights come up, they take shots . . . relapse.

N—Leaving You Three

(faster, more familiar, more routine) x 2

O—Train Wreck in 12 Steps Part One

in blackness. scattered chairs. scattered bodies. the three victims lay in positions that only disaster could have designed. contorted and bent but uniformly still and silent. their bodies shouldn't bend this way. they have bottles near them. sound of trains. louder. louder. collision. boom. lights up. the following is spoken while victims remain in their mutilated and contorted state. this is where the train threw them. this is how they landed.

HER

We admitted we were powerless over alcohol—that our lives had become unmanageable.

(her again)

Just a little.

(her once more)

Legs aren't supposed to bend like this.

HER

What happened?

(her again)

The train derailed.

(her once more)

The train derailed.

HER

The train derailed.

(her once more)

Does your leg do this? *gestures to mangled leg*

(her again)

Sometimes . . .

HER

I was supposed to go feed her cats and dogs. I forgot. People forget.

(her again)

It just depends on how far my body flew before it landed.

(her once more)

That makes sense. I'd guess 200 feet. No . . . 203.

HER

She was gone for two months. Egypt. She had to see Egypt.

(her again)

Why the extra three feet?

(her once more)

Because that makes it worse than last time.

(her again)

I don't remember last time.

HER

"My cats and dogs are dead," she screamed. "Why didn't you feed them?"
She was always too loud on the phone. Her voice is large.

(her again)

panicked. I don't remember last time. Why don't I remember
last time? I don't remember last time.

HER

I just forgot. I forgot to feed your cats and dogs for two months.
Feed your own damn cats and dogs for two months and tell me if it's
something that you would remember if you were me. Feed them yourself.

(her again)

I don't remember last time!

(her once more)

Shhhhhhhhhhh!

HER

I just forgot to feed your cats and dogs for two months. It's nothing. I'm fine.

(her once more)

Shhhhhhhhhhh!

(her again)

I'm fine.

(her once more)

I'm fine.

HER

I'm fine.

(her again)

I'm fine.

(her once more)

I'm fine.

HER

I'm fine.

(her again)

I'm fine.

(her once more)

I'm fine.

HER

I'm fine.

(her again)

I'm fine.

(her once more)

I'm fine.

HER

I'm fine.

*stillness of the bodies until the audience prompts the stage to **ignite**.*

the following are spoken simultaneously until (((((

HER

I killed your pets. Your animals are dead. Postcards from Egypt.

(her again)

I don't remember last time.

(her once more)

203 feet, splattered on the ground.

(((((

blackout. sound of trains. collision. boom. it's happened again.

lights up. bodies still contorted but in different positions on stage.

still. silent. broken.

P—Leaving You Four

(faster, more familiar, more routine) x 10

Q—Train Wreck Two

sound of trains. louder. louder. collision. boom. lights up.

(her once more)

Legs aren't supposed to bend like this.

HER

What happened?

(her again)

The train derailed.

(her once more)

The train derailed.

HER

The train derailed.

(her once more)

Does your leg do this? *gestures to mangled leg*

(her again)

Sometimes . . .

HER

I was supposed to go feed her cats and dogs. I forgot. People forget.

(her again)

It just depends on how far my body flew before it landed.

(her once more)

That makes sense. I'd guess 200 feet. No . . . 204.

HER

She was gone for two months. Egypt. She had to see Egypt.

(her again)

Why the extra four feet?

(her once more)

Because that makes it worse than last time.

laughter leads to train horns leads to . . .

R—Leaving You Five

(faster, more familiar, more routine) x 100

S—Train Wreck Three

sound of trains. louder. louder. collision. boom. lights up.

(her again)

The train derailed.

(her once more)

The train derailed.

HER

The train derailed.

(her once more)

Does your leg do this? *gestures to mangled leg*

(her again)

Sometimes . . .

HER

I was supposed to go feed her cats and dogs. I forgot. People forget.

(her again)

It just depends on how far my body flew before it landed.

(her once more)

That makes sense. I'd guess 200 feet. No . . . 205.

HER

She was gone for two months. Egypt. She had to see Egypt.

(her again)

Why the extra five feet?

(her once more)

Because that makes it worse than last time.

laughter leads to train horns leads to . . .

T—Recovery

HER, (her again), and (her once more) move in unison across the stage chanting various strings of looped text as soundscape from the top of the show returns at full volume. they are battling to be heard. HE is standing behind them. HE pulls them center stage with his eyes. they cannot fight back and begin a frenzied stop motion version of the drinking machine. they manage to

break free and snap back into line and continue crossing the stage. HE follows
closely behind. they feel his pull once they reach the other side of the stage.
they struggle to hold on. they claw the floor, the walls, anything and everything
as the lower part of their body is pulled toward center stage. they are unable
to continue holding on and fly violently stage center. after several attempts to
run in unison in varying directions, they finally break free. HE is sitting center.
they slowly circle the stage and eventually position themselves where they
always are during I'm Leaving You. suitcase and shears in hand.

HER

I'm leaving you.

HE doesn't respond

HER and (her again)

I'm. Leaving. You.

still doesn't respond

HER, (her again), and (her once more)

I'm leaving you!

HER

You were warm. You made me laugh. I could be myself with you. I
could be anything
I wanted to be with you. You'd hold me in your arms and whenever I
thought
I might be losing you, I just looked in your eyes one more time and I
was warm all over.
Warm. But you've changed.

HER, (her again), and (her once more)

I'm leaving you!

she turns to him and holds up shears threatening to cut. he takes a step toward
her and stops. pause. gun cock. blackout.

end

But Is It *Art*? An Ethnotheatre Aesthetic

*This is the danger that arts based researchers, in their dedication
to eradicate cruelties, may become strident, exclusionary, monologic,
and authoritative—and therefore off-putting to readers and self-
defeating. This is the danger that arts based researchers may, . . .
in their zeal to make history, forget to make art.*

—Tom Barone and Elliot Eisner[1]

Notice that the title for this chapter is not "But Is It *Research?*" The title
is "But Is It *Art?*" I agree with Barone and Eisner that topical theatre like
ethnodrama can sometimes, if not most of the time, be short on art.
There's a reason that titles such as *The Laramie Project, The Exonerated,*
and *The Vagina Monologues* have become so well known, and the play *I
Am My Own Wife* won the Tony Award and Pulitzer Prize for Best Drama. Yes, they are all socially conscious works, but they are also *excellent
artistic products.* Ethnodramatists should never forget that our mission is
about substance *and* style, form *and* feeling, research *and* art.

An Ethnotheatre Aesthetic

I was invited by New York University's Program in Educational Theatre
to serve as a respondent at their 2006 forum on ethnotheatre and theatre for social change. I wrote and published an article for their online
journal, *Arts Praxis,* which I adapt in this chapter (Saldaña, 2010a). The
event was an intense and exciting weekend of original ethnodramatic
work directed by NYU faculty that explored conventional and reality[2]
(reality squared) approaches to the art form.

Of all the participant questions posed by NYU forum organizers,
the most intriguing to me was, "Is there an ethnotheatre aesthetic?" My
flip response was, "Yes. Next question. . . ." But an inquiry as rich as this
merits some thoughtful response. My five assertions that follow don't
claim to provide the definitive argument or answers to ethnotheatrical
aesthetics that, for purposes of this chapter, are defined as *significant
accomplishments of artistic quality and merit in the genre.* But I do address

one major theme that suggests an ironic paradox of ethnotheatre: The mounting of ethnographic reality on stage is at its most effective when the production assumes a nonrealistic—read: "theatrical"—style as its presentational framework.

An ethnotheatre aesthetic emerges from theatre artists' creative approaches to stage productions of natural social life.

You would think that the staging of ethnographic fieldwork—the mounting of real life—would suggest if not mandate that our play script adaptations adhere to the tenets of naturalism—or what has been labeled verbatim theatre or conversational dramatism in play production's and performance studies' explorations of human communication, social interaction, and conflict. I once overheard two participants at an international Playback Theatre symposium confess to each other that listening to other people's actual stories can sometimes be "fatiguing" and even "boring." I understand completely, for it is not necessarily the teller on stage sharing her story to the Playback Conductor that is intriguing, but its interpretive re-creation by the Playback Performers. If art is to imitate life, then art needs to do so in an engaging manner for its audiences.

Can the everyday—the mundane—naturally staged, make good theatre? It certainly makes good ethnographic scholarship, for I was quite intrigued to learn that there is actually an academic publication called the *Journal of Mundane Behavior* (which even the editors acknowledge is a rather humorous title). It would be fascinating to peruse their articles with hopes of finding a study with ethnodramatic potential. But ethnodramatist Robin Soans cautions that:

> Some people are boring in a fascinating or amusing way, and others are just boring. And if it's boring, it renders the whole [ethnotheatrical] exercise futile. What's the point of gathering three hundred people in a darkened space merely to tell them something they've heard before, or worse, to send them to sleep? (Hammond & Steward, 2008, p. 33)

Certainly, stories of physical abuse, racial discrimination, natural disaster, war, and sexual identity are "juicier" than those of our mundane routines. The epiphanies of our lives make better monologues than everyday matters—most often. Yet there are times when I have been mesmerized as a reader and audience member by dramatic depictions of the little things in life that I thought no one but me was aware of. Perhaps we need to explore what it would mean to become twenty-first century Chekhovs—to find the drama in the mundane of our contemporary selves, to capture not just the content of our character but also the quirkiness of it. I have always been intrigued by Roberston Davies' (1991) observation that "Theorists of drama may deal in tragedy and comedy, but the realities of life are played more often in the mode of melodrama, farce and grotesquerie" (p. 215).

Nevertheless, naturalism and realism in the hands of theatre artists can sometimes take on new interpretive meaning and become rich opportunities for creative reproduction. The early twentieth century "kitchen sink" dramas were faithful to reality but often uninspiring for a director's conceptual vision. Perhaps it is because most of today's ethnotheatrical artists fear that the occasional dryness of interview transcripts and participant observation field notes needs something more to make it engaging on stage. Our highly visual, mediated culture has raised the bar and reshaped audience expectations for live performance presentations. Perhaps we are *too* creative, and our directorial and scenographic training muddy the naturalistic waters. But this is not a liability; it is an advantage. When the vast repertoire of theatrical forms, genres, elements, styles, and media is applied to the staging of social science research, interesting presentational and representational hybrids emerge.

An ethnotheatre aesthetic emerges from theatre artists' application of available and new theatrical forms, genres, styles, elements, and media onto the ethnodramatic play script and its production.

Playwrights don't "write" ethnodramas, they *adapt* them—both in terms of content and theatricality. I was fortunate as a graduate student to take a playwriting course from the late theatre for youth author, Aurand Harris. I find that several of the principles he taught us are still prominent in my own ethnodramatic play scripts and in those of others. One of the basic approaches to his writing was that each adaptation should be structured with a stylistic theatrical frame. For example, *A Toby Show* is the Cinderella story, but integrates elements of the Chautauqua, Vaudeville, and early twentieth century Toby Theatre in the United States. *Androcles and the Lion* is an adaptation of Aesop's fable, but incorporates characters and elements from the commedia dell'arte along with conventions of the musical. In contemporary ethnodramas, *The Laramie Project* simulates the documentary with reminiscences of story theatre, while *The Exonerated* (on stage) adopts the traditional conventions of reader's theatre. In script form, Anna Deavere Smith's one-woman plays are not structured as narrative monologues but as suites of poetic verse.

Ethnotheatrical artists don't necessarily heighten or skew reality through their imaginative writing and staging, but they seem to endow their productions with aesthetic forms that create hybrids of performative ontologies. The late qualitative researchers Miles and Huberman (1994) wrote that investigators should "think display" when organizing and analyzing their empirical materials. Theatre artists, by default, are well trained to "think display" on stage; thus our ethnodramatic productions are not just representational and presentational exhibitions, they are also analytic acts. Ethnodramas are not play scripts in the traditional sense, but essentialized fieldwork reformatted in performative "data displays." Reality on stage now seems to acquire not a reductive but an exponential quality—hence, reality[2].

Consider an example from the NYU forum on ethnotheatre. Christina Marín's production of José Casas's 14 provided a staged testimonio by Latino/Latinas and whites. Joe Salvatore's An Teorainn/Edge wove interview excerpts with evocative dance-drama. Traditional storytelling sometimes reminiscent of stand-up comedy structured the women's performances in Dana Edell's ViBe Theatre Experience and Nan Smithner's Women's Project. Philip Taylor's Beautiful Menaced Child was plotted with Boalian forms, while Brad Vincent's The Silence at School maintained the elegance of reader's theatre with accompanying media projections. Stephen DiMenna's youth theatre production of Uncensored 2006 gave us the authentic stories of adolescents' experiences in the form of an ensemble revue (with a dash of sketch comedy thrown in). No "neutral" or traditionally realistic productions were offered at the NYU ethnotheatre forum. To freely adapt performance studies scholar Richard Schechner's oft-quoted phrases, the ethnotheatrical presentations were "restoried behavior" and "not-not-real."

The aesthetic possibilities of ethnotheatre are extended further if we can make our productions even more multidisciplinary. A contemporary music equivalent to ethnodrama is Steve Reich's composition, Different Trains. Tape-recorded rhythmic phrases and speech melodies from interviews with his childhood governess, a retired Pullman porter, and Holocaust survivors about trains in America and Europe during World War II, not only served as the inspiration for the music but are also woven into the music itself. Interview excerpts in Different Trains include such phrases as: "from Chicago to New York," "one of the fastest trains," and "they tattooed a number on our arm." Reich explains, "I selected small speech samples that are more or less clearly pitched and then notated them as accurately as possible in musical notation. . . . The piece thus presents both a documentary and a musical reality

. . . that I expect will lead to a new kind of documentary music video theater in the not too distant future" (Reich, 1989, n.p.). Musicals like *Working* and *A Chorus Line* contain some authentic passages of interview text, while New York City's The Civilians and Chicago's Albany Park Theatre Project integrate verbatim interview passages into their productions' song lyrics. Might it be possible in the not-too-distant future to create ethnodramatic oratorio or even opera?

When I first began writing ethnodramas, I was loath to tinker too freely with the authentic words and voices of participants. I felt that theatre's artistic power to creatively *present* would negate attempts to authentically *represent*. But after reading and/or viewing well over 300 scripts and productions I classify as ethnodramatic, I have returned and applied to ethnotheatre my adopted pragmatic advice for selecting appropriate analytic strategies: "Whatever works." I notice that most of the ethnodramas I've read have been written in such diverse dramatic and theatrical forms as the revue, rant, radio drama, performance art, story theatre, reader's theatre, chamber theatre, poetry, expressionism, debate, digital storytelling, participation theatre, simulated lecture, and ritual. It's a bit ironic that slice-of-life scripts about human social reality, constructed with the conventions of realism or naturalism, are actually quite few in number. The ethical conundrum for ethnodramatists to maintain fidelity to our transcripts and fieldnotes should not paralyze us from thinking imaginatively about a research study's staging potential. But ethnotheatrical artists should also acknowledge that, like all rigorous researchers, we have an obligation to our participants and audiences to balance creativity with credibility and trustworthiness.

An ethnotheatre aesthetic emerges from theatre artists' integrity to truthfulness as well as truth.

Oddly enough, I find myself applying a quantitative measure to assess whether a play's qualitative background research and dramatization merit its classification as an ethnodrama (as I define it). A production at my university used interview transcripts of troubled adolescents in a group home as a foundation for devising an original work about their lives. I eagerly awaited and attended the performance, assuming that this was to be a new ethnodramatic work. Though the production was well mounted and realistically performed by the university actors, I sensed unauthentic and implausible dialogue throughout the play. The next day I asked the student playwright, "What percentage of your script contained the actual words said by teenagers the company interviewed and observed?" After a few seconds of reflection he responded, "About forty percent." Therefore, I classified the production as an exemplar of devised theatre that addressed important social issues about youth, but it was not ethnotheatrical.

Autoethnography aside, how much authenticity is necessary for a script to be labeled ethnodramatic? How "real" should reality theatre be? Though abhorrent to some, what percentage of a script's monologue, dialogue, and action should consist of actual excerpts from transcripts, fieldnotes, and documents to justify its classification as an ethnodrama? Screenwriter Peter Morgan (2007) notes that when it comes to historic fiction, and he lacks the necessary information about what is true, the challenge for him is to write what *appears* to be truthful. (As a side note, I've always found it fascinating that the word "hypocrite" comes from the Greek *hypokritēs*, meaning "actor on the stage.")

I admittedly and unapologetically use a subjective level of significance of sorts, balanced with my personal response to the play or production, to assess whether a play is an ethnodrama. A playwright can tell me that his or her script consists of approximately ninety percent verbatim extracts from empirical materials, and I will comfortably label the play ethnodramatic. Anything less than that is considered on a case-by-case basis. I have encountered several exceptions to my rule, and have even been fooled on occasion, so I reserve the right to change this metric and method in the future as the need arises. U.K. ethnodramatist Alecky Blythe refers to this instinctive gauge as her "truthometer" (Hammond & Steward, 2008, p. 96).

Case in point: Some are taken aback when they see Paul Greengrass's (2006a, 2006b) *United 93* in my bibliography of cinematic ethnodramas. (Several film critics erroneously labeled this work a "docudrama.") Half the film portrays the action of the doomed flight inside the airplane on September 11, 2001. How can any of us know with unquestionable certainty what actually happened on board to the passengers, crew, and hijackers, and what they actually said and did before the tragic outcome? I was persuaded by Greengrass's director's commentary that accompanies the film on DVD. On the soundtrack, he notes how several of the actual people who were involved with air traffic control and operations during the tragedy were cast to portray themselves in *United 93*. *The 9/11 Commission Report* was used as a "bible," he says, to faithfully reconstruct the real-time events depicted in the film. Over one hundred interviews with surviving family members, transcripts of frantic phone calls by passengers and crew, and two weeks of intensive rehearsals by the director and cast to create a sense of "plausible truth" (Greengrass, 2006b, p. 101) were used as sources for reconstructing the monologue, dialogue, and action. Meticulously researched screenplay notwithstanding, the emotional power of the film itself, the frightening sense of reality captured by the actors' naturalistic performances, and the director's stark but compassionate vision lead me to conclude that *United 93* is one of the finest, if not the best, ethnodramas ever produced.

A second case in point: One of the most stunning moments for me as an instructor occurred in my Ethnodrama and Ethnotheatre class when we dramatized passages from Michael V. Angrosino's (1994) classic article, "On the Bus with Vonnie Lee." This case study profiles a developmentally disabled adult raised in the southern United States who had a passion for riding the city bus. We experimented with Victor Turner's premise that, to get into the skin of our participants, we needed to act out their stories—ethnodramatic studio exercises we labeled "staging culture."

Angrosino's article begins with a brief descriptive sketch of Vonnie Lee's childhood, one sadly troubled with an alcoholic mother engaged with countless physically and sexually abusive boyfriends. We cast five students in class to portray Vonnie Lee, his two sisters, their mother, and one of the abusive men in their lives. The improvisation began with all actors framed to let their assigned characters ("poor white trash—real crackers," according to Vonnie Lee) take them in directions they felt appropriate as they improvised. The scene was set in the family's home and, after some initiating action, transitioned to discomfort at the harsh dialogue directed by the adults toward the children, which later escalated to the mother yelling drunkenly and obscenely at Vonnie Lee as the boyfriend inappropriately fondled one of the young sisters. The improvisation reached such a peak of violence that the actors and some of the class audience members felt an urgent need to stop the exercise. Upon reflection and processing, the actors and some of their classmates realized that it was not just the cruelty portrayed and experienced by the characters that compelled the students to break out of role, but the stunning realization that they had captured moments that were all too plausible and all too truthful for their comfort.

Victor Turner was right.

An ethnotheatre aesthetic emerges from theatre artists' capacities for thinking theatrically as well as ethnographically.

I cannot state this enough and you cannot read it enough: Stop thinking like a social scientist and start thinking like an artist. I've been privileged to read play script drafts submitted to me by playwrights across

North America these past few years for feedback and revision recommendations. A few of those scripts provide opportunities to discuss how our initial assumptions about writing ethnodrama might steer us in misleading directions.

One play attempted to realistically reconstruct the talk among abused women in a group support session, who were also in rehearsal for a play about their personal experiences. My initial response as a reader was that the dialogue exchanged between them seemed artificial, with a contrived framework for justifying a theatrical presentation. I recommended that the writer "think theatrically" (Wright, 2009) rather than ethnographically, and to consider how the works of African-American playwright Ntozake Shange might be used as inspirational models for reconceptualizing the play. La'Ketta Caldwell's revised draft of *Unclothed* now presents the haunting stories and healing of women who have been emotionally, physically, and sexually abused in a monologic, ceremonial, and dynamic drama. Here is a playwright who trusted her artistic impulses and created a heart-wrenching play with theatricality yet authenticity—a quality I label "ethnodramatic validity" (Saldaña, 2005, p. 32).

Another writer felt compelled to include government statistics related to the social issues he addressed in his play. The numbers were delivered throughout the text by a chorus of men, but this device interrupted the rather nice flows of action that had been developed at that stage in his ethnodramatic comedy-drama. I initially advised the playwright to edit these didactic scenes from his draft since I was more concerned with his characters than the "stats." In discussion, we both acknowledged that the facts about gay population demographics, HIV/AIDS, and other social issues were compelling for traditional research articles but not for a play. In other words, it was good science, but not good drama.

Nevertheless, we felt that the importance of those facts merited audience education and a place in the script—but where and how? We brainstormed ideas and serendipitously hit upon the idea of making the obvious obvious. In the revision, playwright Carlos Manuel, himself a character in the play as the ethnographer, suddenly stops the action of *Vaqueeros*, which portrays the lives of closeted gay Latinos, and presents the statistics as a campy PowerPoint slide presentation with accompanying hard-copy handouts for the audience ("Here, take one and pass 'em on down"). The lesson learned was that important facts—even descriptive statistics—can be delivered humorously and theatrically. Whatever works. . . .

*An ethnotheatre aesthetic emerges from theatre artists'
production and publication of research and creative activity
in the genre to advance the field and to encourage dialogue
among its practitioners.*

Our once-labeled "experimental" and "alternative" (read: marginal-ized) ethnotheatrical work has now earned a respected place in the con-temporary canon of research methodologies. "Ethnodrama" appears as an entry in *The Sage Encyclopedia of Qualitative Research Methods* (Given, 2008). Sage Publications has also produced its *Handbook of the Arts in Qualitative Research* (Knowles & Cole, 2008), which includes chapters on ethnodrama plus other theatrical forms such as reader's theatre, film/video, and community-based presentations.

Quality ethnodramas are still being produced and published, rang-ing from the rigorously researched yet poignant narratives of women with HIV (Sandelowski, et al., 2006) to the multiple performance proj-ects about Hurricane Katrina's aftermath in Louisiana and Mississippi (e.g., Holmes, 2009; Marks & Westmoreland, 2006) to the controversial Wilton, Connecticut High School theatre production of *Voices in Conflict* (Dickinson, 2008). I am uncertain whether ethnotheatre will hold con-tinued promise as a legitimate research-based art form with a potential trajectory of increasing validity and thus full acceptance in education and the social sciences; whether its verbatim theatre forms will contin-ue to produce moderately successful commercial/professional ventures by such playwrights as Robin Soans (2004, 2005, 2007); or whether it is merely a current trend in the history of theatre that may one day be looked back on as an amusing but outdated genre. But reality will never go out of style, correct? It may simply be theatre's presentation and rep-resentation of it that will continue to evolve.

The current trends in qualitative inquiry and theatre for social change have produced not only a body of ethnodramatic work but eth-nodramatic "social work." Mienczakowski's (1995) and Denzin's (2003) oft-cited publications promote an ethnodramatic mission that is primar-ily critical, political, moral, and emancipatory. Certainly, well-crafted ethnotheatrical productions can accomplish these admirable goals with-out didacticism and heavy-handedness. But as an individual reader and audience member of ethnodrama, I am also searching for things I didn't know before, for new knowledge about specific cultural groups, for in-sight and revelation about *me*, not just the generic human condition.

I search for significant trivia, not just big ideas. I search for artful moments, not just activism. And every time I go to the theatre I search for entertainment, not just meaning. Ethnodramatists should acknowledge that their diverse audience members have multiple and sometimes conflicting agendas as they attend and attend *to* the ethnotheatrical event. My personal goal as an artist—because it's also what I want as an audience member—is to develop an ethnotheatre aesthetic that captures on stage a complex rendering of what I label *ethnotainment*: *"Theatre's primary goal is to entertain—to entertain ideas as it entertains its spectators.* With ethnographic performance, then, comes the responsibility to create an entertainingly informative experience for an audience, one that is aesthetically sound, intellectually rich, and emotionally evocative" (Saldaña, 2005, p. 14, emphasis in original).

To recap, an ethnotheatre aesthetic emerges from theatre artists':

- creative approaches to stage productions of natural social life;
- application of available and new theatrical forms, genres, styles, elements, and media onto the ethnodramatic play script and its production;
- integrity to truthfulness as well as truth;
- capacities for thinking theatrically as well as ethnographically; and
- production and publication of research and creative activity in the genre to advance the field and to encourage dialogue among its practitioners.

These assertions weave *truth* and *art*, in all their magnitude, into scripted, performed, and published ethnotheatrical work.

Closure

Theatre artistic director Peter Sellars speaks passionately about the art form, and his charge to all of us is as follows, from his Foreword to Bowles' (1997) anthology of ethnodramas by and about gay and lesbian street youth:

> Theatre was invented to demonstrate utterly and conclusively that you are not superior to any other human being on the planet. We are all very needy. We are carrying more than we know how to bear. And we are mostly not very honest about it—to ourselves, let alone each other. . . . Artists are communicators and their task is to open up and sustain communication in zones of darkness, complexity, confusion and impasse. The formation of new vocabularies, the reformation of old vocabularies, the gift of aligning the imaginative function of our thought processes and emotional life with our actual experience of reality and the ongoing shifting nature of our relationships—these are important services. (pp. vii-viii)

Reality as the inspirational source for dramatic literature is an idea that is over 2,500 years old. But twenty-first century perceptions of reality are multiple, ambiguous, contested, and complex. Ethnodrama and ethnotheatre provide opportunities for artists and audiences to more closely examine how we and others experience life, and to shape those moments into new aesthetic forms that bring us closer to notions of what is real and what is true as we individually and collectively construct them.

Theatre is a democratic forum for multiple and diverse voices and spectators to assemble and experience particular renderings about the human condition. And the wide variety of literary and artistic genres, elements, and styles available to us provide an array of exciting possibilities for representing and presenting social life. This book's primary goal has been to offer readers pragmatic guidance for writing and staging ethnotheatre, but in no way is it intended as the authoritative or definitive work on the subject, despite my assertions throughout as to what I value and believe about social science and art.

At this particular and unstable period in our world history, many theatre artists are asking themselves what is "the theatre of the future." Some are integrating state-of-the-art technology into production work to blur the boundaries between mediated and live performance. Others decline to speculate on the trajectory of "the theatre of the future" because the future is so uncertain and unpredictable. And a few pessimistic others are even proclaiming the death of traditional live theatre as we know it. One of my younger colleagues feared that the economic instability of 2009–2011 and its consequent budgetary cutbacks to theatre production companies would "kill" the art form. But throughout my forty years of theatre practice, I have been surprised and delighted by the creativity and endurance of artists to continue developing exciting new work, whether it be a unique play script or an innovative staging technique. And I have been literally moved to tears as an audience member from honest and truthful performances in minimalist productions mounted in the humblest of performance spaces. I reassured my colleague that as long as people have bodies, voices, and creativity, we will always have theatre. And as long as people live in reality and search for truth, we will always have ethnotheatre.

ENDNOTE

1. In Tom Barone and Elliot Eisner (2012), *Arts Based Research*, p. 128.

RECOMMENDED READINGS AND NETWORKS

Books on Playwriting

These playwriting titles offer contemporary writers practical guidance in the development of original work.

Ayckbourn, Alan. *The Crafty Art of Playmaking* (New York: Palgrave Macmillan, 2009). One of England's most celebrated comic playwrights offers lighthearted but direct guidance on the writing and directing of original plays.

Gutkind, Lee (Ed.). *Keep It Real: Everything You Need to Know About Researching and Writing Creative Nonfiction* (New York: W. W. Norton & Company, 2008). Gutkind and contributors offer valuable guidance on "The ABCs of Creative Nonfiction" such as composite characters, defamation and libel, fact-checking, montage writing, and point of view.

Wright, Michael. *Playwriting in Process: Thinking and Working Theatrically* (2nd ed.). (Newburyport, MA: Focus Publishing, 2009). Wright's text provides excellent exercises (called "etudes") for the development of characters and action.

Professional Associations and Events

Hundreds of professional associations are engaged with research. Following are seven major organizations that sponsor regular events (at the time of this writing) of particular interest to arts-based researchers and ethnodramatists.

The American Alliance for Theatre & Education focuses on drama and theatre with grades K–12 youth and professional theatre for young audiences; several sessions at its annual conferences focus on playwriting, devised work, ethnotheatre, and theatre for social change. Its website is at www.aate.com.

The American Educational Research Association's Special Interest Groups in Arts-Based Educational Research and Arts and Learning sponsors several sessions at annual conferences held throughout the U.S. and Canada; visit www.aera.net to learn more. Also explore the association's Ethical Standards document at http://www.aera.net/up loadedFiles/About_AERA/Ethical_Standards/EthicalStandards.pdf.

The Association for Theatre in Higher Education has focus groups in Performance Studies, Playwriting, and Theatre for Social Change; annual conferences are held throughout the U.S. and Canada. Learn more at www.athe.org.

The Centre for Qualitative Research at Bournemouth University's School of Health & Social Care, U.K., specializes in novel and innovative research methodologies, including performative social science, and hosts a number of annual conferences, workshops, and master classes; visit www.bournemouth.ac.uk/cqr/index.html.

The International Congress of Qualitative Inquiry is an annual multidisciplinary event with an international presence; the conference, which features several sessions on performance and performance studies, is held on the University of Illinois at Urbana-Champaign campus in the U.S. Its website is found at www.icqi.org.

The National Communication Association sponsors annual conventions which include sessions and performances from two of its pertinent divisions—Performance Studies and Theatre; see http://www.natcom.org/.

Performance Studies International creates opportunities for dialogue among artists, activists, and academics; annual events bring together scholars and practitioners worldwide. Visit http://psi-web.org/.

Consent Form

What follows is a *sample* consent form that might be signed between a researcher/playwright and an adult participant for an ethnodramatic project. The form is adapted from one particular university's Institutional Review Board's (IRB) requirements, and additional forms are needed if the participants are from vulnerable population categories such as children or prisoners. Those researcher/playwrights not subject to IRB review should consult with legal counsel for advisement and written contracts.

CONSENT FORM

[title of ethnodramatic play production project]

Introduction

The purposes of this form are to provide you, as a prospective participant, information that may affect your decision whether to participate in this research and play production project, and to record the consent of those who agree to be involved in the project.

Researcher/Playwright

[name, title, and workplace of the researcher/playwright] has invited your participation in a research project that will be written up as a play script for a performed stage production.

Project Purpose

The purpose of the research is to [describe the justification for the research in simple lay language] and to dramatize the findings as a stage production for live performance.

Description of Research and Play Production Project

If you decide to participate, you will join a project involving research of [include a nontechnical explanation of the protocol, such as interviews, participant observation, and so on; discuss that participants can skip questions if the research involves an interview or focus group].

If you say "yes," then your participation will last for [duration of participation] at [location]. You will be asked to [nontechnical description of what will happen to all participants]. Approximately [number] people will be participating in this project [nationally and locally if relevant].

Risks

There are no known risks from taking part in this project, but in any research, there is some possibility that you may be subject to risks that have not yet been identified.

Benefits

The possible/main benefits of your participation in the research are [describe the benefits of participation, or lack of benefits, to the individual participant as well as to the field or society].

or

Although there may be no direct benefits to you, the possible benefits of your participation in the research are [others may benefit by . . .].

Confidentiality

All information obtained in this project is strictly confidential. The results of this research and its scripted performance may also be used in reports, presentations, and publications, but the researcher/playwright will not identify you by your actual name. In order to maintain confidentiality of your records, [name of researcher/playwright] will [indicate specifically how the researcher/playwright will keep the actual names of the participants confidential, how this information will be secured, and who will have access to the confidential information; if the research project involves audio or video tapes, describe when and how they will be destroyed].

or

[In some cases such as a focus group or performance it may not be possible to guarantee confidentiality. The following is an example of what can be stated when confidentiality cannot be guaranteed: "Due to the nature of the project, the research/playwriting team cannot guarantee complete confidentiality of your data. It may be possible that others will know what you have reported." In cases in which confidentiality cannot be guaranteed, this may be a risk to the participant and should be described in the Risks section.]

Withdrawal Privilege

Participation in this project is completely voluntary. It is OK for you to say "no." Even if you say "yes" now, you are free to say "no" later, or withdraw from the project at any time.

[If applicable: Your decision will not affect your relationship with (university) or otherwise cause a loss of benefits to which you might otherwise be entitled.]

[If the participants are students, patients, clients, or employees, advise that participation is voluntary and that nonparticipation or withdrawal from the project will not affect an individual's grade, treatment, care, or employment status, as appropriate.]

[If applicable, participants should be told what will happen to their tapes and/or data if they withdraw.]

Costs and Payments

The researcher/playwright wants your decision about participating in the project to be absolutely voluntary. Your participation may pose some [costs, inconvenience, etc]. In order to [help defray your costs] you may receive [payment, etc.]. [If payment is to be provided to the participant, include amount of payment, method of payment, and schedule for payment, including whether payment will be made in increments or in one lump sum. Discuss issue of payment if participant does not complete the project. In some cases, negotiations may be made for possible script sales and production royalties.]

or

There is no payment for your participation in the project.

Voluntary Consent

Any questions you have concerning the research project, the script, the play production, or your participation, before or after your consent, will be answered by [name of individual, address, and telephone number of the researcher/playwright; the names and contact information of co-investigators can be included as well].

If you have questions about your rights as a participant in this research, or if you feel you have been placed at risk, you can contact the [university IRB unit and phone number].

This form explains the nature, demands, benefits, and any risk of the project. By signing this form you agree knowingly to assume any risks involved. Remember, your participation is voluntary. You may choose not to participate or to withdraw your consent and discontinue participation at any time without penalty or loss of benefit. In signing this consent form, you are not waiving any legal claims, rights, or remedies. A copy of this consent form will be given (offered) to you.

Your signature below indicates that you consent to participate in the above project. [Release statement for videotaping must be inserted here if applicable; for example: "By signing below, you are granting to the researchers the right to use your likeness, image, appearance and performance—whether recorded on or transferred to videotape, film, slides, and photographs—for presenting or publishing this research (or for whatever use)." This can be done as part of the signature line or as a separate signature if there are options for videotaping, photography, use of records, and so on.]

Participant's Signature	Printed Name	Date

Legal Authorized Representative (if applicable)	Printed Name	Date

Researcher's/Playwright's Statement

"I certify that I have explained to the above individual the nature and purpose as well as the potential benefits and possible risks associated with participation in this research and play production project, and have answered any questions that have been raised, and have witnessed the above signature. These elements of informed consent conform to the assurance given by [university and IRB unit] to protect the rights of human subjects. I have provided/offered the participant a copy of this signed consent document."

Signature of Researcher/Playwright: _____

Date: _____

A Selected Bibliography
of Academic Resources in Ethnodrama,
Ethnotheatre, and Arts-Based Research

Scholars from the social sciences, education, health care, and other academic disciplines have contributed a body of literature in book chapters, professional print, and online journals about their ethnodramatic and performance experiences. This appendix includes a selected listing of published works from various fields that can inform fellow academics about resources in their subject areas. Also explore such specialty journals as *Text and Performance Quarterly*, *Women and Performance*, and *Performance Research*.

Arts-Based Research and Methodology

Alexander, B. K. (2005). Performance ethnography: The reenacting and inciting of culture. In N. K. Denzin & Y. S. Lincoln (Eds.), *The Sage handbook of qualitative research*, 3rd ed. (pp. 411–441). Thousand Oaks, CA: Sage.

Cho, J., & Trent, A. (2009). Validity criteria for performance-related qualitative work: Toward a reflexive, evaluative, and coconstructive framework for performance in/as qualitative inquiry. *Qualitative Inquiry 15*(6), 1013–1041.

Curtis, A. (2008). How dramatic techniques can aid the presentation of qualitative research. *Qualitative Researcher 8*, 8–10.

Denzin, N. K. (2001). The reflexive interview and a performative social science. *Qualitative Research 1*(1), 23–46.

—. (2003). Reading and writing performance. *Qualitative Research 3*(2), 243–268.

Donmoyer, R., & Yennie-Donmoyer, J. (1995). Data as drama: Reflections on the use of reader's theater as a mode of qualitative data display. *Qualitative Inquiry 1*(4), 402–428.

Eisner, E. (1997). The promise and perils of alternative forms of data representation. *Educational Researcher 26*(6), 4–10.

Finley, S., & Knowles, J. G. (1995). Researcher as artist/artist as researcher. *Qualitative Inquiry 1*(1), 110–142.

Fisher, K., & Phelps, R. (2006). Recipe or performing art? Challenging conventions for writing action research theses. *Action Research 4*(2), 143–164.

Gray, R. E. (2000). Graduate school never prepared me for this: Reflections on the challenges of research-based theatre. *Reflective Practice 1*(3), 377–390.

—. (2003). Performing on and off the stage: The place(s) of performance in arts-based approaches to qualitative inquiry. *Qualitative Inquiry 9*(2), 254–267.

Gray, R. E., Ivonoffski, V., & Sinding, C. (2002). Making a mess and spreading it around: Articulation of an approach to research-based theater. In A. P. Bochner & C. Ellis (Eds.), *Ethnographically speaking: Autoethnography, literature, and aesthetics* (pp. 57–75). Walnut Creek, CA: AltaMira Press.

Holman Jones, S. (2005). Autoethnography: Making the personal political. In N. K. Denzin & Y. S. Lincoln (Eds.), *The Sage handbook of qualitative research*, 3rd ed. (pp. 763–791). Thousand Oaks, CA: Sage.

Jenkins, M. M. (2010). The personal is the political: Capturing a social movement on stage. *International Review of Qualitative Research 3*(1), 125–148.

Leavy, P. (2008). Performance-based emergent methods. In S. N. Hesse-Biber & P. Leavy (Eds.), *Handbook of emergent methods* (pp. 343–357). New York: Guilford.

Lincoln, Y. S., & Denzin, N. K. (2003). The revolution in presentation. In Y. S. Lincoln & N. K. Denzin (Eds.), *Turning points in qualitative research: Tying knots in a handkerchief* (pp. 375–378). Walnut Creek, CA: AltaMira Press.

Lucas, A. (2006). Performing the (un)imagined nation: The emergence of ethnographic theatre in the late twentieth century. Ph.D. Diss, University of California–San Diego/University of California–Irvine.

Makeham, P. (1998). Community stories: 'Aftershocks' and verbatim theatre. In V. Kelly (Ed.), *Our Australian theatre in the 1990s* (pp. 168–181). Amsterdam: Rodopi.

McCall, M. M., Becker, H. S., & Meshejian, P. (1990). Performance science. *Social Problems 37*(1), 117–132.

Mienczakowski, J. (1995). The theater of ethnography: The reconstruction of ethnography into theater with emancipatory potential. *Qualitative Inquiry 1*(3), 360–375.

—. (1996). An ethnographic act: The construction of consensual theatre. In C. Ellis & A. P. Bochner (Eds.), *Composing ethnography: Alternative forms of qualitative writing* (pp. 244–264). Walnut Creek, CA: AltaMira Press.

—. (1997). Theatre of change. *Research in Drama Education 2*(2), 159–172.

—. (2001). Ethnodrama: Performed research—limitations and potential. In P. Atkinson, A. Coffey, S. Delamont, J. Lofland, & L. Lofland (Eds.), *Handbook of ethnography* (pp. 468–476). Thousand Oaks, CA: Sage.

Mienczakowski, J., & Morgan, S. (2001). Ethnodrama: Constructing participatory, experiential and compelling action research through performance. In P. Reason and H. Bradbury (Eds.), *Handbook of action research: Participative inquiry and practice* (pp. 219–227). London: Sage.

Miller, M. (1998). (Re)presenting voices in dramatically scripted research. In A. Banks & S. P. Banks (Eds.), *Fiction & social research: By ice or fire* (pp. 67–78). Walnut Creek, CA: AltaMira Press.

Norris, J. (2000). Drama as research: Realizing the potential of drama in education as a research methodology. *Youth Theatre Journal 14*, 40–51.

Paget, M. A. (1995). Performing the text. In J. Van Maanen (Ed.), *Representation in ethnography* (pp. 222–244). Thousand Oaks, CA: Sage.

Prendergast, M. (2003). I, me, mine: Soliloquizing as reflective practice. *International Journal of Education and the Arts 4*(1). Retrieved from http://www.ijea.org/v4n1/index.html.

Rivera, J. (2003). 36 assumptions about writing plays. *American Theatre 20*(2), 22–23.

Saldaña, J. (1998). Ethical issues in an ethnographic performance text: The "dramatic impact" of "juicy stuff." *Research in Drama Education 3*(2), 181–196.

—. (1999). Playwriting with data: Ethnographic performance texts. *Youth Theatre Journal 13*, 60–71.

—. (2003). Dramatizing data: A primer. *Qualitative Inquiry 9*(2), 218–236.

Spry, T. (2010). Some ethical considerations in preparing students for performative autoethnography. In N. K. Denzin & M. D. Giardina (Eds.), *Qualitative inquiry and human rights* (pp. 158–170). Walnut Creek, CA: Left Coast Press.

Performance Studies and Theatre

Alexander, B. K. (2000). Skin flint (or, the garbage man's kid): A generative autobiographical performance based on Tami Spry's *Tattoo Stories*. *Text and Performance Quarterly 20*(1), 97–114.

Anderson, M., & Wilkinson, L. (2007). A resurgence of verbatim theatre: Authenticity, empathy and transformation. *Australasian Drama Studies 50*, 153–169.

Becker, H. S., McCall, M. M., Morris, L. V., & Meshejian, P. (1989). Theatres and communities: Three scenes. *Social Problems 36*(2), 93–116.

Case, G. A. (2005). "Tic(k)": A performance of time and memory. In D. Pollock (Ed.), *Remembering: Oral history performance* (pp. 129–142). New York: Palgrave Macmillan.

Conquergood, D. (1991). Rethinking ethnography: Towards a critical cultural politics. *Communication Monographs 58*(2), 179–194.

—. (1998). Beyond the text: Toward a performative cultural politics. In S. J. Dailey (Ed.), *The future of performance studies: Visions and revisions* (pp. 25–26). Annandale, VA: National Communication Association.

—. (2003). Performing as a moral act: Ethical dimensions of the ethnography of performance. In Y. S. Lincoln & N. K. Denzin (Eds.), *Turning points in qualitative research: Tying knots in a handkerchief* (pp. 397–413). Walnut Creek, CA: AltaMira Press.

Conrad, D., McCaw, K., & Gusul, M. G. (2009). Ethnodramatic playwriting as collaborative work. In W. S. Gershon (Ed.), *The collaborative turn: Working together in qualitative research* (pp. 165–184). Rotterdam: Sense Publishers.

Crow, B. K. (1988). Conversational performance and the performance of conversation. *The Drama Review 32*(3), 23–54.

Dening, G. (1996). The theatricality of history making and the paradoxes of acting. In G. Dening, *Performances* (pp. 103–127). Chicago: University of Chicago Press.

Donelan, K., Bird, J., Wales, P., & Sinclair, C. (2009). How did you get here? Exploring ethnographic performance. In J. Shu & P. Chan (Eds.), *Planting trees of drama with global vision in local knowledge: IDEA 2007 dialogues* (pp. 490–499). Prince Edward, Kowloon, Hong Kong: Hong Kong Drama/Theatre and Education Forum.

Eisner, R. S. (2005). Remembering toward loss: Performing *And so there are pieces. . . .* In D. Pollock (Ed.), *Remembering: Oral history performance* (pp. 101–128). New York: Palgrave Macmillan.

Flannery, E. J. (2009). (Ac)knowledging: Eating, living, loving. *Qualitative Inquiry 15*(3), 439–447.

Gingrich-Philbrook, C. (1997). Refreshment. *Text and Performance Quarterly 17*, 352–360.

Goltz, D. B. (2007). Artist's statement: Forgive me, audience, for I know not what I do. *Text and Performance Quarterly 27*(3), 231–235.

—. (2007). Banging the bishop: Latter day prophecy. *Text and Performance Quarterly 27*(3), 236–265.

Gordon, M. (2005). Memory and performance in staging *The Line* in Milwaukee: A play about the bitter Patrick Cudahy strike of 1987–1989. In D. Pollock (Ed.), *Remembering: Oral history performance* (pp. 85–100). New York: Palgrave Macmillan.

Jackson, S. (1993). Ethnography and the audition: Performance as ideological critique. *Text and Performance Quarterly 13*, 21–43.

Jones, J. L. (1996). The self as other: Creating the role of Joni the ethnographer for *Broken Circles*. *Text and Performance Quarterly 16*, 131–145.

—. (2002). Performance ethnography: The role of embodiment in cultural authenticity. *Theatre Topics 12*(1), 1–5.

Jules-Rosette, B., McVey, C., & Arbitrario, M. (2002). Performance ethnography: The theory and method of dual tracking. *Field Methods 14*(2), 123–147.

Kalb, J. (2001). Documentary solo performance: The politics of the mirrored self. *Theater 31*(3), 12–29.

Lathem, L. (2005). Bringing old and young people together: An interview project. In D. Pollock (Ed.), *Remembering: Oral history performance* (pp. 67–84). New York: Palgrave Macmillan.

Lieblich, A. (2006). Vicissitudes: A study, a book, a play: Lessons from the work of a narrative scholar. *Qualitative Inquiry 12*(1), 60–80.

Lincoln, Y. S. (2004). Performing 9/11: Teaching in a terrorized world. *Qualitative Inquiry 10*(1), 140–159.

Madison, D. S. (2003). Performance, personal narratives, and the politics of possibility. In Y. S. Lincoln & N. K. Denzin (Eds.), *Turning points in qualitative research: Tying knots in a handkerchief* (pp. 469–486). Walnut Creek, CA: AltaMira Press.

Miller-Day, M. (2008). Performance matters. *Qualitative Inquiry 14*(8),1458–1470.

Nethercott, S. S., & Leighton, N. O. (1990). Memory, process, and performance. *Oral History Review 18*(2), 37–60.

Park-Fuller, L. (2000). Performing absence: The staged personal narrative as testimony. *Text and Performance Quarterly 20*(1), 20–42.

Passes, A. (2006). Chaos theory—a footnote: an experiment for radio. *Anthropology and Humanism 31*(1), 75–82.

Pelias, R. J. (2002). For father and son: An ethnodrama with no catharsis. In A. P. Bochner & C. Ellis (Eds.), *Ethnographically speaking: Autoethnography, literature, and aesthetics* (pp. 35–43). Walnut Creek, CA: AltaMira Press.

—. (2005). Performative writing as scholarship: An apology, an argument, an anecdote. *Cultural Studies/Critical Methodologies 5*(4), 415–424.

Pelias, R. J., & VanOosting, J. (1987). A paradigm for performance studies. *Quarterly Journal of Speech 73*, 219–231.

Pineau, E. (2000). *Nursing mother* and articulating absence. *Text and Performance Quarterly 20*(1), 1–19.

Pollock, D. (1990). Telling the told: Performing *Like a family*. *Oral History Review 18*(2), 1–36.

Poulos, C. N. (2010). Transgressions. *International Review of Qualitative Research 3*(1), 67–88.

Richards, S. L. (2006). Who is this ancestor? Performing memory in Ghana's slave castle-dungeons (a multimedia performance meditation). In D. S. Madison & J. Hamera (Eds.), *The Sage handbook of performance studies* (pp. 489–507). Thousand Oaks, CA: Sage.

Rouveral, A. J. (2005). Trying to be good: Lessons in oral history and performance. In D. Pollock (Ed.), *Remembering: Oral history performance* (pp. 19–43). New York: Palgrave Macmillan.

Saldaña, J. (2008). *Second chair: An autoethnodrama. Research Studies in Music Education 30*(2), 177–191.

Simhoni, O. (2008). *The false witness: Artistic research on stage. The Qualitative Report 13*(3), 353–378.

Snyder-Young, D. (2010). Beyond an "aesthetic of objectivity": Performance ethnography, performance texts, and theatricality. *Qualitative Inquiry 16*(10), 883–893.

Spaulding, S. B., Banning, J., Harbour, C. P., & Davies, T. G. (2009). Drama: A comparative analysis of individual narratives. *The Qualitative Report 14*(3), 524–565.

Spry, T. (2001). Performing autoethnography: An embodied methodological praxis. *Qualitative Inquiry 7*(6), 706–732.

—. (2003). Illustrated woman: Autoperfomance in "Skins: A daughter's (re)construction of cancer" and "Tattoo stories: A postscript to 'Skins'". In L. C. Miller, J. Taylor, and M. H. Carver (Eds.), *Voices made flesh: Performing women's autobiography* (pp. 167–191). Madison, WI: University of Wisconsin Press.

Stucky, N. (1988). Unnatural acts: Performing natural conversation. *Literature in Performance 8*(2), 28–39.

—. (1993). Toward an aesthetics of natural performance. *Text and Performance Quarterly 13*, 168–180.

—. (2002). Deep embodiment: The epistemology of natural performance. In N. Stucky & C. Wimmer (Eds.), *Teaching performance studies* (pp. 131–144). Carbondale, IL: Southern Illinois University Press.

Turner, V., & Turner, E. (1982). Performing ethnography. *The Drama Review 26*(2), 33–50.

Welker, L. S., & Goodall, H. L., Jr. (1997). Representation, interpretation, and performance: Opening the text of *Casing a promised land. Text and Performance Quarterly 17*, 109–122.

Education

Ajwang´, R. O., & Edmondson, L. (2003). Love in the time of dissertations: An ethnographic tale. *Qualitative Inquiry 9*(3), 466–480.

Bagley, C. (2008). Educational ethnography as performance art: Towards a sensuous feeling and knowing. *Qualitative Research 8*(1), 53–72.

Barone, T. (2002). From genre blurring to audience blending: Reflections on the field emanating from an ethnodrama. *Anthropology and Education Quarterly 33*(2), 255–267.

Belliveau, G. (2006). Engaging in drama: Using arts-based research to explore a social justice project in teacher education. *International Journal of Education & the Arts 7*(5). Retrieved from http://www.ijea.org/v7n5/v7n5.pdf.

—. (2007). Dramatizing the data: An ethnodramatic exploration of a playbuilding process. *Arts & Learning Research Journal 23*(1), 31–51.

Boran, K. (1999). *Rising from the ashes: A dramaturgical analysis of teacher change in a Chicago public high school after probation.* Unpublished doctoral dissertation, National-Louis University.

Campbell, G., & Conrad, D. (2006). *Arresting change: Popular theatre with young offenders.* In L. A. McCammon & D. McLauchlan (Eds.), *Universal mosaic of drama and theatre: The IDEA 2004 dialogues* (pp. 375–391). Ottawa: IDEA Publications and IDEA 2004.

Chappell, D. (2006). Banned book ethnographies: A project with 8th graders. *Teaching Artist Journal 4*(3), 182–189.

Conrad, D. (2005). Rethinking 'at risk' in drama education: Beyond prescribed roles. *Research in Drama Education 10*(1), 27–41.

—. (2006). Entangled (in the) sticks: Ethical conundrums of popular theater as pedagogy and research. *Qualitative Inquiry 12*(3), 437–458.

Cozart, S. C., Gordon, J., Gunzenhauser, M. G., McKinney, M. B., & Petterson, J. A. (2003). Disrupting dialogue: Envisioning performance ethnography for research and evaluation. *Educational Foundations 17*(2), 53–69.

Diamond, C. T. P., & Mullen, C. A. (2000). Rescripting the script and rewriting the paper: Taking research to the "Edge of the Exploratory." *International Journal of Education and the Arts 1*(4). Retrieved from http://www.ijea.org/v1n4/index.html.

Downey, A. L. (2008). No child left untested: Docudrama in six scenes. *Youth Theatre Journal 22*, 47–66.

Finley, M. (2003). Fugue of the street rat: Writing research poetry. *International Journal of Qualitative Studies in Education 16*(4), 603–604.

Finley, S. (2000). "Dream child": The role of poetic dialogue in homeless research. *Qualitative Inquiry* 6(3), 432–434.

—. (2001). From the streets to the classrooms: Street intellectuals as teacher educators, collaborations in revolutionary pedagogy. In K. Sloan & J. T. Sears (Eds.), *Democratic curriculum theory and practice: Retrieving public spaces* (pp. 113–126). Troy, NY: Educators International Press.

Finley, S., & Finley, M. (1999). Sp'ange: A research story. *Qualitative Inquiry* 5(3), 313–337.

Gallagher, K. (2007). Theatre pedagogy and performed research: Respectful forgeries and faithful betrayals. *Theatre Research in Canada 28*(2), 105–119.

Goldstein, T. (2008). Multiple commitments and ethical dilemmas in performed ethnography. *Educational Insights 12*(2). Retrieved from http://www.ccfi.educ.ubc.ca/publication/insights/v12n02/pdfs/goldstein.pdf.

Goldstein, T., & Wickett, J. (2009). Zero tolerance: A stage adaptation of an investigative report on school safety. *Qualitative Inquiry 15*(10), 1552–1568.

Gouzouasis, P., Henrey, J., & Belliveau, G. (2008). Turning points: A transitional story of grade seven music students' participation in high school band programmes. *Music Education Research 10*(1), 75–90.

Lewis, P. J. (2011). Collage journaling with pre-service teachers: A reader's theatre in one > collage act. *International Review of Qualitative Research 4*(1), 51–58.

Meyer, M. J. (1998). *Transitional wars: A study of power, control and conflict in executive succession—theatre as representation.* Unpublished doctoral dissertation, McGill University.

—. (2001). Illustrating issues of power and control: The use of dramatic scenario in administration training. *Educational Management and Administration 29*(4), 449–465.

—. (2001). Reflective leadership training in practice using theatre as representation. *International Journal of Leadership in Education 4*(2), 149–169.

Rex, L. A., Murnen, T. J., Hobbs, J., & McEachen, D. (2002). Teachers' pedagogical stories and the shaping of classroom participation: "The dancer" and "Graveyard shift at the 7–11." *American Educational Research Journal 39*(3), 765–796.

Rogers, D., Frellick, P., & Babinski, L. (2002). Staging a study: Performing the personal and professional struggles of beginning teachers. In C. Bagley & M. B. Cancienne (Eds.), *Dancing the data* (pp. 53–69). New York: Peter Lang Publishing.

Saldaña, J. (1998) "Maybe someday, if I'm famous . . .": An ethnographic performance text. In J. Saxton & C. Miller (Eds.), *Drama and theatre in education: The research of practice, the practice of research* (pp. 89-109). Brisbane: IDEA Publications.

—. (2010). Writing ethnodrama: A sampler from educational research. In M. Savin-Baden & C. H. Major (Eds.), *New approaches to qualitative research: Wisdom and uncertainty* (pp. 61–69). London: Routledge.

Sallis, R. (2003). Ethnographic performance in an all boys school. *NJ: Drama Australia Journal 27*(2), 65–78.

—. (2008). From data to drama—The construction of an ethnographic performance. *NJ: Drama Australia Journal 31*(2), 7–20.

Sparkes, A. C. (2002). Ethnodrama. In A. C. Sparkes, *Telling tales in sport and physical activity* (pp. 127–148). Champaign, IL: Human Kinetics.

Thorp, L. (2003). Voices from the garden: A performance ethnography. *Qualitative Inquiry 9*(2), 312–324.

Walker, R., Pick, C., & MacDonald, B. (1991). "Other rooms: Other voices"—A dramatized report. In C. Pick and B. MacDonald (Eds.), *Biography, identity and schooling: Episodes in educational research* (pp. 80–93). Washington, DC: Falmer Press.

White, V., & Belliveau, G. (2010). Whose story is it anyway? Exploring ethical dilemmas in performed research. *Performing Ethos 1*(1), 85–95.

Health Care

Colantonio, A., Kontos, P. C., Gilbert, J. E., Rossiter, K., Gray J., & Keightley, M. L. (2008). After the crash: Research-based theater for knowledge transfer. *Journal of Continuing Education in the Health Professions 28*(3), 180–185.

Dupuis, S. L., Gillies, J., Mitchell, G. J., Jonas-Simpson, C., Whyte, C., & Carson, J. (2011). Catapulting shifts in images, understandings, and actions for family members through research-based drama. *Family Relations 60*(1), 104–120.

Eakin, J. M., & Endicott, M. (2006). Knowledge translation through research-based theatre. *Healthcare Policy 2*(2), 54–59.

Keen, S., & Todres, L. (2007). Strategies for disseminating qualitative research findings: Three exemplars. *Forum: Qualitative Social Research 8*(3). Retrieved from http://www.qualitative-research.net/index.php/fqs/article/view/285/625.

Kontos, P. C., & Naglie, G. (2006). Expressions of personhood in Alzheimer's: Moving from ethnographic text to performing ethnography. *Qualitative Research 6*(3), 301–317.

McIntyre, M. (2009). Home is where the heart is: A reader's theatre. *The Canadian Creative Arts in Health, Training and Education Journal*. Retrieved from http://www.cmclean.com/archives/CCAHTE-Journal-7-McIntyre.html.

McIntyre, M., & Cole, A. (2008). Love stories about caregiving and Alzheimer's disease: A performative methodology. *Journal of Health Psychology 13*(2), 213–225.

Mienczakowski, J., Smith, L., & Morgan, S. (2002). Seeing words—hearing feelings: Ethnodrama and the performance of data. In C. Bagley & M. B. Cancienne (Eds.), *Dancing the data* (pp. 34–52). New York: Peter Lang.

Mitchell, G. J., Dupuis, S., Jonas-Simpson, C., Whyte, C., Carson, J., & Gillis, J. (2011). The experience of engaging with research-based drama: Evaluation and explication of synergy and transformation. *Qualitative Inquiry 17*(4), 379–392.

Mitchell, G. J., Jonas-Simpson, C., & Ivonoffski, V. (2006). Research-based theatre: The making of *I'm still here!*. *Nursing Science Quarterly 19*(3), 198–206.

Mulcahy, C. M., Parry, D. C., & Glover, T. D. (2009). Between diagnosis and death: A performance text about cancer, shadows, and the ghosts we cannot escape. *International Review of Qualitative Research 2*(1), 29–42.

Mullen, C. A., Buttignol, M., & Diamond, C. T. P. (2005). Flyboy: Using the arts and theater to assist suicidal adolescents. *International Journal of Education & the Arts 6*(5). Retrieved from http://ijea.asu.edu/v6n5.

Nimmon, L. E. (2007). ESL-speaking immigrant women's disillusions: Voices of health care in Canada: An ethnodrama. *Health Care for Women International 28*(4), 381–396.

Nisker, J., Martin, D. K., Bluhm, R., & Daar, A. S. (2006). Theatre as a public engagement tool for health-policy development. *Health Policy 78*, 258–271.

Pardue, K. T. (2004). Introducing reader's theater! A strategy to foster aesthetic knowing in nursing. *Nurse Education 29*(2), 58–62.

Parry, D. C., & Glover, T. D. (2011). Living with cancer? Come as you are. *Qualitative Inquiry 17*(5), 395–403.

Rosenbaum, M. E., Ferguson, K. J., & Herwaldt, L. A. (2005). In their own words: Presenting the patient's perspective using research-based theatre. *Medical Education 39*(6), 622–631.

Rossiter, K., Gray, J., Kontos, P., Keightley, M., Colantonio, A., & Gilbert, J. (2008). From page to stage: Dramaturgy and the art of interdisciplinary translation. *Journal of Health Psychology 13*(2), 277–286.

Saldaña, J. (2010). Ethnodramas about health and illness: Staging human vulnerability, fragility, and resiliency. In C. McLean & R. Kelly (Eds.), *Creative arts in interdisciplinary practice: Inquiries for hope & change* (pp. 167–184). Calgary: Detselig Enterprises.

Sandelowski, M., Trimble, F., Woodard, E. K., & Barroso, J. (2006). From synthesis to script: Transforming qualitative research findings for use in practice. *Qualitative Health Research 16*(10), 1350–1370.

Saunders, C. M. (2008). Forty seven million strong, weak, wrong, or right: Living without health insurance. *Qualitative Inquiry 14*(4), 528–545.

Schipper, K., Abma, T. A., van Zadelhoff, E., van de Griendt, J., Nierse, C., & Widdershoven, G. A. M. (2010). What does it mean to be a patient research partner? An ethnodrama. *Qualitative Inquiry 16*(6), 501–510.

Schneider, B. (2005). Mothers talk about their children with schizophrenia: A performance autoethnography. *Journal of Psychiatric and Mental Health Nursing 12*(3), 333–340.

Shapiro, J., & Hunt, L. (2003). All the world's a stage: The use of theatrical performance in medical education. *Medical Education 37*(10), 922–927.

Smith, C. (2008). Performing my recovery: A play of chaos, restitution, and quest after traumatic brain injury. *Forum: Qualitative Social Research 9*(2), Art. 30, http://www.qualitative-research.net/index.php/fqs/article/view/410/889.

Smith, C. A. M., & Gallo, A. M. (2007). Applications of performance ethnography in nursing. *Qualitative Health Research 17*(4), 521–528.

Stuttaford, M., Bryanston, C., Hundt, G. L., Connor, M., Thorogood, M., & Tollman, S. (2006). Use of applied theatre in health research dissemination and data validation: A pilot study from South Africa. *Health 10*(1), 31–45.

Ethnic and Cultural Studies

Bates, D., Chase, N., Ignasiak, C., Johnson, Y., Zaza, T., Niesz, T., Buck, P., & Schultz, K. (2001). Reflections: Writing and talking about race in middle school. In J. Shulz & A. Cook-Sather (Eds.), *In our own words: Students' perspectives on school* (pp. 127–148). Lanham, MD: Rowman & Littlefield.

Bhattacharya, K. (2009). Negotiating shuttling between transnational experiences: A de/colonizing approach to performance ethnography. *Qualitative Inquiry 15*(6), 1061–1083.

Bui, D.-M. T. (2001). Six feet tall: A one-person performance. *Cultural Studies/CriticalMethodologies 1*(2), 185–189.

Cho, G. M., & Kim, H. (2005). Dreaming in tongues. *Qualitative Inquiry 11*(3), 445–457.

de Guevara, L. (2006). Theatre and drama for empowerment: The immigrant experience. In L. A. McCammon & D. McLauchlan (Eds.), *Universal mosaic of drama and theatre: The IDEA 2004 dialogues* (pp. 321–324). Ottawa: IDEA Publications and IDEA 2004 World Congress.

Fine, M., Roberts, R. A., Torre, M. E., Bloom, J., Burns, A., Chajet, L., Guishard, M., & Payne, A. (2004). *Echoes of Brown: Youth documenting and performing the legacy of Brown v. Board of Education.* New York: Teachers College Press.

Goldstein, T. (2001). Hong Kong, Canada: Playwriting as critical ethnography. *Qualitative Inquiry 7*(3), 279–303.

—. (2002). Performed ethnography for representing other people's children in critical educational research. *Applied Theatre Researcher* (3) (Online). Available at www.gu.edu.au/centre/atr/opt6/frameset1b3.html.

Gubrium, A. C., & Mazhani, T. (2009). Sharing race, the personal, and the political from multiple social locations at an HBCU. *Qualitative Inquiry* 15(3), 448–466.

Jenkins, M. M. (2010). Ethnographic writing is as good as ten mothers. *Qualitative Inquiry* 16(2), 83–89.

—. (2010). The fabulous ruins of Detroit: Selected excerpts. *Qualitative Inquiry* 16(2), 90–103.

Kondo, D. (1995). Bad girls: Theater, women of color, and the politics of representation. In R. Behar & D. A. Gordon (Eds.), *Women writing culture* (pp. 49–64). Berkeley, CA: University of California Press.

Kotarba, J. A. (1998). Black men, black voices: The role of the producer in synthetic performance ethnography. *Qualitative Inquiry* 4(3), 389–404.

Moreira, C. (2008). Life in so many acts. *Qualitative Inquiry* 14(4), 590–612.

Park, H.-Y. (2009). Writing in Korean, living in the U.S.: A screenplay about a bilingual boy and his mom. *Qualitative Inquiry* 15(6), 1103–1124.

Pifer, D. A. (1999). Small town race: A performance text. *Qualitative Inquiry* 5(4), 541–562.

Rodriguez, K. L., & Lahman, M. K. E. (2011). *Las comadres*: Rendering research as performative. *Qualitative Inquiry* 17(7), 606–612.

Wang, W. J. (2006). The subversive practices of reminiscence theatre in Taiwan. *Research in Drama Education* 11(1), 77–87.

West-Olatunji, C. A., Baker, J. C., & Brooks, M. (2006). African-American adolescent males: Giving voice to their educational experiences. *Multicultural Perspectives* 8(4), 3–9.

Women's Studies

Bloom, L. R., Reynolds, A., Amore, R., Beaman, A., Chantem, G. K., Chapman, E., Fitzpatrick, J., Iñiguez, A., Mozak, A., Olson, D., Teshome, Y., & Vance, N. (2009). *Identify this . . . A reader's theatre of women's voices. International Review of Qualitative Research* 2(2), 209–228.

Carver, M. H. (2003). Risky business: Exploring women's autobiography and performance. In L. C. Miller, J. Taylor, & M. H. Carver (Eds.), *Voices made flesh: Performing women's autobiography* (pp. 15–29). Madison, WI: University of Wisconsin Press.

Ellis, C., & Bochner, A. P. (1992). Telling and performing personal stories: The constraints of choice in abortion. In C. Ellis & M. G. Flaherty (Eds.), *Investigating subjectivity: Research on lived experience* (pp. 79–101). Newbury Park, CA: Sage.

Gannon, S. (2004). Out/performing in the academy: Writing 'The Breast Project'. *International Journal of Qualitative Studies in Education* 17(1), 65–81.

Minge, J. M. (2006). Painting a landscape of abortion: The fusion of embodied art. *Qualitative Inquiry 12*(1), 118–145.

Montano, L. M. (2003). Death in the art and life of Linda M. Montano. In L. C. Miller, J. Taylor, & M. H. Carver (Eds.), *Voices made flesh: Performing women's autobiography* (pp. 265–281). Madison, WI: University of Wisconsin Press.

Lesbian and Gay Studies

Chapman, J., Sykes, H., & Swedberg, A. (2003). Wearing the secret out: Performing stories of sexual identities. *Youth Theatre Journal 17*, 27–37.

Dillard, S. (2000). *Breathing Darrell*: Solo performance as a contribution to a useful queer methodology. *Text and Performance Quarterly 20*(1), 74–83.

Goldstein, T. (2004) Performed ethnography for anti-homophobia teacher education: Linking research to teaching. *The Canadian On-Line Journal of Queer Studies in Education, 1*(1). Retrieved from http://jqstudies.oise. utoronto.ca/journal/viewarticle.php?id=13&layout=html.

—. (2006). Toward a future of equitable pedagogy and schooling. *Pedagogies: An International Journal 1*(3), 151–169.

Honeychurch, K. G. (1998). Carnal knowledge: Re-searching (through) the sexual body. In W. E. Pinar (Ed.), *Queer theory in education* (pp. 251–273). Mahwah, NJ: Lawrence Erlbaum Associates.

Taylor, J. (2003). On being an exemplary lesbian: My life as a role model. In L. C. Miller, J. Taylor, & M. H. Carver (Eds.), *Voices made flesh: Performing women's autobiography* (pp. 192–214). Madison, WI: University of Wisconsin Press.

REFERENCES

Ackerman, E., & Sanchez, KJ. (2010). *ReEntry.* New York: Playscripts, Inc.

Ackroyd, J., & O'Toole, J. (2010). *Performing research: Tensions, triumphs and trade-offs of ethnodrama.* Stoke on Trent: Trentham Books.

Allen, C. J., & Garner, N. (1997). *Condor Qatay: Anthropology in performance.* Prospect Heights, IL: Waveland Press.

Angrosino, M. V. (1994). On the bus with Vonnie Lee: Explorations in life history and metaphor. In J. Creswell (2007) (Ed.), *Qualitative inquiry and research design: Choosing among five approaches* (pp. 251–263). Thousand Oaks, CA: Sage.

Bailey, S. (2010). *Barrier-free theatre.* Enumclaw, WA: Idyll Arbor.

Barone, T., & Eisner, E. W. (2012). *Arts based research.* Thousand Oaks, CA: Sage.

Blank, J., & Jensen, E. (2004). *The exonerated.* New York: Faber and Faber.

—. (2010). *Aftermath* (acting edition). New York: Dramatists Play Service.

Boal, A. (1998). *Legislative theatre.* New York: Routledge.

Bowles, N. (Ed.). (1997). *Friendly fire: An anthology of 3 plays by queer street youth.* Los Angeles: A.S.K. Theater Projects.

Brown, P., & the Workers Cultural Action Committee. (2001). *Aftershocks.* Sydney: Currency Press.

Brown, P. (2010). Ethics, ownership, authorship. In P. Brown (Ed.), *Verbatim: Staging memory & community* (pp. 109–112). Strawberry Hills NSW, Australia, Currency Press.

Burke, G. (2007). *The national theatre of Scotland's* Black Watch. London: Faber and Faber.

Carson, J. (2009). *Liars, thieves and other sinners on the bench.* New York: Theatre Communications Group.

Chang, H. (2008). *Autoethnography as method.* Walnut Creek, CA: Left Coast Press.

Chapman, J., Swedberg, A., & Sykes, H. (2005). *Wearing the secret out.* In J. Saldaña (Ed.), *Ethnodrama: An anthology of reality theatre* (pp. 103–120). Walnut Creek, CA: AltaMira Press.

Cizmar, P., Filloux, C., Kriegel, G., Mack, C. K., Margraff, R., Smith, A. D., Yankowitz, S. (2009). *Seven* (acting edition). New York: Dramatists Play Service.

Cosson, S. (Ed.). (2010). *The Civilians: An anthology of six plays*. New York: Playscripts, Inc.

Cosson, S., & Friedman, M. (2003). *Gone missing*. In S. Cosson (2010) (Ed.), *The Civilians: An anthology of six plays* (pp. 35–68). New York: Playscripts, Inc.

Cozart, S. C., Gordon, J., Gunzenhauser, M. G., McKinney, M. B., & Petterson, J. A. (2003). Disrupting dialogue: Envisioning performance ethnography for research and evaluation. *Educational Foundations 17*(2), 53–69.

Crossley, M. (2007). Narrative analysis. In E. Lyons & A. Coyle (Eds.), *Analysing qualitative data in psychology* (pp. 131–144). London: Sage.

Davenport, K. (2009). *My first time*. New York: Samuel French, Inc.

Davies, R. (1991). *Murther & walking spirits*. New York: Viking.

Davis, C. S., & Ellis, C. (2008). Emergent methods in autoethnographic research: Autoethnographic narrative and the multiethnographic turn. In S. N. Hesse-Biber & P. Leavy (Eds.), *Handbook of emergent methods* (pp. 283–302). New York: Guilford Press.

Davis, D. (1993). *Telling your own stories*. Little Rock: August House.

Delany, S. L., Delany, A. E., & Hearth, A. H. (1993). *Having our say: The Delany sisters' first 100 years*. New York: Delta.

Denzin, N. (1997). *Interpretive ethnography: Ethnographic practices for the 21st century*. Thousand Oaks, CA: Sage.

—. (2003). *Performance ethnography: Critical pedagogy and the politics of culture*. Thousand Oaks, CA: Sage.

Dickinson, B. (2008). *Voices in conflict*. New York: Playscripts, Inc.

Ehrenreich, B. (2002). *Nickel and dimed: On (not) getting by in America*. New York: Owl Books.

Ellis, C. (2008). *Revision: Autoethnographic reflections on life and work*. Walnut Creek, CA: Left Coast Press.

Filewod, A. (2009). The documentary body: Theatre workshop to banner theatre. In A. Forsyth & C. Megson (Eds.), *Get real: Documentary theatre past and present* (pp. 55–73). New York: Palgrave Macmillan.

Finley, M. (2000). *Street rat*. Grosse Pointe, MI: Greenroom Press.

Finley, S., & Finley, M. (1999). Sp'ange: A research story. *Qualitative Inquiry 5*(3), 313–337.

Gibson, W. (1999). *American primitive (John & Abigail): The words of John and Abigail Adams* (acting edition). New York: Dramatists Play Service.

Given, L. M. (2008). *The Sage encyclopedia of qualitative research methods*. Thousand Oaks, CA: Sage.

Gray, R. E., & Sinding, C. (2002). *Standing ovation: Performing social science research about cancer*. Walnut Creek, CA: AltaMira Press.

Grbich, C. (2007). *Qualitative data analysis: An introduction.* Thousand Oaks, CA: Sage.

Greengrass, P. (2006a). *United 93* [DVD]. United States: Universal.

—. (2006b). *United 93: The shooting script.* New York: Newmarket Press.

Haehnel, A. (2010). *What I want to say but never will.* New York: Playscripts, Inc.

Hammond, W., & Steward, D. (Eds.) (2008). *Verbatim verbatim: Contemporary documentary theatre.* London: Oberon Books.

Hare, D. (2004). *Stuff happens.* New York: Faber and Faber.

Higgins, C., Cannan, D., & Turnbull, C. (1984). *The Ik.* Woodstock, IL: Dramatic Publishing.

Hochschild, A. R. (2003). *The managed heart: Commercialization of human feeling* (2nd ed.). Berkeley: University of California Press.

Holden, J. (2005). *Nickel and dimed* (acting edition). New York: Dramatists Play Service.

Holmes, J. (2009). *Katrina: A play of New Orleans.* London: Methuen.

Kaufman, M., & Members of the Tectonic Theater Project. (2001). *The Laramie project* (acting edition). New York: Dramatists Play Service.

Kestecher, N. (2010). Unreality radio. In J. Biewen & A. Dilworth (Eds.), *Reality radio: Telling true stories in sound* (pp. 108–115). Chapel Hill, NC: University of North Carolina Press.

Knowles, J. G., & Cole, A. L. (Eds.). (2008). *Handbook of the arts in qualitative research: Perspectives, methodologies, examples, and issues.* Thousand Oaks, CA: Sage.

Liamputtong, P. (2009). *Qualitative research methods* (3rd ed.). Victoria: Oxford University Press.

Madison, D. S. (2005). *Critical ethnography: Method, ethics, and performance.* Thousand Oaks, CA: Sage.

Mann, E. (1996). *Having our say: The Delany sisters' first 100 years* (acting edition). New York: Dramatists Play Service.

—. (2000). In conversation: Emily Mann. *Theatre Topics 10*(1), 1–16.

Marks, M., & Westmoreland, M. (2006). *The Katrina project: Hell and high water.* New York: Playscripts, Inc.

McCammon, L., & Saldaña, J. (2011). Lifelong impact: adult perceptions of their high school speech and/or theatre participation. Unpublished report.

McLeod, J., & Thomson, R. (2009). *Researching social change.* London: Sage.

Mears, C. L. (2009). *Interviewing for education and social science research: The gateway approach.* New York: Palgrave Macmillan.

Mienczakowski, J. (1995). The theater of ethnography: The reconstruction of ethnography into theater with emancipatory potential. *Qualitative Inquiry 1*(3), 360–375.

Miles, M. B., & Huberman, A. M. (1994). *Qualitative data analysis* (2nd ed). Thousand Oaks, CA: Sage.

Miller, S. (2006). *My left breast.* New York: Playscripts, Inc.

Morgan, P. (2007, February 25). *ABC News: Perspective* [Radio broadcast]. Washington DC: American Broadcasting Corporation.

Mulcahy, C. M., Parry, D. C., & Glover, T. D. (2009). Between diagnosis and death: A performance text about cancer, shadows, and the ghosts we cannot escape. *International Review of Qualitative Research 2*(1), 29–42.

Nathan, R. (2005). *My freshman year: What a professor learned by becoming a student.* New York: Penguin Books.

Nelson, A. (2002). *The guys.* New York: Random House.

—. (2003). *The guys* (acting edition). New York: Dramatists Play Service.

Norris, J. (2010). *Playbuilding as qualitative research: A participatory arts-based approach.* Walnut Creek, CA: Left Coast Press.

Packer, G. (2008). *Betrayed.* New York: Faber and Faber.

Park, H.-Y. (2009). Writing in Korean, living in the U.S.: A screenplay about a bilingual boy and his mom. *Qualitative Inquiry 15*(6), 1103–1124.

Park-Fuller, L. (2003). A clean breast of it. In L. C. Miller, J. Taylor, & M. H. Carver (Eds.), *Voices made flesh: Performing women's autobiography* (pp. 215–236). Madison, WI: University of Wisconsin Press.

Patterson, W. (2008). Narratives of events: Labovian narrative analysis and its limitations. In M. Andrews, C. Squire, & M. Tamboukou (Eds.), *Doing narrative research* (pp. 22–40). London: Sage.

Peshkin, A. (1986). *God's choice: The total world of a fundamentalist Christian school.* Chicago: University of Chicago Press.

Poulos, C. N. (2008). *Accidental ethnography: An inquiry into family secrecy.* Walnut Creek, CA: Left Coast Press.

—. (2010). Transgressions. *International Review of Qualitative Research 3*(1), 67–88.

Reich, S. (1989). *Different trains [CD and jacket notes].* New York: Elektra/Asylum/Nonesuch Records.

Rickman, A., & Viner, K. (Eds.). (2006). *My name is Rachel Corrie.* New York: Theatre Communications Group.

Robinson, J. (2010). Encounters in child care. In J. Ackroyd & J. O'Toole (Eds.), *Performing research: Tensions, triumphs and trade-offs of ethnodrama* (pp. 105–121). Stoke on Trent: Trentham Books.

Rukulak, J. (2001). *The writer's block: 786 ideas to jump-start your imagination.* Philadelphia: Running Press.

Saldaña, J. (1998a). Ethical issues in an ethnographic performance text: The "dramatic impact" of "juicy stuff." *Research in Drama Education 3*(2), 181–196.

—. (1998b). "Maybe someday, if I'm famous . . .": An ethnographic performance text. In J. Saxton & C. Miller (Eds.), *The research of practice, the practice of research* (pp. 89–109). Victoria, BC: IDEA Publications.

—. (2002). Finding my place: The Brad trilogy. In H. F. Wolcott, *Sneaky kid and its aftermath: Ethics and intimacy in fieldwork* (pp. 167–210). Walnut Creek, CA: AltaMira Press.

—. (Ed.). (2005). *Ethnodrama: An anthology of reality theatre.* Walnut Creek, CA: AltaMira Press.

—. (2006). This is not a performance text. *Qualitative Inquiry 12*(6), 1091–1098.

—. (2008). *Second chair:* An autoethnodrama. *Research Studies in Music Education 30*(2), 177–191.

—. (2009). *The coding manual for qualitative researchers.* London: Sage.

—. (2010a). Reflections on an ethnotheatre aesthetic. *Arts Praxis 2.* Retrieved from http://steinhardt.nyu.edu/music/artspraxis/2/reflections_on_an_ethnotheatre_aesthetic.

—. (2010b). Writing ethnodrama: A sampler from educational research. In M. Savin-Baden & C. H. Major (Eds.), *New approaches to qualitative research: Wisdom and uncertainty* (pp. 61–69). London: Routledge.

Saldaña, J., Finley, S., & Finley, M. (2005). *Street rat.* In J. Saldaña (Ed.), *Ethnodrama: An Anthology of reality theatre* (pp. 139–179). Walnut Creek, CA: AltaMira Press.

Sandelowski, M., Trimble, F., Woodard, E. K., & Barroso, J. (2006). From synthesis to script: Transforming qualitative research findings for use in practice. *Qualitative Health Research 16*(10), 1350–1370.

Saunders, C. M. (2008). Forty seven million strong, weak, wrong, or right: Living without health insurance. *Qualitative Inquiry 14*(4), 528–545.

Smith, A. D. (1993). *Fires in the mirror: Crown Heights, Brooklyn and other identities.* New York: Anchor Books.

—. (1994). *Twilight: Los Angeles, 1992.* New York: Anchor Books.

—. (1997). *Fires in the mirror: Crown Heights, Brooklyn and other identities* (acting edition). New York: Dramatists Play Service.

—. (2000). *Talk to me: Listening between the lines.* New York: Random House.

—. (2003). *Twilight: Los Angeles, 1992* (acting edition). New York: Dramatists Play Service.

Snyder-Young, D. (2010). Beyond an "aesthetic of objectivity": Performance ethnography, performance texts, and theatricality. *Qualitative Inquiry 16*(10), 883–893.

Soans, R. (2004). *The Arab-Israeli cookbook.* Twickenham: Aurora Metro Press.

—. (2005). *Talking to terrorists.* London: Oberon Books.

—. (2007). *Life after scandal.* London: Oberon Books.

Sun, N. (2008). *No child . . .* (acting edition). New York: Dramatists Play Service.

Thoms, A. (Ed.). (2002). *with their eyes.* New York: HarperTempest.

Tillmann-Healy, L. M. (1996). A secret life in a culture of thinness: Reflections on body, food, and bulimia. In C. Ellis & A. P. Bochner (Eds.), *Composing ethnography: Alternative forms of qualitative writing* (pp. 78–108). Walnut Creek, CA: AltaMira Press.

Toth, J. (1993). *The mole people: Life in the tunnels beneath New York City.* Chicago: Chicago Review Press.

Turner, V. (1982). *From ritual to theatre.* New York: PAJ Publications.

Ukaegbu, V., & Ewu, J. (2010). Performing histories—Voices of black rural community. In J. Ackroyd & J. O'Toole (Eds.), *Performing research: Tensions, triumphs and trade-offs of ethnodrama* (pp. 169–185). Stoke on Trent: Trentham Books.

Vanover, C., & Saldaña, J. (2005). *Chalkboard concerto: Growing up as a teacher in the Chicago public schools.* In J. Saldaña (Ed.), *Ethnodrama: An anthology of reality theatre* (pp. 62–77). Walnut Creek, CA: AltaMira Press.

Wager, D. C. (2008). *In conflict.* New York: Playscripts, Inc.

Weigler, W. (2001). *Strategies for playbuilding: Helping groups translate issues into theatre.* Portsmouth, NH: Heinemann.

Wolcott, H. F. (2002). *Sneaky kid and its aftermath: Ethics and intimacy in fieldwork.* Walnut Creek, CA: AltaMira Press.

Wright, D. (2004). *I am my own wife: Studies for a play about the life of Charlotte von Mahlsdorf.* New York: Faber and Faber.

Wright, M. (2009). *Playwriting in process: Thinking and working theatrically* (2nd ed.). Newburyport, MA: Focus Publishing.

Wright, P. (1999). The thought of doing drama scares me to death. *Research in Drama Education 4*(2), 227–237.

About the Author

Johnny Saldaña is a professor of theatre at Arizona State University's School of Theatre and Film in the Herberger Institute for Design and the Arts. He is the author of *Longitudinal Qualitative Research: Analyzing Change Through Time* (AltaMira Press, 2003), *Ethnodrama: An Anthology of Reality Theatre* (AltaMira Press, 2005), *The Coding Manual for Qualitative Researchers* (Sage Publications, 2009), and *Fundamentals of Qualitative Research* (Oxford University Press, 2011).

Saldaña has published articles in such journals as *Youth Theatre Journal, Stage of the Art, Teaching Theatre, Research in Drama Education, Research Studies in Music Education, Multicultural Perspectives, Journal of Curriculum and Pedagogy*, and *Qualitative Inquiry*. He has also published chapters on research methods in longitudinal qualitative inquiry and ethnodrama for such titles as *Arts-Based Research in Education, Handbook of the Arts in Qualitative Research, Handbook of Longitudinal Research, New Approaches to Qualitative Research, Creative Arts in Interdisciplinary Practice*, and entries for *The Sage Encyclopedia of Qualitative Research Methods*.

Mr. Saldaña's methods in longitudinal qualitative inquiry, ethnodrama, coding, and qualitative data analysis have been applied and cited by researchers internationally to explore diverse topics in education, the arts, sociology, human development, business, government, and health care.

For e-mail correspondence, contact: Johnny.Saldana@asu.edu.